James N Bookstover

Indian massacres and tales of the red skins

An authentic history of the American Indian from 1492 to the present time

plished by the proper means, and the rumor spread like wildfire that the white chief could bring the dead to life. These incidents so amazed and frightened Powhatan and his people that they came in from all quarters returning stolen property.

In the latter part of 1609 Captain Smith met with a terrible accident by the firing of a bag of gunpowder. He was so fearfully torn and burned that he leaped into the river, and was with difficulty rescued from drowning. He was obliged to go to England to procure medical assistance, and was never after able to revisit the colony which he had helped to found.

After his departure things went rapidly to ruin, and there was a general revolt of the Indians. In 1613, Pocahontas was captured and held as a hostage. While she was at Jamestown a young Englishman, John Rolfe, became passionately attached to her, and on the first of April they were married. They excited great attention everywhere, even at court, where Captain Smith made a speech about her before the queen. This interesting little woman died in 1617, as she was about to revisit America. She was known as Rebecca after her baptism and conversion to the Christian religion. She left one child, Thomas Rolfe, who afterward lived in Virginia, and to whom many old Virginia families still trace their origin. Powhatan, her father, died a year later.

INDIAN MASSACRES.

Great distress was experienced from want of food, and every means was resorted to in order to procure it from the Indians. Powhatan had come to despise the Jamestown colony, owing to a foolish coronation scene by Newport, who had recently arrived from England with a crowd of useless adventurers.

The splendor of the articles of coronation fairly turned the head of Powhatan, who became treacherous toward Smith and tried to kill him when he came to barter for corn. But the daring captain performed prodigies of valor in repelling attacks single-handed. His Indian angel, the friendly little Pocahontas, came at night to warn him of an attack. Powhatan decoyed Smith and his "old fifteen" into his house, and was profuse in his offers of provision and friendship; but in the meantime an ambuscade had surrounded the house. Smith was urged to come out to the door to receive his presents; but he saw that "the bait was guarded with at least two hundred men, and thirty lying under a great tree (placed athwart as a barricade), each with his arrow ready to shoot." Smith, perceiving the plan to betray him, sprang upon the king, seizing him by the hair, and, holding a pistol to his breast, led him forth; where, making a terrible speech before the people, he succeeded in gaining peace and provisions.

Several incidents occurred about this time which tended to establish the power of Smith over the savages. One was the explosion of a quantity of gun-powder which the Indians were trying to dry upon a plate of armor as they had seen the English do. Another was the affair of the pistol and the charcoal. An Indian had stolen one of these weapons: his two brothers were seized by Smith as pledges; one of them was sent in search of the pistol, and told that his brother would be hanged in twelve hours if it were not returned. The one who was retained was placed in a dungeon. Smith, pitying the poor, naked savage, sent him some food and some charcoal for a fire. Toward midnight the brother returned with the weapon, but the poor fellow in the dungeon was found stupefied by the charcoal and terribly burned. The lamentations of the brother were so touching that Smith promised him, if he would abstain from future thefts, that he would restore the captive to life. This was accom-

preparations were now made to give a still more forcible impression. Messengers were sent to inform the Indian monarch that the great captain of the seas had reached Jamestown, and would make a visit to his royal friend and ally.

Powhatan received the officers with the greatest distinction. He declined any petty traffic, but requested Newport to bring forward at once all the goods that he had brought for trade, expressing his willingness to give full return. His desire was complied with, Newport wishing to outdo the king in generosity; but the result hardly equalled his expectation, for the cunning savage valued his corn at such a rate that the English thought it cheaper in Spain. A few blue beads in the possession of Smith caught the eye of Powhatan, and aroused his curiosity and avarice. The wary captain pretended to be loth to part with them, as being of a rare substance worn by the greatest kings in the world. To obtain them, Powhatan readily paid an immense quantity of corn. The trade in blue beads, after this, became a royal monopoly.

On the 2nd day of June 1608, Smith set out upon his exploration of Chesapeake bay. His companions numbered fourteen and their boat was an open barge. As they coasted along the eastern shore, everywhere the greatest astonishment and fright were manifested by the savages. The discharge of the guns invariably filled them with terror. Before reaching the head of the bay Smith was compelled to turn back, owing to the fatigue of his men, who were unaccustomed to such exposure.

On the 24th of July a second expedition up the Chesapeake was undertaken. Encountering a fierce tribe belonging to the redoubtable Iroquois or Six Nations of what was afterward New York state, they pacified them and obtained some of their shields, with which they fortified their boat; reminding one in this of Stanley, the African explorer, who did the same in his immortal descent of the Congo river. Upon one occasion, while Smith was exploring the Rappahannock river, he was attacked by a party of Rappahannocks, who were so cunningly disguised with bushes that they were supposed to be a natural growth of trees on the shore. On these two voyages Chesapeake bay was surveyed and an accurate chart of the entire country drawn up.

CAPT. SMITH RESCUED BY POCAHONTAS.—(SEE PAGE 19).

from death: whereat the Emperor was contented he should live.

Of late years strong doubt has been entertained as to the truth of Captain Smith's story about Pocahontas.

After two days of friendly intercourse, Smith was informed that he might return in safety to Jamestown; but as a prelude to the conveyance of this satisfactory intelligence, Powhatan was at much pains to get up a theatrical scene that should terrify his prisoner. Left alone in a large cabin, Smith's ears were saluted by frightful noises from behind a mat partition, and, soon Powhatan, with hundreds of attendants, in hideous disguises, made his appearance. He appointed twelve Indians to guide him to the settlement, requesting that a grindstone and two great guns should be sent back by them in return for liberty. Captain Smith felt little security or ease until he was safely restored to his companions at Jamestown. Two demi-culverins, together with a millstone, were proffered to the guides; but, seeing the terrible effect of a discharge of stones among the branches of an ice-covered tree, the poor savages were greatly terrified, and accepted divers toys in place of so weighty and dangerous a present.

So reduced were the settlers at this time, that all must have perished with starvation but for the intercourse established by Smith between them and the people of Powhatan. Every four or five days, his noble and generous little protectress, Pocahontas—she was then only about ten years of age—would make her appearance, accompanied by attendants laden with provisions. Part of these supplies came as presents from the king or his daughter; for the rest, the price paid in toys and articles of use was left entirely at Smith's discretion.

Captains Newport and Nelson now arrived from England with two ships, laden with necessaries and articles of traffic. Rejoiced at the arrival of friends and provisions, the colonists allowed the sailors to hold what intercourse they pleased with the natives, and the consequence was that the market was soon spoiled by the irregularity of prices offered by the English for Indian commodities. Smith had possessed Powatan and his people with extravagant ideas of the power and majesty of Newport, whose speedy arrival he predicted, and triumphal progress with their illustrious captive, among the tribes on the Rappahanock and Potomac rivers, and elsewhere. At Pamaunkee, a solemn incantation was performed with a view to ascertain his real feelings toward them. Having seated him upon a mat before a fire, in one of the larger cabins, all retired, and presently there came skipping in a great grim fellow, all painted, with a hellish voice and a rattle in his hand. He sprinkled a circle of meal about the fire, and commenced his conjuration. Six more similar devils then entered, and having danced about him for a time, sat down and sang a wild song. The chief conjuror next laid down five kernels of corn, and proceeded to make an extravagant oration. At the conclusion they all gave a short groan, and then laid down three grains more. The operation was continued till they had twice incircled the fire and was then varied by using sticks instead of corn. Three days were spent in these wearisome barbarities, each day being passed in fasting, and the nights being as regularly ushered in with feasts. Smith was, after this, entertained with the best of cheer at the house of a brother to the king. He still observed that not one of the men would eat with him, but the remains of the feast were given him to be distributed among the women and children.

The great monarch of the country, Powhatan, at this period, was holding his court on the bank of York river, and thither Smith was conveyed to await the royal pleasure. The reception of so important a captive was conducted with suitable solemnity and parade. Powhatan sat upon a raised seat before a fire. He was about sixty years of age, of noble figure, and commanding presence. A young girl sat on each side of the king, and marshalled around the room were rows of warriors and women, bedecked with beads, feathers and paint. Smith's entrance was hailed by a shout; the queen brought him water to wash, and he was magnificently entertained. Having ended his repast, a long consultation was held, when two great stones were brought before Powhatan; then as many as could, laid hands on the captive, dragged him to them, and thereon laid his head, and being ready with their clubs to beat out his brains, Pocahontas, the king's dearest daughter, when no entreaty could prevail, got his head in her arms, and laid her own upon his to save him

shot the two Englishmen as they were sleeping by the canoe; and, to the number of over two hundred, surrounded the gallant captain, who, accompanied by one of his guides, was out with his gun in search of game. Binding the Indian fast to his arm, with a garter, as a protection from the shafts of the enemy, Smith made such good use of his gun that he killed three of his assailants and wounded several others. The whole body stood at some distance, stricken with terror at the unwonted execution of his weapon, while he slowly retired toward the canoe. Unfortunately, attempting to cross a creek with a miry bottom, he stuck fast, together with his guide, and, becoming benumbed with cold, he threw away his arms, and surrendered himself. Delighted with their acquisition, the savages took him to the fire, and restored animation to his limbs by warmth and friction. He immediately set himself about conciliating the king, and presenting him with an ivory pocket compass, proceeded to explain its use. Perhaps with a view of trying his courage, they bound him to a tree, and all made ready to let fly their arrows at him, but were stayed by a sign from the chief. They then carried him to Orapaks, where he was well fed, and treated with kindness. When they reached the town, a strange savage dance was performed around the chief and his captive, by the whole body of warriors.

Although the Indians would not, as yet, eat with their prisoner, he was so feasted that a suspicion arose in his mind that they "would fat him to eat him." One of the old warriors, whose son had been wounded at the time of the capture, was with difficulty restrained from killing him. The young Indian was at his last gasp, but Smith, wishing to send information to Jamestown, said that he had there a medicine of potent effect. The messengers sent on this errand made their way to Jamestown, carrying a note from Smith. They returned, bringing with them the articles requested in the letter, to the wonder of all that heard it, for they thought he could either divine, or the paper could speak.

A plan was at that time on foot to make an attack upon the colony, and such rewards as were in their power to bestow—"life, liberty, land and women"—were proffered to Smith by the Indians, if he would lend his assistance. They made a

CHAPTER III.

VIRGINIA INDIANS—ADVENTURES OF CAPT. JOHN SMITH.

In 1584 Sir Walter Raleigh, under a patent from Queen Elizabeth, sent out two small vessels, which duly arrived at the island of Roanoke, where the voyagers were royally entertained by Wingina, King of the country, and his wife. Sir Walter christened the land Virginia in honor of the queen.

Sir Richard Grenville visited Virginia in 1585 and left over 100 men to form a settlement at Roanoke. All returned, however, within a year.

The most complete account of the aboriginal inhabitants of Virginia, particularly those who dwelt in the eastern portion of that district upon the rivers and the shores of Chesapeake Bay, is contained in the narrative of Captain John Smith. This bold and energetic pioneer, joined his fortunes to those of Bartholomew Gosnoll and his party, who sailed from England on the 19th of December, 1606, and soon became leader in the colony he brought from the mother-country.

Smith, with a barge and boat's crew, undertook an exploration of the sources of the Chickahominy, which empties into James river, a few miles above Jamestown. After making his way for about fifty miles up the stream, his progress was so impeded by fallen trees and the narrowness of the channel, that he left the boat and crew in a sort of bay, and proceeded in a canoe, accompanied only by two Englishmen and two Indian guides. The men left in charge of the boat, disregarding his orders to stay on board till his return, were set upon by a great body of natives, and one of their number, George Cassen, was taken prisoner. Having compelled their captive to disclose the intentions and position of the captain, these savages proceeded to put him to death in a most barbarous manner, severing his limbs at the joints with shells, and burning them before his face. As they dared not attack the armed company in the boat, all hands then set out in hot pursuit of Smith.

Coming upon the little party among the marshes, they

him with whatever weapon came to hand. When the time arrived, Vitachuco, who was seated at the general's table, rallying himself for a desperate effort, sprang upon his host, and endeavored to strangle him. "This blade," says the Portugese narrator, "fell upon the general; but before he could get his two hands to his throat, he gave him such a furious blow with his fist upon the face that he put him all in a gore of blood." De Soto would have doubtless perished by the unarmed hands of the muscular chief had not his attendants despatched the assailant.

All the other prisoners followed their cacique's example. Catching at the Spaniards' arms, or the " pounder wherewith they pounded the maize," each set upon his master therewith, or on the first that fell into his hands. They made use of the lances or swords they met with, as skilfully as if they had been bred to it from childhood; so that one of them, with sword in hand, made head against fifteen or twenty men in the open place, until he was killed by the governor's halberdiers. Another desperate warrior, with only a lance, kept possession of the room where the Indian corn was stored, and could not be dislodged. He was shot through an aperture in the roof. The Indians were at last overpowered, and all who had not perished in the struggle, were bound to stakes and put to death. Their executioners were the Indians of Paracoxi, who shot them with arrows.

De Soto, about the last of November, sent a detachment back to the bay of Espiritu Santo, with directions for two caravels to repair to Cuba, and the other vessels, which had not already been ordered home, to come round by sea and join him at Palache. Twenty Indian women were sent as a present to the general's wife, Donna Isabella.

De Sota died upon the Red river, and those of his companions who escaped death from exposure, disease, or savage weapons, years after the events above described, made their way down the Mississippi to the gulf, and thence reached the Spanish provinces of Mexico.

of the dead were deposited, to defend them from attacks of wolves. His vigilance and resolution, in dispatching a wolf, which had seized the body of a child of one of the principal chiefs, aroused a kindly feeling toward him, and he was well used for three years. At the end of that time Hiriga, having been worsted in a fight with Moscoso, a hostile chief, thought it necessary or expedient to make a sacrifice of his Christian subject to the devil. Forewarned of this danger by his former benefactress, Ortiz fled in the night toward the country of Moscoso. Upon first meeting with the subjects of this chief, he was in great danger from the want of an interpreter to explain whence he came, and what was his errand; but, at last, finding an Indian who understood the language of the people with whom he had lived, he quieted the suspicions of his hosts, and remained with them in friendship no less than nine years. Moscoso, hearing of the arrival of De Soto, generously furnished his captive with an escort, and gave him free permission to return to his countrymen.

De Soto now concluded to send his vessels back to Cuba, and, leaving a strong guard in Hiriga's country, proceeded northward to Vitachuco. The treacherous chief pretended friendship, but prepared for an overwhelming attack. The vigilance of John Ortiz, however, averted the catastrophe. The cacique, or chief, was secured, and his army routed. Many of the fugitives were driven into a lake, where they concealed themselves by covering their heads with the leaves of water-lilies. The lake was surrounded by the Spanish troops, but such was the resolution of the Indians, that they remained the whole night immersed in water, and, on the following day, when the rest had delivered themselves up, being constrained by the sharpness of the cold they had endured in the water, twelve still held out, resolving to die rather than surrender. Chilled and stupefied by exposure, these were dragged ashore by some Indians of Paracoxi, belonging to De Soto's party, who swam after them, and seized them by the hair.

Although a prisoner, with his chief warriors reduced to the condition of servants, Vitachuco did not lay aside his daring purposes of revenge. He managed to circulate the order among his men, that on a day appointed, while the Spaniards were at dinner, every Indian should attack the one nearest

sessed themselves of the nearest village, where were the headquarters of the Hiriga, the chief.

At the inland extremity of the town stood the temple devoted by the Indians to religious observances. Over the entrance was the wooden figure of a fowl, having the eyes gilded—placed there for the purpose of ornament. Clearings were now made around the village to give free scope to the cavalry, and parties were sent out to explore the country, and to make prisoners who should serve as guides or hostages. The remembrance of outrages committed upon himself and his people by Narvaez, had so embittered Hiriga against the whites, that no professions of friendship and good will could appease his hatred. In the tangled forests the Indians were found to be no contemptible opponents. Their bows and arrows were so effective that coats of mail did not prove a sufficient protection against their force. The arrows were headed, as usual, with stone, or with fish-bones; those which were made of canes or reeds produced the deadliest effect.

A party, under Gallegos, scouring the country a few miles from the camp attacked a small body of Indians, and put them to flight; but, as a horseman was charging with his lance at one of the number, he was amazed to hear him cry out: "Sirs, I am a Christian; do not kill me, nor these poor men, who have given me my life." Naked, sun-burned, and painted, this man was scarcely distinguishable from his wild associates. His name was John Ortiz, and he had lived with the Indians twelve years, being one of the few followers of Narvaez who escaped destruction. Since the disastrous failure of that expedition he had made his way to Cuba in a small boat, and had returned again to Florida in a small vessel sent in quest of the lost party. The Indians enticed a few of the crew on shore, and made them prisoners. Ortiz was among the number, and was the only one who escaped immediate death. After amusing themselves by various expedients to terrify and torment their captive, the savages, by the command of Hiriga, bound him to four stakes, and kindled a fire beneath him. He was preserved, even in this extremity, by the compassionate entreaties and persuasions of a daughter of the chief. His burns having been healed, he was deputed to keep watch over the temple where the bodies

The Indians of Florida showed a great degree of resolution and desperate valor, in defending their homes against the murderous Spaniards. Unappalled by the terrible execution of the unknown weapons of their enemies, who, mounted upon horses (hitherto unknown in the country) and clad in defensive armor, presented a novel spectacle to their wondering eyes, they disputed the invaded territory inch by inch.

Pamphilo de Narvaez, in April 1528, with a commission from Charles the Fifth to conquer and take possession, landed four hundred men and forty or fifty horses at East Florida. Penetrating the wilderness, they crossed the country to Appalache. Finding no gold, and but little provision at this town, from which they drove out the inhabitants, the Spaniards shaped their course toward Aute, only to find it burned and deserted by its inhabitants. Many of the party having already perished, the rest, hopeless of making further progress by land, set to work to construct boats in which they might reach a port of safety. With singular ingenuity they prepared tools from the iron of their accoutrements; and, with no further materials than were furnished by the productions of the forest, and the manes, tails, and skins of their horses, five small boats were built. They embarked and set sail, but nearly all perished, either by famine or by the dangers of the sea. Only a handful of the number were ever heard from, among whom was Alvar Funez Cabeza de Vaca. With only four companions he kept on his course to the West, and, after years of peril, reached the Spanish settlements of Mexico.

The next Spanish expedition to Florida was that of Fernando de Soto, who with seven ships of his own providing, and accompanied by from six hundred to one thousand warlike and energetic adventurers, many of whom were of noble rank, he set sail, in April 1538. Upward of a year was spent, mostly upon the island of Cuba, before the fleet set sail for the Florida coast. In May 1539, the vessels came to anchor off Tampa Bay, and a large division of soldiers, both horse and foot, were landed. The Indians had taken the alarm, and, although the smoke of their fires had been seen from ship-board in various directions, all had fled from the district, or lay concealed in the thickets. Some skirmishes took place near the point of landing, and the Spaniards speedily pos-

CHAPTER II.

FIRST TROUBLES WITH WHITE MEN—FLORIDA INDIANS.

Little is known of the history of American Indians previous to the discoveries by Spaniards. It was unfortunate that these early voyagers were mostly hard-hearted men. In almost every instance of first contact with the aborigines deeds of violence were unnecessarily committed by the invaders. If they did not kill, they generally managed to entice a few of them aboard their ships, and conveyed them to Europe as vouchers of the truth of their reports. Columbus, on his first voyage in 1492, carried away a number of natives to Spain. Only seven survived the sea voyage, and these were presented to King Ferdinand. The blood of several Indians was shed by Columbus' crew. Sebastian Cabot gave three Newfoundlanders to Henry VII. In 1508 the French discovered the St. Lawrence and on their return carried off several Indians to Paris.

The adventures of Spaniards with the Indians of Florida are among the earliest, chronologically, and are very thrilling in interest. Juan Ponce de Leon, governor of Porto Rico, was led by Indian fables in 1512 to search the low islands of the coast for a fountain that should bestow perpetual youth. All of North America, to the northward and eastward of Mexico, went by the name of Florida, before English settlements were made upon the coast. Failing in his first search, Leon undertook a second expedition into the unknown world, in hopes of finding mines of the precious metals, but was killed in a fight with the natives.

The perfidious Luke Valasquez de Ayllon, in 1518, visited Florida, to procure gold and slaves. The kindly natives, whom he tempted on board, were shut under hatches, and conveyed to Cuba. Returning again to the country, he and his party were justly punished for their treachery, nearly all of them being slain by the inhabitants, who, mindful of former injuries, rose upon them unawares. Those who had been carried into servitude mostly perished, by voluntary starvation, grief and despair.

tions of the shell being much the most **valuable**. The great labor in preparing it was the boring, **which was** effected by a sharp flint. When we consider the **slow nature of** such a process, **we can scarcely** credit the accounts **given of the** immense quantities of wampum that were procured by the white colonists, while it retained its value in exchange for European commodities, or which were exacted as **tribute**, in atonement for national offences. With this "wompompeague" they paid tribute, redeemed captives, satisfied for murders and other wrongs, purchased peace with their potent neighbors, as occasion required; **in a word**, it answered on all occasions, with them, as gold **and silver** doth with us. They delighted much **in having and using** knives, combs, scissors, hatchets, hoes, guns, needles, awls, looking-glasses and such like necessaries which they purchased of the English **and** Dutch with their "**peague**," and then sold them their peltry **for** their "wompeague."

The principal articles of food used by the aborigines were **the** products of the chase, fish, beans, some species of squashes **and** pumpkins, and maize or Indian Corn. Wild rice, growing **in rich** wet land in the interior of the country, furnished a wholesome and easily gathered supply of farinaceous food to the tribes of the temperate portion of the United States. Shell fish were a very important addition to the resources of those who dwelt near the sea-coast, and in the interior, various species of wild roots, and certain nutritious bark supplied the failure of the cultivated crop, and furnished the means to eke out a subsistence when the hunt was unsuccessful or the last year's stores had been consumed before the season of harvest. The use of milk was entirely unknown to the Indians until the white man taught them its value.

as to effectually **resist wind and** weather, however stormy and cold.

Some of these wigwams **were of** great **size, being from fifty** to a hundred **feet** in length, **but** the generality **were** of dimensions suitable **to a** single family. **Their** bedding consisted of mattresses disposed in bunks attached to the **walls,** or upon low movable couches. Bear **and** deer skins furnished additional covering. Their other **furniture and** household utensils were simple in the extreme. Clay or earthern **pots,** wooden platters, bowls and spoons, and pails ingeniously **fashioned** of birch bark, served their purpose for cookery and **the table.** They were skilled in basket-making.

In many of their towns and villages, **the** wigwams were **set in** orderly rows, with an open space **or** court near the **centre; while the** whole was surrounded by a strong palisade, having but **one or** two narrow entrances.

The **clothing of the** Indians consisted mostly of skins, dressed **with no little skill.** Leggins of deer skins, with a hand's **breadth of the material** hanging loose at the side seam, and often **highly** ornamented with fringe and embroidery; moccasins of buck, **elk, or** buffalo skin; and a garment of various fashion, from a simple cincture about the loins, **to a** warm and ornamental mantle **or** coat, completed the **equipment** of the **men.**

The women wore a short frock, reaching to the knees; **their** covering **for the** legs and feet was similar to that worn by the men. Ornamental mantles, covered with neatly arranged feathers, were in vogue. Colored porcupine quills were in general **use,** both for stitching and ornamenting the clothing and other equipments.

A **fondness** for gay colors and gaudy decorations **was conspicuous** in all the tribes. From pocone **and other roots** a **brilliant red** paint **or** dye was prepared, with which and other pigments, **as charcoal,** earths, and extracts from the barks of certain trees, they painted their bodies, either to make a terrible impression on their enemies, or simply to bedeck themselves in becoming manner in the eyes of their friends. The usual savage custom of wearing pendants at the ears was common.

The **"qua-hog" or** round **clam** furnished **the** principal

he would undergo the extremes of toil, exposure, hunger and privation, was marvelous.

Our museums throughout the country teem with specimens of the primitive instruments used by Indians for offence or defence. Arrow heads were made of triangular bits of wrought flint, quartz, or other stone. Larger pieces of the same material served for lances and tomahawks. How the arrow and lance heads could have been attached with any degree of firmness to the wood, seems almost incomprehensible. A species of glue assisted in accomplishing this object, but the shank or portion of the stone that entered the wood is in some of the specimens so short and ill defined that it seems impossible that it should have been held firm in its place by such means. A handle was commonly affixed to the "tom-hog" or tomahawk by inserting it in a split sapling, and waiting for the wood to grow firmly around it, after which, it was cut off at the requisite length.

The Indian bow was shorter than that formerly used in England, and was so stiff as to require great strength or skill to bend it. It became a much more effective weapon after the introduction of steel or iron arrow-heads. Clubs, sometimes studded with flints, with the bow and tomahawk, constituted the principal weapons of the race. Daggers of flint or bone, and shields of buffalo-hide, were in use among some of the Western tribes.

The habitations and clothing of the Indians varied greatly with the temperature of the climate. In the warm regions of the South, a slight covering proved sufficient, while to resist the severity of a New England winter very efficient precautions were taken. The usual manner of building their wigwams was by fixing a row of poles firmly in the ground in the form of a circle, and then bending and confining the tops together in the centre. A hole was left for the smoke of the fire to escape, at the top of the cabin; every other part being warmly and closely covered with matting. A tight screen hung over the doorway, which was raised when any one entered, and then allowed to fall into its place.

A species of matting was prepared by peeling the bark from trees, and subjecting it, packed in layers, to a heavy pressure. With this material, or with mats woven from rushes, etc., the walls of the huts were so closely thatched,

al familiarity with scenes like those witnessed at the execution of a prisoner by the American savages, they would experience no horror at the sight. We need not seek further than the history of religious and political persecutions in Europe, or the cruelties practise l on reputed witches in our own country, to satisfy us that the character of the Indians will suffer little by comparison with that of their contemporaries of our own race.

Among some of those nations which included an extensive confederacy, where a system of government had become settled by usage, and the authority of the chief had been strengthened by lon gsubmission to him and his predecessors, an arbitrary monarchy seems to have prevailed; but among the smaller tribes, the authority of the chief was rather advisory than absolute. There was generally a king who held hereditary offices, and exercised the powers of a civil governor by virtue of his descent, while to lead the warriors in battle, the bravest, most redoubted and sagacious of the tribe was elected. These two chief offices were not unfrequently united in the same person, when the lawful sachem, from a spirit of emulation or from natural advantages, showed himself worthy of the position.

All matters of national interest were discussed at a solemn council, consisting of the principal men of the tribe, and at which great decorum and formality were observed. As the debate proceeded, the whole conclave, whenever a remark from the orator speaking excited their approbation, would give expression to their approval by a guttural ejaculation.

A natural instinct of retributive justice ordained that the crime of murder should be punished by the hand of the deceased person's nearest relative.

The institution of marriage among the American Indians in their palmy days was by no means so restrictive a system as that adopted by enlightened nations. It was for the most part dissoluble at the pleasure of the parties, and polygamy was extensively practiced. As with other barbarous nations the woman was compelled to undergo the drudgery of daily labor, while her lord and master lounged indolently about the village, except at times when his energies were called forth for hunting or war. When once engaged in these pur

premature or excessive **labor, but** their erect posture and slender figure give them the appearance of a tall race. Their limbs are well formed, but calculated rather for agility than strength, **in** which **they** rarely equal the more **vigorous** of European nations. **They** generally have small feet.

The most distinguishing peculiarities **of** the race **are the** reddish or copper color **of** the skin; the prominence of the **cheek-bone;** and the **color** and quality of the hair. This is not absolutely straight, **but** somewhat **wavy, and** has **not inaptly** been compared to the mane of the **horse**—less from its coarseness than from its glossy hue and **the** manner in which it **hangs.** Their eyes are universally dark. The women are rather short, with broader faces, and **a greater** tendency to obesity than the men, **but** many **of them** possess a symmetrical figure, with an agreeable **and** attractive countenance.

It was formerly quite a general **impression** that the Indians were destitute of beards. This error resulted from the almost universal custom prevalent among them of eradicating what they esteemed a deformity. Tweezers, made of **wood** or muscle-shells, served to pluck out the hairs as **soon as** they appeared; and, after intercourse with the whites **commenced,** a coil of spiral wire was applied to the same **use.** It was esteemed greatly becoming among **the men to** carry **this** operation still further, and to lay bare **the whole** head, with the exception of a top-knot, **or** ridge like **the comb** of a cock, in which feathers or porcupine quills **were** fantastically interwoven.

The Indians are naturally taciturn, but fond of set speeches. Their oratory is of **no** mean **order,** and is distinguished for a pithiness, a quaintness, and occasionally a vein **of dry** sarcasm, which have never been surpassed. The most pleasing traits in the character of these **strange** people are their reverence for **age,** their affection **for** their children, their high notions of honor, and their **keen** sense of justice. The great stigma upon the whole race **is** their deliberate and systematic cruelty in the treatment **of** captives. **It is hard** to account for this, **but it** really appears, upon **investigation,** to be rather a national custom, gradually reaching a climax, than to have arisen from any innate love of inflicting pain. It is perfectly **certain that,** if the children of the most en-

inal people, or most likely two aboriginal peoples, had existed in what is now the United States for an indefinite period extending over many hundreds and perhaps thousands of years. The colonists of this country found the native Indians divided into numerous tribes, speaking different dialects. East of the Mississippi, the chief of these, with their probable number about A. D. 1650 were: the Algonquin tribes, 90,000; the Sioux or Dakotas, 3,000; the Huron Iroquois, 17,000; Catawbas, 3,000; Cherokees, 12,000; Uchees 1,000; Natchez, 4,000; and Mobilians, 50,000—about 180,000 all told.

The Indians, before receiving instruction concerning the white man's God, generally believed in the existence of a Supreme Deity, embodying a principle of universal benevolence, and that to him their gratitude was due for all natural benefits. On the other hand, they stood in fear of a spirit of evil, whose influence upon human affairs they considered as being more direct and familiar. To this being, known among many tribes as Hobamocko, much more assiduous devotion was paid than to the Great Spirit, it being far more essential in their view to deprecate the wrath of a terrible enemy, than to seek the favor of one already perfectly well disposed toward his creatures. Beside these two superior deities, a sort of fanciful mythology invested every notable object with its tutelary divinity, and bestowed on each individual his guardian spirit. A general idea that the good would be rewarded, and the bad punished, was entertained. A pleasant land was fabled, in which the hunter, after death, should pursue his favorite employment, in the midst of abundance, and a stranger forever to want or fear. Their heaven was as far removed from the sensual paradise of the Mahometans, as from the pure abstractions of an enlightened religion. Ease, comfort, and a sufficiency for the natural wants, seemed all-sufficient to these simple children of nature, to render an eternity delightful.

The general appearance of a North America Indian can be given in few words; the resemblance between those of different tribes being full as close as between different nations of either of the great families into which the human race has been arbitrarily divided. They are about of the average height which man attains when his form is not cramped by

CHAPTER I.

ORIGIN OF NORTH AMERICAN INDIANS—THEIR CUSTOMS, RELIGION AND PECULIARITIES.

Perhaps the Indian, as far as color goes, has the clearest title of all the races of the earth as the lineal descendant of Adam, the first man, (whose name signified red dirt), God having chosen such material for his formation. This, however, is only speculation.

The native races of northern Asia and the Indians of America are classed as belonging to the same Mongoloid variety of the human race; but whether America was originally peopled from Asia, or Asia from America, is a problem which pre-historic research has not yet solved. The strongest proof that our Indians are from Asia is afforded by the fact that the nomadic tribes of Alaska are related to the Kamhatkans, who even now pass and repass Behring Straits. A tribe was found in Alaska who spoke the language of Kamhatka, and many tribes on both sides of the Straits were identical in manners and customs. Other similarities established were those of features and complexion; religion, dress and ornaments; marriages, methods of warfare, dances, sacrifices, funeral rites, festivals and beliefs concerning dreams; games, naming of children, dwellings and forms of government.

Columbus, when he touched land in 1492, believed he had reached India, and consequently he called the natives Indians. How long the Continent had been peopled before his discovery is unknown, but ancient remains, such as the mounds in the Mississippi valley, the pre-historic copper mines south of Lake Superior, and the shell-mounds (kitchen middings) along the sea coasts, attest the fact that an aborig-

The assertion that "truth is stranger than fiction" is again verified in this little volume, the contents of which have been collated from historical *facts* about Indians from time immemorial in America down to the present day—far surpassing the blood-curdling stories evolved from the imagination of sensational novel writers. All the bloody massacres and Indian wars with our aborigines are here succinctly transcribed for the benefit of those who have not the time or data or research, yet crave the exciting and horrible in literature. It is not the intention of the compiler to inflame the mind of Young America, or provide that kind of mental pabulum that creates a desire to go West to fight the Red Men. Hence he advises the putting away of all guns, for all the remaining savages in this country are now corraled on reservations under the eyes of Government soldiers, and there is small possibility of there ever being occasion again to record parallel Indian horrors with those here presented.

TALES OF THE RED SKINS:

AN

AUTHENTIC HISTORY OF THE AMERICAN INDIAN FROM 1492 TO THE PRESENT TIME.

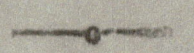

PUBLISHED BY A. D. PORTER,
NEW YORK
1895.

James N Bookstover

Indian massacres and tales of the red skins
An authentic history of the American Indian from 1492 to the present time

ISBN/EAN: 9783744748742

Printed in Europe, USA, Canada, Australia, Japan

Cover: Foto ©ninafisch / pixelio.de

More available books at **www.hansebooks.com**

CHAPTER IV.

NEW ENGLAND INDIANS—THE PURITANS AND THEIR THRILLING EXPERIENCES WITH RED MEN.

ON the 6th of September, 1620, the Mayflower, freighted with forty-one adventurous enthusiasts, sailed from Plymouth in England; and on the 9th of the following November arrived on the barren shores of Cape Cod. A few days afterward a reconnoitering party caught sight of a small number of the natives, who, however, fled at their approach. On the 8th of December, a slight and desultory action occurred, the Indians attempting to surprise the Pilgrims by night. They were, however, discomfited and compelled to retreat. On the 11th of December the little band landed, and fixed their first settlement at Plymouth.

In the month of March a peaceful communication was established with the natives, through the intervention of Samoset. He introduced Tisquantum, or Squanto, who was one of the twenty-four kidnapped by Thomas Hunt, **in 1614. By** his knowledge of the country and coast, and his acquaintance with their language, Squanto became of great service to the colonists, and continued their friend until his death in 1622, while he was on his passage down the coast for the purpose of purchasing corn and other necessaries. Much of romantic interest attaches to the history and adventures of this serviceable Indian, both during his captivity and after his restoration to his own country. Escaping by the assistance of certain kindly-disposed monks, from Spain, where he, with his companions, had been sold in slavery, he reached England, and was taken into the employment of a London merchant. He was brought back to Patuxet, the Indian name of the country in which the pilgrims first landed, by Captain Thomas Dermer, who sailed in the employ of Sir Ferdinando Gorges, during the summer preceding the arrival of the Mayflower. After his introduction by Samoset, he remained with his new allies, instructing them in the mode of raising corn and in the best **methods** of fishing. By the friendly influence of Squanto and Samoset, who acted as interpreters, a league of amity and mutual protection was affected between the colony and the powerful sachem Massasoit, father of the still more celebrated Philip.

In 1622, two ships were sent over from England by Thomas Weston, with a considerable number of colonists. A new settlement was formed by them on Massachusetts Bay, known as Weston's colony. They were mostly idle and improvident fellows who had much difficulty in obtaining anything to eat. It was charged against them that they once hanged an innocent and comparatively worthless member of the community in order to spare the life of an able-bodied man who had stolen some corn from the Indians and whose life the savages demanded.

In 1623, all the Indians of Eastern Massachusetts, excepting those under the immediate control of their faithful ally, Massasoit, made a league to extirpate the colony at Wessagusset and probably that at Plymouth also. The plot was betrayed by Massasoit, who sent Hobomok, rival interpreter of Squanto, to tell the Plymouth people of it. Captain Miles Standish, with eight men, set out for Wessagusset to crush this conspiracy by one terrible blow. In conjunction with Weston's men this little company overpowered the Indians, killing six of their number, among them Chief Wittawamet.

In April of 1637, an attack was made upon the village of Wethersfield, by a body of Pequots, assisted by other Indians of the vicinity, whose enmity had been excited by some unjust treatment on the part of the white inhabitants. Three women and six men of the colonists were killed and cattle and other property destroyed. Two young girls, daughters of Abraham Swain, were taken and carried into captivity. Their release was afterward obtained by some Dutch traders, who inveigled a number of Pequots on board their vessel, and threatened to throw them into the sea if the girls were not delivered up. During the time that these prisoners were in power of the Indians, they received no injury, but were treated with uniform kindness, a circumstance which, with many others of the same nature, marks the character of the barbarians as being by no means destitute of the finer feelings of humanity.

The settlers on the Connecticut now resolved upon active operations against the Pequot tribe. Although the whole number of whites upon the river, capable of doing military service, did not exceed three hundred, a force of ninety men was raised and equipped. Captain John Mason, a soldier by profession, and a brave one, was appointed to the command of the expedition.

The Pequot camp was upon the summit of a high rounded hill, still known as Pequot hill, in the present town of Groton, and was considered by the Indians as impregnable. The English, under Mason, resolved on a night attack upon the palisaded Pequots, who were sunk in sleep after a great feast and dance. The alarm was given by the barking of a dog, and the cry "Owannux, Owannux!" was raised, this being the Indian name for the English. Mason and his men rushed through the narrow brush-filled opening in the palisades and fell upon the Pequots with fury. Presently Mason resolved to fire the wigwams; the dry material caught like tinder and the flames held carnival everywhere. The Pequots fought desperately, but their bow-strings snapped from the heat and a general massacre ensued. About four hundred men, women and children were destroyed (most of them burned), with a loss of but two killed on the part of the English.

There are preserved some thrilling legends, more or less reliable, concerning the early warfare of the famous Iroquois, or Six Nations, whose sway at one time extended over what are now the Middle states, their principal seat being in the beautiful lake region of New York. The bands composing the Six Nations were the Oneidas, Cayugas, Onondagas, Mohawks, Senecas and Tuscaroras. No other American tribes ever produced so many renowned warriors and orators as the Iroquois. Their chief enemies were the Delawares, Appalachians and Cherokees. One of the Indian legends is to the effect that chief Piskaret of the Adirondacks started off alone into the enemy's country, using every precaution to avoid detection—reversing his snow-shoes and pursuing the most unfrequented routes. Upon reaching an Iroquois village he murdered and scalped for two successive nights; on the third a watch was set at every lodge. Piskaret knocked one of the watchmen on the head, and then fled, hotly pursued; but he was fleeter of foot than any man of his time, and, always managing to keep just in sight of his pursuers, he enticed them to a great distance from their village. At night, while they were asleep, overcome with fatigue, he murdered the entire number and bagged their scalps.

The principal settlements of the Delaware Indians lay between the Hudson and the Potomac. That these savages had many noble traits of character all the world knows through the prominence given to them by the treaty of William Penn, who came over in 1682. The grand treaty-council was held just above Philadelphia. The comparatively mild character of the Delawares may be judged by the esteem and veneration in which they held their famous chief, Tammany. This man was so beloved by both Indians and whites, that, after his death, he was actually canonized as St. Tammany. Throughout the Revolutionary War his day was celebrated with great respect, both by the army and civilians, until Jefferson's administration.

The fame of this great chief extended even among the whites. His festival was celebrated on the first day of May, at which time a numerous society of his votaries walked together in procession through the streets of Philadelphia (their hats decorated with bucks' tails), and proceeded to a handsome place out of town, which they called the wigwam, where, after a long talk, and the calumet of peace and friendship had been duly smoked, they passed the day in festivity and mirth. After dinner Indian dances were performed on the green in front of the wigwam; the calumet was again smoked and the company separated. Since that time Philadelphia, New York and other towns have had their Tammany societies. Tammany halls and the old relic of Indian greatness have degenerated into an organization for political purposes.

CHAPTER V.

KING PHILIP'S WAR—DESTRUCTION OF BROOKFIELD AND DEERFIELD
—SHOCKING BARBARITY.

The war of the New England colonies with King Philip was the most important as well as the most dangerou**s to** their existence of all the Indian contests in that part of the country. Philip was the son of the chief Massasoit, and succeeded his brother Alexander as leader of his tribe. Whatever were the motives which actuated him in the war of extermination (whether revenge for his brother's death or jealousy of the increasing power of the whites, it is certain that he had brooded over his plan in secret for years.

Long-continued and extensive negotiations were entered into by him with surrounding tribes. On the 24th of June, 1675, the first attack was made at Swanzey, when about eight or nine men were killed. The alarm was given to Boston, and a detachment of men sent out under Captains Henchman and Prentice. These united with the Plymouth **force** under Captain Benjamin Church and Major Cutworth. **They** took up their quarters in **a** house in Swanzey. After some skirmishing, the region was cleared of the Indians. One white was killed, and a Mr. Gill struck by **a ball** that would have proved fatal, but for a singular defensive armor, in the shape of **a quantity** of thick **brown** paper which he had inserted under his clothes.

Captain Church was a brave and energetic man, and figured prominently in **this** war. At the outbreak he was living as a solitary pioneer-colonist in the country. He was in the habit of taking Indian captives, **whom** he put through a sort of taming process by treating them **with** kindness and generosity. Thus, he soon had about him **a** devoted bodyguard of soldiers, who served him with the greatest enthusiasm.

On the 18th of July, 1675, the united forces of **the colonists** drove Philip with his warriors into **a swamp near Pocasset**. After some skirmishing the whites withdrew. It **was said** that a vigorous attack here might have ended the war.

The story of the destruction of Brookfield by the Nipmucks

is a thrilling one. The terrified inhabitants of this village had collected in a single house that stood upon a rising knoll of ground. They had fortified their place of refuge as well as they were able by piling logs and hanging feather beds against the walls. The troops under Wheeler and Hutchinson (who had come here for the purpose of a treaty, but had, instead, been treacherously fired upon) also entered this house, which was then closely besieged by the Indians, who shot burning arrows upon the roof, and, attaching rags dipped in brimstone to long poles, fired them and thrust them against the walls.

From Monday, the 2nd of August, till Wednesday evening these attempts continued. Finally, they filled a cart with combustible materials, and, attaching long sets of poles to it, so that it could be operated from a distance, they sent it forward blazing against the building. But a timely shower of rain extinguished the flames and saved the besieged whites. Assistance reached them that night. Major Willard, with forty-six men, effected an entrance into the house, and the Indians retired, after the destruction of a large part of the town.

In this war the Narragansetts, the old friends of the English, had remained neutral, or had at least pretended to do so. But, on what seems insufficient grounds, the colonists resolved to wage war against them, it being alleged that they had aided and abbetted the enemy. Accordingly, a very large body of English under command of Josias Winslow, governor of the colony of Plymouth (Church also taking part), moved down upon the Narragansetts in the middle of the winter. A guide was found who piloted them to the chief fort of the enemy, which was situated on an island in the midst of a large swamp.

The entire village was surrounded by a strong palisade, and the only means of approach was by crossing the marsh upon an immense fallen tree. File after file of soldiers was swept from this narrow bridge by the fire of the Indians. At last an entrance was effected. Church, who had been wounded, tried to dissuade the general from firing the wigwams, since on such a bitterly cold night they would need their shelter and warmth themselves, the nearest refuge from the snow-storm which was impending being some sixteen miles distant. But his advice was unheeded and a terrible scene ensued.

Large numbers of old men, women and children were burned alive in their huts. The colonists lost eighty killed and one hundred and fifty wounded. Beside the unnumbered wretches who perished in the huts by the flames, it is supposed that about five hundred warriors were killed and seven hundred wounded.

Upon one occasion the English permitted a young Narragansett captive to be tortured to death by their Indian allies, partly that they might not displease these confederates, and also that they might have ocular demonstration of savage cruelty. The victim had killed and scalped many Englishmen, as he acknowledged, and they thought fit to let him suffer, although the sight brought tears to their eyes. The Mohegans cut round the joints of his fingers and toes successively, and then broke them off. They compelled him to dance and sing in this condition until he had wearied both himself and them, and then broke his legs. Sinking in silence on the ground, he sat till they finished his miseries by a blow.

The capture of Philip and the close of the war was in the month of August, 1676. Church was worn out with hard service, but, at the urgent request of the government, consented to pursue Philip to the death. With a company of men he marched to Pocasset, and then made a flying trip to Rhode Island to visit his wife, who fainted with joy at seeing him alive.

But scarcely had the first greeting been given, when a messenger brought word that Philip was at his old quarters at Mount Hope Neck. Church, bidding his wife good-bye, immediately mounted his horse that he had just left at the door, and set off at full speed. The king, dejected in spirits and reduced to the utmost straits, was encamped upon a spot of dry land in the swamp. Church distributed a portion of his force so as to command the avenues of escape; the remainder he ordered to beat up Philip's head-quarters. The Indians, startled by the first fire of the guns, rushed into the swamp. Philip passed within easy shooting range of two of the attacking party—an Englishman and an Indian; the gun of the former snapped; but the latter shot the king through the heart as, half naked and flinging his accoutrements behind him, he advanced at full speed. His body was quartered and insulted; his hand was given to Alderman, the Indian who shot him; and the head was long exposed at Plymouth, where grim and harsh old Mather says exultingly that he with his own hand displaced the jaw from the skull of "that blasphemous leviathan."

Annawan, Philips bravest chief, escaped the massacre, but was pursued by Church to Rhode Island. He was tracked to Squannaconk Swamp, in the southeastern part of Rehoboth, an old Indian having turned traitor and piloted the English to his lair, which they found to be on a ledge of steep rocks which stood over the marsh. The only way to approach it was by climbing down from above.

It was night when Church arrived there; stopping the guide with his hand, he crawled to the edge of the rock and looked down upon the scene below. Annawan's hut consisted of a tree felled against the wall of rock, with birch bushes piled up against it. Fires were lit without, over which meat was roasting and kettles were boiling, and the light revealed several companies of the enemy. Their arms were stacked together and covered with a mat. In close proximity to them lay old Annawan and his son; an aged squaw was pounding corn in a mortar, and, as the noise of her blows continued, Church, preceeded by the guide and his daughter, and followed by his Indian allies, let himself down by the bushes and twigs which grew in the crevices of the rocks. With his hatchet in his hand he stepped over the young Annawan, who drew himself into a heap with his blanket over his head, and reached the guns. The old chief sat up, crying out "Howoh!" but, seeing he was taken, lay down again in silence. All submitted. Annawan ordered his women to prepare supper for Church and his men, and they supped together harmoniously. Then all fell asleep, except the leaders, who lay looking at each other for nearly an hour; when Annawan arose and brought the regalia of Philip, which he presented on his knees to Church, saying: "Great captain, you have killed Philip and conquered his country; for I believe that I and my company are the last that war against the English. The war is ended by your means. These things belong to you."

He then handed him two broad belts richly worked in wampum, one of which, fringed with red hair from the Mohawks' country, reached from the shoulders nearly to the ground. He also gave him two horns of powder and a red cloth blanket. He said that Philip was accustomed to ornament his person with this regalia upon state occasions.

The chief facts of this long and eventful conflict with Philip are thus summarized by Baylies: "In this war, which lasted but little more than a year and a half, six hundred Englishmen were killed; thirteen towns in Massachusetts, Plymouth and Rhode Island were destroyed, and almost every family had lost a relative; six hundred dwellings had been burned; a vast amount in goods and cattle had been destroyed, and a great debt created. But the result of the contest was decisive; the enemy was extinct, the fertile wilderness was opened and the rapid extension of settlements evinced the growing prosperity of New England."

Up to the time of Philip's war the people of Maine and New Hampshire had but little to complain of in the conduct of the Indians of their country. But after the date of the opening of hostilities in 1675 they were of course continually under suspicion; in fact, from that time there were many uprisings and massacres in these two colonies. Captain Church was sent against them, and he waged the war with his usual energy and more than his accustomed cruelty. In the summer of 1689 the Indians made an attack on Dover, where Major Waldron was in command with a considerable force. The savages were burning to avenge a wanton insult and injury inflicted upon them, the major having kidnapped and sent to Boston two hundred Indians, of whom eight or ten were hanged and and the rest sold as slaves. The attack was made at night. Two old squaws, having obtained permission to sleep in the garrisoned houses, arose at night and unbarred the doors, when the savages rushed in and completely overpowered the troops, among the captives being Major Waldron. Although eighty years of age, he defended himself with desperate bravery, but was finally struck down by a blow from behind. Bruised and mangled, he was placed in a chair on a table, and the savages gathered round glutted their long-cherished hatred by torturing him.

One of their charges against him was that he had cheated

them in trading transactions. It was reported among them that he used to estimate the weight of his fist to be a pound; also, that his accounts were not crossed out according to agreement. As they gashed his naked breast, each said, "I cross out my account." They would then cut a joint from his finger, with the question: "Wi'l your fist weigh a pound now?" These fiendish barbarities continued until he fainted from loss of blood, when he was placed out of misery for ever.

In January, 1699, the war with the French being over, the Indians of Maine and New Hampshire concluded a treaty with the colonies. But in May, 1702, war was again declared, and all the old difficulties broke out again with renewed bitterness. One of the most famous episodes of the wars with these Northeastern Indians was Lovewell's fight. The engagement took place near Saco Pond, in Maine, the Indian in command being Pangus, chief of the Pequawkets. His men numbered eighty, while Lovewell had but thirty-four.

The cruel and barbarous murders committed by the Indians in these regions had indused the general court of Massachusetts to offer a bounty of five hundred dollars for each Indian's scalp brought in. Lovewell, with forty men, coming upon a small body of Indians sleeping round their fires, killed and scalped all of them; then, with their trophies mounted on hoops, they marched in triumph to Boston and received five thousand dollars.

Lovewell left Dunstable on the 16th of April, 1725. Early on the following morning, while at prayers, they heard the report of a gun. Leaving their packs, they pressed forward to meet the Indians. Pangus discovered the packs, and thereby learning the inferior strength of the enemy, boldly advanced and provoked battle. On the morning of the 8th, Ensign Wyman discovered an Indian who was returning from a hunt, having in one hand some fowls which he had killed, and in the other two guns. Perceiving that his hour had come, he levelled a gun at Captain Lovewell and mortally wounded him, though he did not immediately fall, but was able to lead his men in the second engagement, which occurred soon after when they had returned to the place where they had left their packs. Here the Indians fell upon them from an ambuscade. They held up ropes and asked the English if they would surrender; they replied by charging and firing, thus **driving** back the savages, who, however, soon rallied and, in turn, forced the English to retreat. Lovewell now fell. The fight continued obstinately until night, the Indians howling, yelling and barking like dogs, **and the** English cheering each other with huzzas. Pangus, chief of the red men, and Powan, another chief, were slain. Fourteen of the English escaped from the battle ground at midnight, and, although fifty miles from any settlement, succeeded in reaching their friends.

One Solomon Keyes, who had received three wounds from the Indians, had a remarkable escape. **Thi**nking to crawl away and die in some spot where the Indians could not scalp him, he crept along the shore of the pond and found a canoe, into which he rolled himself **and** was floated away by the **wind.** To his amazement, he found that during the night he had **been** drifted to within a short distance of the fort called Ossipee, which Lovewell's men had built as a refuge. Here he found a few companions, and, eventually recovering from his wounds, returned home with them.

Another sadly memorable event of the wars of the northern New England settlers with the Indians was the destruction of Deerfield in Massachusetts, which event formed part of a deep-laid plan of the Canadian French and the Indians for laying waste the entire frontier. The scheme was, however, but partially successful. Deerfield had been palisaded and **t**wenty soldiers quartered there in different houses. But **these** guards forgot their duty. The snow afforded easy access over the fortifications to the town, and the conquest of the place was made with the greatest ease.

The story is given in the words of the Rev. John Williams: "On Tuesday, the 29th of February, 1703-4, not long before break of day, the enemy came in like a flood upon us, our watch being unfaithful—an evil whose awful effects, in the surprisal of our fort, should bespeak all watchmen to avoid, if they would not bring the charge of blood upon themselves. They came to my house in the beginning of the onset, and by their violent endeavors to break open doors and windows with axes and hatchets awakened me out of sleep; on which I leaped out of bed, and, running toward the door, perceived the enemy making their entrance into the house. I called to awaken two soldiers in the chamber, and, returning toward my bedside for my arms, the enemy immediately brake into my room, I judge to the number of twenty, with painted faces and hideous acclamations. I reached up my hands to the bed-tester for my pistol, uttering a short petition to God, expecting a present passage through the valley of the shadow of death. Taking down my pistol, I cocked it and put it to the breast of the first Indian who came up, but my pistol missed fire. I was seized by three Indians, who disarmed me and bound me, naked as I was, in my shirt, and so I stood for near the space of an hour."

In the mean time the work of destruction went on. Forty-seven person were killed, and the entire town burned, with the exception of one house, which stood next to Mr. Williams', and in which seven men withstood the entire force of three hundred French and Indians. Mr. Williams continues: "About sun an hour high we were all carried out of the house for a march, and I saw many of the houses of my neighbors in flames, perceiving the whole fort, one house excepted, to be taken. We were carried over the river to the foot of the mountain, about a mile from my house, where we found a great number of our neighbors, men, women and children, to the number of one hundred, nineteen of whom were afterward murdered by the way and two starved to death near Coos in a time of great scarcity or famine the savages underwent there. When we came to the foot of our mountain they took away our shoes and gave us Indian shoes to prepare us for our journey."

At this point a few English who had escaped, and a few from Hatfield, attacked the Indians and pressed them hard —so much so that the French leader sent a command to have the captives slain. Luckily, however, the messenger was killed on the way.

They now commenced a journey of three hundred miles through a trackless wilderness, consuming forty days in its accomplishment. Boughs of trees formed the only beds of women and little children; the latter were, in general, treated well, probably because they desired to obtain ransom for them. At the first encampment some of the Indians became intoxicated, and in their fury killed Mr. Williams' man.

On the second day's march occurred the death of Mrs. Williams. On the occasion of the capture in Deerfield, she received a terrible shock through the murder of two of her children at her own door, together with a black woman belonging to the family. At the upper part of Deerfield meadow it became necessary to cross Green river. The Indian who captured Mr. Williams was unwilling that he should speak to the other captives; but on the second day he had another master, who allowed him both to speak to his wife and to help her along. This was their last meeting; she very calmly told him that she was dying.

Having now reached the river, and Mr. Williams' old master returning, the two were separated. In crossing the stream, which was very rapid and about two feet deep, Mrs. Williams became thoroughly wet by falling down. Her husband learned this and other subsequent facts concerning her from others, he himself being farther on in the van. Directly after she had emerged from the water she felt unable to proceed, and the wretch whose captive she was slew her with one stroke of his hatchet.

Others were killed and many died from exposure. It was debated whether they should not take the life of Mr. Williams also, but his master prevailed upon them not to do so. A young woman who was unable to proceed without continually falling down, was told by her master that she must die. She obtained leave to talk a few moments with her minister, Mr. Williams, and, then returning, was executed.

In 1706 fifty-seven of these Deerfield people were sent in a flag-ship to Boston, but many never left Canada. The Jesuits made strenuous endeavors to convert Mr. Williams and others; their efforts were successful with his daughter Eunice, who afterward married an Indian (by whom she had several children), and passed her life in a wigwam. After her marriage, dressed in the Indian garb, she visited her friends at Deerfield, and was kindly received by them, but all attempts to regain her proved unavailing.

CHAPTER VI.

WAR WITH THE SIX NATIONS.—HORRIBLE MASSACRES AND TORTURES.

The colonial wars with the Iroquois, or Six Nations, were numerous and bloody. The principal Indian leaders were Shingis and Captain Jacobs, whose head-quarters were at Kittanning, on the Allegheny river. In 1756, Colonel John Armstrong, with three hundred men, proceeded against them, the attack beginning on the 8th of September. The savages fought desperately in their log cabins, and when told that they would be burned if they did not surrender, one of them replied that he did not care, as he could kill four or five before he died. As the fire approached them, some began to sing, while others, darting from the flames, were shot. Captain Jacobs was killed. Shingis was reputed to be one of the most famous, daring and cruel warriors of his time. He was a terror to the whole frontier of Pennsylvania.

One of the great conflicts of this epoch occurred in 1775 at Lake George, between the French and Indians, under General Dieskau, and the English, under General William Johnson (superintendent of Indian affairs in America) and the brave Mohawk chief, Hendrick. After a stubborn fight the French were defeated. General Dieskau was found wounded and leaning against a stump for support. Supposing that his captors wanted plunder, he put his hand in his pocket to draw out his watch; but one of the soldiers, mistaking it for a movement to secure his pistol, shot him again in the hips. He lived to reach England, but died soon afterward. It is related that, before the battle, upon General Johnson consulting the opinion of Hendrick upon the advisability of detaching a certain portion of his force, and asking him if he thought the number sufficient, he replied: "If they are to fight, they are too few; if they are to be killed, they are too many." Hendrick was killed in the engagement.

One of the noblest chiefs of the Iroquois, the most magnanimous and friendly Indian of the times, was the famous Logan. He took no part in the French wars of 1760, except to act as peace-maker. It was the murder of members of his family that roused his fury against the whites, the circumstances of this brutal outrage being as follows: In the spring of 1774 some Englishmen were exploring lands about Wheeling, Ohio, for the purpose of settling there. The Indians were said, or thought, to have robbed them; the land-jobbers, regarding this as a demonstration of hostility, and learning that there were two savages on the river above, sent against them Captain Michael Cresap, who succeeded in killing them, and directly afterward several more, among whom were members of the family of Logan.

In a short time from this another brutal murder occurred, by which Logan lost a brother and sister. Two wretches near Wheeling, named Greathouse and Tomlinson, with thirty others, resolved to massacre a party of Indians who were assembled on the opposite shore of the Ohio river, and bent on revenge for the murder of their two friends. Greathouse, enticing a part of them to drink rum with him at his house across the stream, murdered them all in his house after they had become considerably intoxicated. The remaining **savages**, hearing of the slaughter of their friends, sent over **two** canoes manned with warriors; but being fired **into by an** ambushed party of the whites, they were obliged to retreat and seek a place of safety.

After an ominous lull, Logan, with eight followers, suddenly appeared on the Muskingum, where he was least expected, and, attacking some men who were at work in a field, killed one and took two prisoners. Nothing could possibly show **the** humanity and gentleness of Logan more than his kind treatment of one of these men, notwithstanding the deep and terrible injuries which he had received at the hands of the English. He not only instructed the prisoner, whose name was Robinson, how to run the gauntlet with the least possible harm, but, when he was tied to the stake to be burned, **cut** the cords that bound him, and afterward had him adopted into an Indian family. This man subsequently became Logan's scribe.

Other tribes now joined in the war. The **Shawnese** took the field under their famous chief Cornstalk and the Delawares also assisted, being justly provoked by the cold-blooded murder of their inoffensive old chief, Bald Eagle. This old man was accustomed to wander **up** and down among the whites, visiting at those houses where he was best entertained. As he was ascending the Kanawha alone in his canoe one day, he was foully murdered by a man who had suffered many wrongs from the Indians. Placing the aged chief upright in his canoe, he let it drift down the river with the current. For a long time no one suspected that he was dead; but when at last the deed was discovered, the most fierce resentment dwelt in the breasts of his tribe.

When the news of the breaking out of hostilities was received the Virginia legislature was in session. Governor Dunmore at once issued orders for the assembling of three thousand men, one half of whom were to march for the mouth of the Great Kanawha, under the command of General Andrew Lewis; and the remainder, under the governor in person, were to proceed to some point on the Ohio above the former, in order to fall upon the Indian towns between while the warriors should be drawn off by the approach of Lewis in the opposite direction. He was then to pass down the Ohio and form a junction with General Lewis at Point Pleasant, whence they were to march according to circumstances.

On the 11th of September the forces under General Lewis, amounting to eleven hundred men, commenced their march from Camp Union for Point Pleasant on the Great Kanawha, distant one hundred and sixty miles. The country between was a trackless wilderness; the army was piloted by Captain Matthew Arbuckle; all the baggage was transported by pack-horses, and the expedition consumed nineteen days on the march.

Before General Lewis could learn the whereabouts of Governor Dunmore, he was attacked by a large force of the Indians, and the famous battle of Point Pleasant was fought. The savages were said to cover four acres of ground as closely as they could stand side by side.

The general, upon learning of the approach of the enemy, gave orders to his brother, Colonel Charles Lewis, to advance with two regiments and reconnoitre. The foe was soon encountered; the colonel was mortally wounded, and his regiment driven back; but another coming up, the Indians were forced to retreat behind a breastwork of logs and brush which they had constructed. They had chosen their ground well, and, in the event of a victory on their part, not an Englishman would have escaped from the narrow neck of ground on which the battle was waged. They had stationed men on both sides of the river to prevent any that might attempt flight by swimming from the apex of the triangle made by the confluence of the two rivers. The battle was obstinately contested. Colonel Fleming conducted himself with great bravery, notwithstanding he had received two balls through the left wrist.

The entire line of the Indian breastworks now became one blaze of fire, which lasted the rest of the day. Here the Indians under Logan, Cornstalk, Elinipsico, Red Eagle and other mighty chiefs of the tribes of the Shawanese, Delawares, Mingoes, Wyandots and Cayugas, amounting, as was supposed, to fifteen hundred warriors, fought as men will ever do for their country's wrongs with a bravery which could only be equalled.

At length the day was decided by three companies of the English getting in the rear of the Indians and rushing down upon them. They, supposing that reinforcements were at hand, at once fled across the Ohio and set out for their villages on the Scioto. A stratagem employed by the English in this fight was the holding out of a hat from behind a tree to be fired at, and dropping it at the first shot; when the Indian, running from his shelter to scalp his supposed victim, was easily picked off. The troops of Governor Dunmore marched to Chillicothe, where, much against the desire of the soldiers, a treaty with the Indians was entered into.

Not long after the treaty of Chillicothe, Logan was foully murdered as he was returning home from Detroit. Previous to his death he had forfeited his manhood by excessive drinking.

The great chief, Cornstalk, was barbarously killed in the fort at Point Pleasant, to which he had come for the purpose of notifying his white friends of the impending storm of war that was about to break upon them, and which he was unable to avert. His son, Elinipsico, prompted by deep filial affection, had traveled far to see him. (Cornstalk, Red Hawk and others had been detained in the fort as hostages after they had given their friendly warning.) On the day following the arrival of Elinipsico an Englishman was murdered by the Indians near at hand and the body was brought over to the fort; whereupon an infuriated band of men, with a certain Captain Hall at their head, cried out, "Let us kill the Indians in the fort!" As the murderers approached, Elinipsico discovered agitation, which, when Cornstalk saw, he said, "My son, the Great Spirit has seen fit that we die together, and has sent you to that end. It is his will, and let us submit." They shot him through with seven bullets. He fell and died without a struggle.

The colonial wars with Pontiac, chief of the Ottawa nation, in the region of the present Michigan and Wisconsin, also claim the attention of the reader. In 1760, Major Rogers marched into Pontiac's domain. He had always declared a willingness to have the English settle in his dominions, provided his rights as sovereign were respected; and it seems probable that the breaking out of the hostilities was due to the indiscreet treatment of him by the English.

Under the rule of this great chief were the Miamis, Ottawas, Chippewas, Wyandots, Pottawatomies, Mississagas, Shawanese, Ottagamies and Winnebagoes. He was a person of great intellect; as an instance of his superior understanding it may be mentioned that he issued bills of credit, all of which he afterward redeemed. They consisted of pieces of the inner bark of trees, on which was pictured the object which he wished to obtain. The government stamp, so to speak, was the figure of an otter drawn, under the article desired, on each piece of the bark; this animal was the escutcheon of his nation.

The first outbreak occurred at Fort Michillimackinac. Traders had several times warned commanding officer Etherington of the unfriendliness of the Indians; but he refused to listen to the stories, and threatened to send as a prisoner to Detroit the next man who should come to him with such false rumors. Gradually, the Indians assembled around the fort until their number amounted to four hundred; but slight attention was paid to them, however. On the 4th of June, which was the king's birthday, the savages began to play in front of the fort a game called *baggatiway*, similar to the national diversion in Canada called lacrosse. In the ardor of the sport, the ball was tossed over the pickets of the fort; this occurred several times, that suspicion might be averted. The last time, however, when a large body had rushed in after the ball, the word was given, and, dispersing rapidly in all directions, they took possession of the fort with scarcely any difficulty. Seventy of the garrison were killed and the remaining twenty retained as slaves.

Pontiac was the instigator of this affair; and indeed, in a few days after the massacre he was in possession of all the garrisons in the West except three. Detroit alone was cut off from assistance. The story of the narrow escape of this city is most thrilling. When Pontiac arrived with his braves he brought many women and children with him, as well as goods for traffic, for the purpose of quieting suspicion. Having encamped, he sent word to Major Gladwin that he wished to trade, but would first like to hold a council with him. Assent was given, and the next morning appointed for the meeting, no distrust having been aroused. The plot, however, was revealed by a squaw, who had made for Major Gladwin a pair of moccasins out of a curious elk skin. Being much pleased with them, he requested her to make another pair for him to present to a friend, and to keep what was left to convert into a pair of shoes for herself. She was then paid for her work and dismissed, but was afterward found loitering within the gates. Being asked what she wanted, she did not reply, and she was again summoned before the major, when, after much confusion and trepidation, she revealed the following plot for the massacre of the garrison on the morrow.

Each chief was to come to the council with such a piece cut from the end of his gun that it could be concealed under his blanket; also, as many as possible, armed in the same manner, were to enter outside, ostensibly for the purpose of trading. The woman was sent away and the news imparted to the men. In the morning all, being prepared, nervously awaited the hour for the meeting. At ten o'clock Pontiac appeared with thirty-six chiefs and a train of warriors. He observed, with some uneasiness, the unusual spectacle of troops marching from place to place, and some investing, or at least facing, the council-house, but was reassured upon being told that it was only parade. The council began by a speech from Pontiac. The signal for attack was known to be the presentation of a wampum peace belt to Major Gladwin in a certain manner. As Pontiac reached this part of his speech, and was about to offer the belt, the officers around the major half drew their swords from their scabbards, the soldiers clutched their guns more firmly, and the chiefs saw at once that they had been betrayed. Pontiac turned as pale as it is possible for an Indian to do, and the chiefs exchanged glances of the utmost astonishment. Pontiac, however, having regained his composure, finished his speech as though nothing had occurred. When Major Gladwin began his reply he at once charged the treachery upon Pontiac, who endeavored to excuse himself, but the major stepped quickly to the nearest chief, and, pulling aside his blanket, revealed the short gun. Of course nothing further could be said, and they were told to leave the fort instantly, as the soldiers could with difficulty be restrained from cutting them to pieces.

On the following day the Indians began a furious attack. They endeavored to set on fire the stockade, and in several places commenced to cut it with axes, so as to form a breach. Major Gladwin finally instructed the men not only to permit the opening to be made, but to assist them by cutting away on the inside. As soon as the passage was effected the Indians rushed forward to enter it; but at that moment a brass four-pounder was discharged at the opening from within, and made dreadful havoc among them. After this they contented themselves with blockading the fort.

There was much difficulty in relieving Detroit, owing to its great distance from the other extreme western forts. At length, on the 29th of July, 1763, Captain Dalyell arrived with succor. Shortly after, sallying forth with two hundred and forty-seven men, he was attacked by the Indians in ambush, and what is known as the battle of Bloody Bridge was fought. This engagement derived its name from the bridge where the attack was made. The main body of the English effected a retreat, but they left the bridge actually blocked up with their dead, showing the desperate character of the struggle.

It seemed almost impossible for any ship bringing aid to escape the detection of Pontiac. Upon one occasion a schooner laden with provisions appeared near the fort, and Pontiac determined to attempt its capture. The vessel

INDIAN MASSACRES. 45

tacked short about, followed by the canoes, the savages pertinacious as hornets, often coming so close to the vessel as to be severely burned by the powder from the guns. They had picked off nearly all the crew, and were at length clambering over the sides of the vessel and up the shrouds, when the captain, being determined not to fall into their hands alive, commanded the gunner to fire the magazine. A Huron chief, understanding a little English, overheard the order and communicated it to the rest, whereupon they precipitately fled the ship in the greatest alarm, and the remnant of the crew were then enabled to bring the vessel safely to the fort. This schooner had been sent from Niagara with a force of eighteen, twelve of whom were Mohawk Indians. So gratified was Major Gladwin by the bravery of the men in rescuing the garrison from the horrible and certain fate of starvation that he caused silver medals, descriptive of the event, to be struck and presented to each of the survivors.

The fame of these wars of Pontiac spread even to Europe. Finally, General Bradstreet, with three thousand men, took the field against him. Thereupon the chief sued for peace, which was granted, and he afterward became apparently a firm friend of the whites. The manner of his death is not certainly known.

CHAPTER VII.

HOSTILITIES ON THE FRONTIER.—RESCUE OF CAPTIVES.—THRILLING SCENES.

During hostilities at Fort Detroit, Fort **Pitt had** been closely besieged by Indians. After Pontiac abandoned the siege at the former place, it was decided by the English (in July, 1763) to send relief to Fort Pitt, which was situated on a point of land made by the junction of the Monongahela with the Ohio. Captain Ecuyer had suffered severely from the galling fire of the Indians, as well as from the great floods which had nearly destroyed the foundations of his fort. He was two hundred miles from any settlement, and could send no word of his danger. General Amherst appointed Colonel Henry Bouquet leader of the relief expedition, and the forces (consisting of about five hundred men) were to rendezvous at Carlisle, Pa. As soon as the Indians learned that the colonel was en route, they broke up the siege and resolved to waylay him. Accordingly, on the 4th of July, they made an attack from an ambuscade at a place called Bushy Run. The English, embarrassed by their convoy of horses laden with flour, were being much distressed and harassed by the savages when the night closed in and forced them to desist from fighting. But the same scene was again enacted, until Colonel Bouquet bethought him of a stratagem which undoubtedly was the means of saving his force from destruction. He feigned a retreat, and the Indians rushed forward into a circle prepared for them by sending one of the wings of the army around a hill where they were unperceived by the enemy, who, being now attacked on all sides, were completely vanquished. In this battle fifty whites and sixty Indians were killed. In a few days Colonel Bouquet arrived at Fort Pitt.

The next year, the depredations of the Indians upon the settlements continuing, it was resolved to send out a still larger force and awe the Indians into submission. Colonels Bradstreet and Bouquet were appointed to co-operate—the former proceeding by way of the great lakes and falling upon the rear of the Wyandots, Ottawas and Miamis, while

the latter set out from Carlisle with a force of fifteen hundred men. On reaching Fort Pitt, various conferences were held with the crafty redskins, who were thoroughly frightened and expressed a desire for peace, finding they had no trifler to deal with in the person of Colonel Bouquet, who, while stern and exacting, was magnanimous as well, and desirous of avoiding the shedding of blood.

He had been sent word by Bradstreet that he had concluded a peace with the Delawares and Shawanese; but Colonel Bouquet would place no reliance upon the good faith of the Indians, and told them so. He demanded of them, in the first place, to prove their sincerity by permitting to return to him in safety two messengers whom he was about to send to Colonel Bradstreet. In the meantime he moved on to Tuscarawas, and, finding here his messengers safely returned, he gave notice that he would hold a council with the chiefs.

At this meeting the Indians in the most abject manner sued for peace. The colonel dismissed them, saying that he would confer with them the next day. At the appointed time, after recounting to them all their outrages and treachery, he gave them twelve days in which to deliver up their captives. He demanded that all prisoners should be surrendered, "Englishmen, Frenchmen, women and children; whether adopted, married, or living among them under any denomination or pretence whatsoever; and to furnish horses, clothes and provisions to carry them to Fort Pitt." When these terms had been complied with they were to be informed of the conditions of peace.

Moving forward to the Forks of Muskingum, in what is now the state of Ohio, Colonel Bouquet caused houses to be built for the reception of the captives; and by the 9th of November two hundred and six had been delivered into his hands, of whom ninety were Virginians and one hundred and twenty-six Pennsylvanians, one hundred and twenty-five being women and children.

The meeting of the adult prisoners with their friends and relatives, many of whom were with the army, was a scene that beggars description. Of the children, many clung to their adopted Indian mothers, and at first refused to depart with their real parents. A number of the Indians declined to be separated from their white captives, and followed the army on its return to Philadelphia. Thus, having completely humbled the Indians and obtained their promise to send, in the spring, one hundred more captives who were off on distant hunting expeditions, hostages being taken to secure the faithful performance of this stipulation, Colonel Bouquet returned to Pennsylvania.

In the year 1782 was committed the diabolical murder of the inoffensive Christian Indians of Gnadenhuetten, Salem and Schonbrunn in Ohio. In February a party of Sandusky Indians had massacred a family consisting of a man, his wife and five or six children. The settlers on the Pennsylvania frontier concluded that either the Moravian Indians at Gnadenhuetten were the guilty parties, or that the murderers were quartered among them. Accordingly, organizing themselves into a band of eighty or ninety men, mounted and provisioned, they set out for Gnadenhuetten under the command of David Williamson. It should here be mentioned that these praying Indians, as they were called, had, the previous autumn, narrowly escaped destruction, having been carried off to Detroit by the notorious Captain Pike (an Indian) by command of the governor at that fort. However, since it was found impossible to prove any wrong against them, they had been released, and were now (the 6th of March) out in the fields gathering in the Indian corn which they had left in the fields the autumn previous when they were taken away.

The white guerillas informed them that it was their purpose to remove them to Fort Pitt for safety. Much pleased, they at once laid down their arms. Those at Salem were then summoned, and all were placed in guarded houses. Colonel Williamson, then drawing up his men in line, put the question whether the Indians should be taken prisoners to Fort Pitt or put to death, requesting those who favored the former movement to step forward and form a new line. Only sixteen or eighteen men are said to have advanced. The savages, in the meantime, having a presentiment of their fate, were praying, singing hymns and exhorting one another to remain firm. In a short time the two buildings were converted into slaughter houses, filled with the mangled and bleeding bodies of these innocent people—gray-haired men, women and tender children; none were spared the fatal wounds of the tomahawk, club, spear and scalping-knife, but two young lads who escaped by feigning death, and creeping unobserved into a cellar.

CHAPTER VIII.

REMINISCENCES OF DANIEL BOONE—HIS HAIR-BREADTH ESCAPES.

The exploits of Daniel Boone in Kentucky form one of the most interesting chapters in the history of Indian wars, both on account of his thrilling and romantic adventures in a land of enchanting beauty and fertility, and from the noble personal character of this hero. He was born in 1735 near Bristol, on the Delaware river. His ancestors were from Devonshire, England. Both his grandfather (George Boone) and his father (Squire Boone) had large families, and were characterized by a love of the freedom and advantages to be found in newly-settled lands. It was this roving and independent spirit that led George Boone to emigrate to America, and that influenced his son, Squire Boone, to remove from Pennsylvania to North Carolina. This characteristic was inherited in full by Daniel. He was eighteen years of age when his father went to their new home; and as early as 1764 he had visited the eastern border of Kentucky, which was not far from his dwelling-place on the banks of the Yadkin.

In 1767, John Findlay, with a companion, discovered and traversed the lonely region of Central Kentucky and Tennessee, and brought to the Carolina settlers glowing accounts of the country. Among his listeners was Boone, who was now married, and who, with his instinctive dislike of crowded settlements, had left his father and settled in a log cabin in the Yadkin Valley as its first resident. But already others were coming in, and he therefore listened eagerly to the description of the beautiful lands to the westward.

On the first of May, 1769, with a small company of comrades, Boone started on his first expedition into that region, which was hereafter to be the scene of actions that were to make him immortal. They found the country beautiful with flowers, green grass and pleasing prospects, and abounding with buffaloes and all varieties of game.

Near the Kentucky river, Boone and a friend named Stewart were taken captive by the Indians, but escaped on the seventh day. Daniel and his brother erected a small cabin, and remained here all winter, Stewart having been killed by the savages, and the remainder of the party having returned to Carolina. In May, Squire Boone set out alone to return to the settlements for the purpose of procuring two horses and ammunition, thus leaving Daniel alone and (as he says) without bread, **salt or sugar**; deprived of the company of his fellow-creatures, **or even** a horse or dog; alone in the **vast wilderness and five hundred miles from the nearest settlement**. For three months he continued his solitary existence, going on exploring expeditions, and often so fearful of the approach of the Indians that he dared not sleep in his cabin. **At length** his brother returned with the **horses, and the two explored** the region between the Cumberland and the Green **rivers**. When they again reached the Kentucky river they resolved to make their future home there.

After a time they revisited North Carolina, but **only** with the intention **to return and inherit this goodly land** which they had seen and admired. A company did actually start; but among the **mountains seven young men of their party, having strayed from the rest**, encountered the Indians, who killed six **of them, including one** of the sons of Boone. This so disheartened the little band that they turned aside to the **settlements** on Clinch river, in Virginia. During **the next year (1773-74)** Boone performed various services as guide and **explorer for** the Virginia government.

In the autumn of 1774 the singular Transylvania Company was formed. Eight private gentlemen, at the head of whom was Richard Henderson, conceived and carried out the bold scheme of purchasing from the Cherokee Indians a large **tract** of country in the West. A council was held, and the **red men** ceded to them all that region between the Kentucky and Cumberland rivers. With this remarkable self-constituted government Daniel Boone entered into relations, consenting to act as guide and leader of a small colony to be planted in the newly-purchased territory. This advance guard was to make a road through the wilderness, and Colonel Henderson would follow with pack mules and wagons. **When** within fifteen miles of the present Boonesborough the pioneers were attacked by **the** savages and four men were **killed**.

Upon reaching the banks of the Kentucky the first duty was to build a **fort, and this was accomplished** by Boone with his characteristic thoroughness. This structure subsequently became the great tower of defence for the young and struggling colony. It was a wonderful work for that time and place, and filled the Indians with alarm and dismay. The houses inside the enclosures appear to have been ranged along the pickets contiguously, in order to strengthen the defence. It was rather unfortunate that the clearing was no larger than the fort, as the woods would afford shelter to the enemy. In two months and a half the structure was completed, and was no doubt regarded with feelings of pride by all.

Boone now returned to North Carolina for his family, Mrs. Boone being the first woman to brave the perils of the wilderness. Colonel Henderson soon arrived with forty men; the clearing of land began and a land-office was opened. Soon there were four settlements and forts in the region, and in 1775 all the pioneers, in the capacity of a legislature, assembled in the open air at Boonesborough in response to a call to form a state! This was certainly the most extraordinary legislature that ever met. They, however, with the parliamentary formalities, passed bills and transacted business with all possible gravity.

The first difficulty with the Indians was the capture, on July 14th, 1776, of three young girls, two of whom were the daughters of settlers who had come in, and the other the daughter of Boone. They had carelessly crossed in a canoe to the opposite side of the Kentucky river (the fort being on the bank of that stream) at a late hour in the afternoon. The merry girls, playing and splashing in the water, permitted the canoe to drift to the opposite side. Lurking there, were five hideous savages, one of whom, crawling stealthily down the bank, seized the rope attached to the boat and drew it away out of sight of the fort. The shrieks of the maidens were heard; but the canoe was the only one, and none dared risk the chance of swimming the river, lest a large body of Indians might be concealed in the woods. Boone was absent at the time, but the next morning he and others were on the track of the Indians, and came up with them just as they were kindling a fire to cook their meal. Firing on them, they wounded or killed two, and routed the remainder so suddenly that they had no time either to injure the " brokenhearted" girls or to take their moccasins and tomahawks with them.

One of Boone's bravest and most fearless scouts was Simon Kenton. Eight times did he run the gauntlet, three times he was tied to the stake and once nearly killed by a blow from an axe. At one time, when he had taken an Indian horse, he was seized and **beaten** by his captors until their arms were tired; they then proceeded to secure him in the following manner for the night: Being placed on his back, his legs were drawn apart and each foot lashed firmly to stakes driven into the ground. A pole was then laid across his breast, his hands tied to each end and his arms lashed round it with thongs. Finally, a strap was passed round his neck and the end secured to a stake in the ground, his head being stretched back to prevent his choking.

This being the time of the Revolutionary War, the savages used frequently to visit their British employers and allies at Fort Detroit. To this place Kenton was taken, and there won, by his deportment, the interest of the wife of an Indian trader named Harvey.

A little romance followed, for this lady promised to assist the escape of Kenton and two other Kentuckian captives, and the opportunity soon presented itself. On the 3rd of June, 1779, the Indians assembled near the fort to have a "spree," which meant to get gloriously drunk on British whisky. They stacked their guns near Mrs. Harvey's house. When it was dark she stole silently out, and, selecting three of the weapons, hid them in a patch of peas in her garden. Hastening to Kenton, she told him what she had done, and instructed him to come with the others at midnight to her palisaded garden, where they would find a ladder, by means of which they could climb over and secure the guns. She also told him of a hollow tree at some distance from the town in which she had concealed such articles of clothing, food, ammunition, etc., as they would require on their journey. At the appointed time the captives appeared at the garden. No time was to be lost, as the yells of the drunken savages could be heard and daylight would soon appear. Taking an affectionate leave of his benefactress, Kenton set out with his companions and escaped safely to Kentucky.

One of the great needs of the colonists was salt. Boone headed an expedition to the Blue Licks for the purpose of making it by evaporating in kettles the water of the famous salt springs situated there. The undertaking was successful as far as the immediate object of it was concerned, but was otherwise disastrous, since all the party were captured except the three who had gone to the fort with the salt which had been manufactured during the month in which they were not disturbed by the redskins. This was the beginning of the long and remarkable captivity of Boone, of which I shall presently speak.

Before the capture the following famous incident is said to have occurred: Boone, while hunting in the woods near the Licks, came upon two Indians. Perceiving that it was useless to think of attempting a retreat, he slipped behind a tree to let them come within rifle-shot, and then exposed himself; the foremost levelled his gun; at the flash Boone, who well knew how to dodge bullets, again stepped behind the tree. In the same manner the next Indian was induced to throw away his bullets, and while they were trying, with eager, trembling hands, to reload, he was upon them and succeeded in shooting one of them dead.

The two antagonists, now on equal grounds, the one unsheathing his knife, the other raising his tomahawk, rushed toward the body of the Indian lying between them. Boone caught the well-aimed tomahawk of his foe on the barrel of his rifle; and, being at close quarters, with only the slain savage intervening, as the redskin, in poising his weapon, exposed himself to attack, he plunged his knife up to the hilt into his body. This occurrence is commemorated in sculptured stone in a group placed over the northern door of the Capitol at Washington.

After the Indians had captured Boone, he took what proved to be the wisest course, submitted quietly and ingratiated himself in their favor, and, when they met the rest of the party at the Licks, signed to them also to surrender. Reposing the greatest confidence in him, they did as directed, and this, no doubt, was the means of saving the fort; for if the savages had not been conciliated here, but had fought and been victorious, they would certainly have gone on to attack this structure, as this had been a part of their programme.

They were Shawanese from Chillicothe, and thither they immediately returned, taking Boone with them.

They next conducted their illustrious captive, by a long journey, to Detroit, to exhibit him to their friends and gratify their vanity. The comrades of Boone were delivered up to Commandant Hamilton at Detroit, who offered the Indians a large ransom **for** their prisoner; **but** they would not accept it. The taciturn, quiet, gentle and unassuming nature of this hero pleased the savages, and they purposed adopting him into their tribe. He was formally adopted by a distinguished old chief named Blackfish, who had recently lost a son, and remained with the tribe four months.

The ceremony of adoption was a severe ordeal. By a painful process his hair was plucked from the head, leaving only a scalp-lock tuft, which was dressed up in feathers and rib**bons.** He was then thoroughly washed and taken to the council-house, where a speech was made to him, and finally he was generously overspread with paint, the ceremony concluding with a feast and pipe-smoking. His captors did not entirely trust him, but carefully counted the bullets given him for hunting, so that he could not conceal any for future use; but Boone outwitted them by halving the balls and using light charges of powder.

At length, when he saw four hundred and fifty warriors **painting,** pow-wowing and otherwise preparing for an expedition against Boonesborough, he determined to escape if possible. Having always carefully concealed from them his accurate knowledge of the Shawanese dialect, he thus learned all their plans. They had ascertained that during his absence the fort had fallen out of repair, and anticipated an easy subjugation of it. Although appearing to evince no interest in their preparations, and having seemingly become an adopted son of the tribe, the heart of Boone was secretly filled with anguish at the thought of his wife and children, whom he believed to be at the fort, although they, with the exception of one daughter, had in reality returned to the home of his father-in-law.

On the 16th of June he arose very early, went out to hunt **and** never returned. The flight of Boone to the fort on the Kentucky river, one hundred and sixty miles away, is one of the most thrilling adventures to be found in **the annals of**

Indian warfare. Four hundred and fifty fleet-footed warriors were on his track, stung to fury by his ingratitude, and by the consciousness that he possessed their secrets. In this remarkable flight Boone occupied four days, during which he had but one regular meal, which consisted of a turkey that he had shot after crossing the Ohio river.

So disconcerted were the Indians by his escape that they were unable to recover from their surprise for three weeks. In the meantime Boone had strengthened the fort in anticipation of the certain siege that was to come. The Indians soon arrived, four hundred and fifty strong, under command of Captain Du Quesne and Blackfish. Boone despatched a messenger to Colonel Arthur Campbell for assistance, and then used every device to gain time. During a truce of two days the besieged were strangely permitted to bring into the fort water and provisions.

After a treacherous attempt to seize Boone and eight others, during a council, hostilities began. A siege had now opened which lasted nine days and nights without intermission. The enemy, from their shelter in the woods, poured in a steady hailstorm of lead against the fort; but they did but little damage to any one, and the one hundred and twenty-five pounds of bullets which were picked up outside of the fort at the close of the siege had been thrown away to little purpose.

The garrison fought heroically, having only two men killed and four wounded; one of the former was the victim of a negro who had deserted from them, carrying with him the skill in shooting which he had acquired in the fort. This renegade had climbed a tree and was firing into the building, when Boone, marking him and taking advantage of a moment when he exposed his head, sent a bullet toward him. After the battle the negro was found dead with a ball in his head, the shot of Boone having been made at a distance of five hundred and twenty-five feet. At length the siege was raised, and the Indians returned in deep chagrin at their failure to secure Boone.

The terrible blow which the whites received in August 1782, at the battle of Blue Licks, is too familiar to render necessary more than mere allusion to it here. The number of settlers slain in that battle was seventy-seven, among whom was a son of Boone. A word as to the latter years of Boone, who experienced the usual fate of great benefactors. He lost his farm in Kentucky, owing to some quibble about the title; and afterward, when he had removed to Missouri and had been granted a large tract of land, he was deprived of that also by the United States authorities. These despicable acts of injustice will ever be a stain upon the escutcheons of Kentucky and the United States, notwithstanding the fact that he did finally receive from the United States government a petty grant of eight hundred acres in Missouri, upon which he lived until his death. He died in 1820 at the age of eighty-six, and was buried in the grave he had designated. In 1845 the legislature caused his remains to be brought to Frankfort, Ky.

CHAPTER IX.

WARS OF NEW ENGLAND AS TOLD BY JUDGE PENHALLOW, WHO DIED AT PORTSMOUTH IN 1726.

A RECORD of nearly all the horrible deeds committed by various tribes of Indians in New England early in the 18th century, was kept by Samuel Penhallow, a Christian gentleman and a judge of the Massachusetts superior court, and hence were not overdrawn. We give some excerpts from his history:

February 8th, 1704, Joseph Bradley's garrison of Haverhill was unhappily surprised by a small band of Indians, who skulking at a distance, and seeing the gates open and none on the sentry, rushed in and became masters thereof. The housewife perceiving the misery that was attending her, and having boiling soap on the fire, scalded one of them to death. The sentinel within was slain, and she with several others were taken; which was the second time of her captivity. But that which heightened her affliction was being **with child**, and yet obliged to travel in a deep snow, **under a** heavy burden, and many days together without subsistence, excepting a few bits of skin, ground-nuts, bark of trees, wild onions, and lily roots. Nevertheless she was wonderfully supported, and at last safely delivered; but the babe soon perished for want of nourishment, and by the cruelty of the Indians, who, as it cried, threw hot embers in its mouth. After a year's bondage, she was sold to the French for eighty livres, and then redeemed by her husband.

May 13th, about break of day, a company of French and Indians fell on a fortified house, at Pascomuck, afterward Easthampton, Mass., where no watch being kept, the people were alarmed in their beds, by the noise of the enemy's rushing on the house; and before the inhabitants could rise, the Indians had shot those that first appeared, killing some and wounding others. The surprised people made what resistance they could, firing briskly on the enemy; but the house being soon set on fire, they were forced to yield themselves prisoners. The enemy soon drew off, but fearing a pursuit, dismissed one of the wounded, with this caution, that if the English followed them, they would slay the prisoners; but the unfortunate messenger in returning back, was slain by another Indian. On the same morning, another party attacked a farm house, two miles off; but the fury of the dogs so alarmed the inhabitants, that they instantly got up and fired several guns, to very good advantage, which prevented any further attempt. As for those at Pascomuck, they were immediately pursued; three made an escape, eight were rescued, nineteen slain, and three carried to Canada.

In the same month intelligence came from Albany that a number of hostile Indians were up the Connecticut river at a place called Cowassuck. A company from Northampton went after them. Not far from the place, a spy was sent out with green leaves for a cap and vest, to prevent his discovery and to find the enemy. When evening came on, the searchers moved toward the river, and soon perceived a smoke at about half a mile's distance, where it was afterward found they had taken up their lodging. About two o'clock in the morning, the wigwam where they lay was reached. The ground was so covered with dry sticks and brush, for the space of five rods, that it could not be passed without making such a crackling, as to alarm the enemy, and give them time to escape. A very small cloud arose, fortunately which gave a smart clap of thunder, and a sudden shower of rain. And this opportunity was embraced to run through the thicket within sight of the wigwam. The enemies were awake; but, however, being unwilling to lose any time, the attacking party crept on hands and knees till within three or four rods of them. Then arising they ran to the side of the wigwam, and fired in upon them: and flinging down guns, surrounded them, and with clubs and hatchets knocked down several. But after all diligence, two of their number made their escape, one mortally wounded.

The Indians commenced their attack on Lancaster on the 31st of July, early in the morning. In their first onset, they killed Lieut. Nathaniel Wilder, near the gate of his own garrison; and on the same day, three others, viz. Abraham How, John Spaulding and Benjamin Hutchins, near the same garrison.

On the 8th of August, as several persons were busy in spreading flax, on a plain, about eighty rods from the house of Mr. Thomas Rice, and a number of boys with them, a number of Indians, seven or ten, suddenly rushed down a woody hill near by, and knocked on the head Nahor Rice, the youngest boy, and seized Asher and Adonijah, sons of Mr. Thomas Rice, and two others, Silas and Timothy, sons of Mr. Edmund Rice, and carried them away to Canada. The persons engaged in spreading flax, escaped safely to the house. Asher, in about four years, returned, being redeemed by his father. His brother, Adonijah, grew up in Canada, and married there. Silas and Timothy mixed with the Indians; lost their mother tongue, had Indian wives, and children by them; and lived at Cagnawaga. The last became the third of the six chiefs of the Cagnawagas.

On the 15th of October following, eighteen Indians **fell on** Cape Neddick, where they took four children of Mr. **Stover's** at a little distance from the garrison. The youngest, not able to travel, was knocked on the head, the other three were car**ried** captive; but being attacked by Lieut. March, and losing one of their company, they killed a second child in way of revenge.

Col. Schuyler from time to time was of eminent service to his country, who advised of 270 men coming to attack Dunstable on the 3rd of July. They fell on a garrison that had twenty troopers posted in it. They had been ranging the woods in the vicinity, and came toward night to this garrison; apprehending no danger, turned their horses loose, piled their arms and harness in the house, and began a carousal, to exhilarate their spirits after the fatigues of the day. A party of Indians had lately arrived in the vicinity, and on that day had designed to attack both Wells' and Galusha s garrisons. One of their number had been stationed to watch each of these houses, to see that no assistance approached, **and no** alarm was given. A short time previous to the approach of the cavalry, the Indian stationed at Wells' had retired to his party, and reported that all was safe. At sunset, a Mr. Cumings and his wife went out to milk their cows, and left the gate open. The Indians, who had advanced undiscovered, started up, shot Mrs. Cumings dead upon the spot, and wounded her husband. They then rushed through the open gate into the house, with all the horrid yells of conquering savages, but stared with amazement on finding the

room filled with soldiers merrily feasting. Both parties were **completely amazed,** and neither acted with much propriety. The soldiers, so suddenly interrupted in their jovial entertainment, found themselves called to fight, when entirely destitute of arms, and incapable of obtaining them. The greater part were panic-struck, and unable to fight or fly. Fortunately, all were not in this sad condition: some six **or** seven courageous souls, with chairs, clubs, and whatever they could seize upon, furiously attacked the advancing foe. The Indians who were as much surprised as the soldiers, had but little more courage than they, and immediately took to their heels for safety; thus yielding the house, defeated by **one** quarter their number of unarmed men. The trumpeter, who was in the upper part of the house at the commencement of the attack, seized his trumpet and began sounding an alarm, when he was shot dead by an Indian on the stairway. He was the only one of the party killed. The savages **disappoi**nted in this part of their plan, immeditely proceeded to Galusha's, two miles distant; took possession of, and burnt it. One **woman** only **escaped.** She sought refuge in the cellar, and concealed herself under a dry cask. After hastily plundering the house, and murdering, as they supposed, all who were in it, the Indians set it on fire and immediately retired. The woman in this critical situation, attempted to escape by the window, but found it too small: she however succeeded in losening the stones till she had opened a hole sufficient to admit of her passage, and with the house in flames over her head, she forced herself out, and crawled into the bushes, not daring to rise for fear she should be discovered. In the bushes she lay concealed until the next day **when** she reached one of the neighboring garrisons.

Joseph English, who was a **friend** Indian, was much distinguished for his attachment to the white inhabitants. In a preceding war with the Indians, he had been taken prisoner from the vicinity of Dunstable and carried to Canada, from whence, by his shrewdness and sagacity, he effected his escape, with one English captive, and returned to his friends in Dunstable. The Indians had for a long time endeavored to retake him, for he was peculiarly obnoxious to them. While he was accompanying Capt. Butterfield and his wife on a visit to their friends, they pursued him, and just as he was upon the point of gaining a thicket, they shot him through the thigh, which brought him to the ground, and they afterward dispatched him with their tomahawks.

On the 8th of July, five Indians, a little before night, fell on an out house in Reading, where they surprised a woman with eight children; the former with the three youngest were instantly dispatched, and the others they carried captive; but one of the children unable to travel, they knocked on the head, and left in the swamp concluding it was dead, but a while after it was found alive. The neighborhood being alarmed, got ready by the morning and coming on their track, pursued them so near that they recovered three of the children, and put the enemy in such a terror that they not only quitted their plunder and blankets, but the other captives also. Several strokes were afterward made on Chelmsford, Sudbury and Groton, where three soldiers as they were going to public worship, were way laid by a small party, who killed two and made the other a prisoner.

At Exeter, a company of French Mohawks, who some time kept lurking about Capt. Hilton's garrison, took a view of all that went in and out; and observing some to go with their scythes to mow, laid in ambush till they laid by their arms, and while at work, rushed on at once, and by intercepting them from their arms, killed four, wounded one, and carried three captive; so that out of ten, two only escaped.

Rebecca Taylor was going to Canada, on the bank of Montreal river, when she was violently insulted by Sampson, her body master, who without any provocation was resolved to hang her; and for want of rope, made use of his girdle, which when he had fastened about her neck, attempted to hoist her up on the limb of a tree (that hung in the nature of a gibbet,) but in hoisting her, the weight of her body broke it asunder, which so exasperated the cruel tyrant that he made a second attempt, resolved that if he failed in that to knock her on the head; but before he had power to effect it, Bomaseen came along, who seeing the tragedy on foot, prevented the fatal stroke.

A child of Mrs. Hannah Parsons, of Wells, the Indians, for want of food, determined to roast alive, but while the fire was kindling, and the sacrifice preparing, a company of French Mohawks came down the river in a canoe with three dogs, which somewhat revived these hungry monsters, expecting to make a feast upon one of them. So soon as they got ashore, the child was offered in exchange; but despising the offer, they tendered a gun, which was readily accepted, and by that means the child was preserved from a horrible death.

Samuel Butterfield, who being sent to Groton as a soldier, was with others attacked as they were gathering in the harvest; his bravery was such, that he killed one and wounded another, but being overpowered by strength, was forced to submit; and it happened that the slain Indian was a Sagamore, and of great dexterity in war, which caused matter of lamentation, and enraged them to such a degree that they vowed the utmost revenge; some were for whipping him to death, others for burning him alive; but differing in their sentiments, they submitted the issue to the squaw widow, concluding she would determine something very dreadful, but she answered: "If by killing him you can bring my husband to life again, I beg you study what death you please, but, if not, let him be my servant;" which he accordingly was, during his captivity, and had favor shown him.

Of all the Indians ever known since King Philip, never any appeared so cruel and inhumane as Assacambuit, that insulting monster who, by the encouragement of the French, went over to Paru, and being introduced to the king, lifted up his hand in the most arrogant manner imaginable, saying "this hand of mine has slain one hundred and fifty of your Majesty's enemies, within the territories of New England," etc. His impudent speech was so pleasing to that bloody monarch that he forthwith knighted him, and ordered eight livres a day to be paid him during life; which so exalted the wretch as at his return, to exert a sovereignty over the rest of his brethren, by murdering one, and stabbing another, which so exasperated those of their relations, that they sought revenge, and would instantly have executed it, but that he fled his country, and never returned after.

At Casco, Indians intercepted a fishing boat sailing between the islands, in which were five men, three of whom they killed, and took the other two. August 10th, 1707, they waylaid the road between York and Wells, and as four horsemen were riding in company with Mrs. Littlefield, who had

the value of sixty pounds with her, were all slain except one, who made his escape.

On the 18th of August, as two women in Northborough, Mass., were out a short distance from the fort gathering herbs, the Indians discovered and pursued them. One Mrs. Mary Fay got safe into the fort; the other, Mary Goodenow, a young and unmarried woman, was taken and carried over the brook into the edge of Marlborough, and there, a little south of the great road, and nigh to Sandy Hill, she was killed and scalped. The enemy were pursued and overtaken in what is now Sterling, where an obstinate engagement took place, in which John Farrar and Richard Singletary, were killed. The Indians at length fled, leaving some plunder and some of their packs, in one of which the scalp of Mary Goodenow was found.

A most afflicting stroke was at Oyster river, where thirty French Mohawks, who appeared like so many furies with their naked bodies painted like blood, and observing some at work hewing timber, and others driving a team, they fell violently upon them with such hideous noise and yelling as made the very woods to echo. At the first shot, they killed seven, and mortally wounded another.

On April 12th, 1709, a scout fell on Deerfield, and took Mehuman Hinsdell, as he was driving a cart, which was the second time of his captivity. And on May 6th, another party within three miles of Exeter, surprised several as they were going to a saw-mill. A few days after, Capt. Wright of Northampton, with several English, and two Natick Indians, adventuring to the lake, within forty miles of fort La Motte, killed and wounded two or three of the French Mohawks; and on their return up French river, met with another body of the enemy in canoes, on whom they fired, and overset, killed and wounded several of them. In this company, was William Moody, who being now alone with but one Indian in a canoe, was encouraged by the English to kill said Indian, and make his escape, which he attempted, but overset the canoe in the struggle, and then Moody swam toward the English for relief, whereupon, Lieut. John Wells, with one or two more, ran down the bank and helped him ashore. In the meantime, a number of the enemy came to the bank, and wounded John Strong, and killed the lieutenant, who had been a man of very good courage, and well spirited to serve his country, and so the loss of him was much lamented. Hereupon, Moody unhappily resigned himself again into the enemy's hands, who most inhumanly tortured him, by fastening him a stake, and roasting him alive, whose flesh they afterward devoured.

On the 20th of July, 1710, six men were making hay in the meadows, when the Indians, who had been watching an opportunity to surprise them, sprang suddenly upon them, dispatched five, and took the other, John White, prisoner. White, spying a small company of his people at a distance, jumped from the Indian who held him, and ran to join his friends; but the Indian fired after him, and wounded him in the thigh, by which he fell; but soon recovered and running again, he was again fired at, and received his death wound. This was the last mischief done by Indians at Brookfield.

August 2nd, between forty and fifty French and Indians fell on Winter Harbor, where they killed a woman and took two men. The week after, they came with a far superior number, killed three, and carried away six, one of the slain they barbarously skinned, and made themselves girdles of his skin.

June 1st, 1712, Indians at Spruce Creek shot John Pickernell as he was locking his door, and going to the garrison; they also wounded his wife and knocked a child on the head, which they scalped, yet afterward it recovered. Two days after they were seen at Amesbury, then at Kingston, where they wounded Ebenezer Stevens and Stephen Gilman, the latter of which they took alive and inhumanly murdered. After this, they killed one at Newichawanick, and on July 18th, fell on a company at Wells, where they slew another and took a negro captive, who afterward made his escape. The Sabbath after they endeavored to intercept the people at Dover as they came from worship; upon which a scout was sent in pursuit, but made no discovery. Yet in the intermitting time, they took two children from Lieut. Heard's garrison, and not having time to scalp them, cut off both their heads and carried them away.

In 1720, Capt. Thomas Baker of Northampton, in the county of Hampshire, in Massachusetts, set out with a scouting party of thirty-four men, passed up Connecticut river, and crossed the height of land to Pemigewasset river. He there discovered a party of Indians, whose sachem was called **Walternummus**, whom he attacked and destroyed. Baker and the sachem levelled and discharged their guns at each other at the same instant. The ball from the Indian's gun grazed Baker's left eyebrow, but did him no injury. The ball from Baker's gun went through the breast of the sachem. Immediately upon being wounded, he leaped four or five feet high, and then fell instantly dead. The Indians fled to the river; Baker and his party pursued, and destroyed every one of them. They had a wigwam on the bank of the river, which was nearly filled with beaver. Baker's party took as much of it as they could carry away, and burned the rest. Baker lost none of his men in this skirmish. It took place at the confluence of a small river with the Pemigewasset, between Plymouth and Campton, which afterward had the name of Baker's river.

As Deacon Joseph Stevens and four of his sons were making hay in a meadow, at Rutland, on the 14th of August, 1723, they were surprised by five Indians. The father escaped in the bushes; two of the sons were slain, and two were made prisoners. Two of the five Indians waylaid a Mr. Davis and son, who that afternoon were making hay in the meadow not far off, but weary of waiting, they were returning to the others, and met Rev. Joseph Willard in their way, who was armed. One of the Indian's guns missed fire, the others did no execution. Mr. Willard returned the fire and wounded one of them, mortally; the other closed in with Mr. Willard; but he would have been more than a match for him, had not the other three come to his assistance and killed Mr. Willard.

April 17th, 1724, William Mitchel, of Scarborough, was shot as he was ploughing in the field. They then fell on a sloop a Kennebunk, which belonged to Lynn, and killed the whole company. But the greatest stroke was on Capt. Winslow, who with sixteen men in two whale-boats, went from St. George's to the Green Islands, which the enemy frequented on the account of fowling. But on their return, they were ambuscaded by two or three companies of them that lay on each side the river. The first that fell was Sergeant Harvey, who commanded the other boat; for by keeping too near the shore, he gave the enemy the greater advantage: however, he returned the shot with as much bravery as could be expected, till overpowered by a multitude. Capt. Winslow, who was considerably ahead and out of danger, perceiving the engagement, courageously returned back to their assistance. But before he could give them any relief, **he was surrounded** with about thirty canoes, who made a hideous yelling; but he gave them **no answer** but from the muzzles of his guns. A smart engagement followed, which held till night: when finding his thigh broken, and most his men slain, he was obliged to **hasten** ashore; but there also he found himself unhappily waylaid. They fell on him with utmost fury, yet his courage continued until the last; for he rested himself on his other knee, and killed an Indian before they had power to slay him. He was the grandson of Governor Winslow of Plymouth.

Sylvanus Nock, **a worthy elder of** the church at Oyster river, soon after this, was **slain as he was** on horseback. Myles Thompson, **of Berwick**, was the same day also killed by another party, and his son was carried captive. A few days **after,** they again beset Capt. Penhallow's garrison where they took three as they were driving their cows to pasture, and at their drawing off killed a great many cattle. **Another party** fell on Kingston, where they took Peter Colcord, Ephraim Severns, and two of Mr. Stevens' children, **wh**om they carried to Canada; but by the unwearied pains and expense of Mr. Stevens, he in a little time purchased his children. Colcord, about six months after, made his escape **and got unto** his friends, but did not survive long.

May 24th, they shot George Chesley as he was returning from public worship, with whom was Elizabeth Burnum, who was mortally wounded. Three days after, they went to Perpooduck, where they killed one and wounded another, and then marched to Saco, where they slew David Hill, a friend Indian. On the same day, another party went to Chester, where they took Thomas Smith, with another whom they pinioned, but soon after, they made their escape.

The frontiers alarmed **at** these outrages, two companies **of** volunteers went from New Hampshire on a bounty act, (one hundred pounds a scalp,) and it happened that Moses Davis, as he was weeding his **corn,** went unto a brook to drink, where he saw three Indian packs, upon which he informed the troops that were then coming out. **He, with his son,** went before as guides, but by an ambushment, were **both shot dead.** The English then fired on them, who killed one, and wounded two more, but could not find either of the latter, although they tracked them by their blood some way. The assembly of New Hampshire then sitting, ordered **the** aforesaid sum of one hundred pounds to be paid.

The next damage they did, was at Groton, but were so closely pursued, that they left several of their packs behind. About which time, news came to Deerfield of a body of Indians discovered up Connecticut river. Capt. Thomas Wells **rallied** a company of men, and went in quest of them, but **made no** further discovery, till, upon their return home, about four miles from Deerfield, three of the company (supposing themselves out of danger, **rode at** some distance before the rest, and unhappily fell into an ambushment of the enemy near **a** swamp, and were all three killed by them. But the company **behind** hearing the guns, rode up with all speed, **and came upon** the enemy while they were scalping the slain; and firing **upon** them, wounded several. Upon which the enemy fled into the swamp, and the English dismounting their horses, ran in after them, and tracked them a considerable way by the blood of the wounded, but found none. However, they recovered ten packs, and heard afterward that two died of their wounds, and a third lost the use of his arm. Another company fell on Spurwink, where they mortally wounded Solomon Jordan, as he was coming **out of** the garrison. Next day, July 18th, Lieut. Bean went in quest of them, and came up with a scout of thirty, whom he engaged and put to flight, leaving twenty-five packs, twelve blankets, a gun, a hatchet, and sundry other things behind them.

The enemy not finding so great encouragement in attacking our frontiers as they expected, were now resolved to turn pirates, and accordingly intercepted several of our fishery as they went in and out the harbors for wood, water, or in case of storms, and accordingly made up a fleet of fifty canoes, who designed at first for Mohegen, but going through the Fox Islands, and seeing several vessels at anchor, surprised eight with little or no opposition; in which were forty men, twenty of whom they put to death, reserving the skippers and best sailors to navigate for them. After this, they took fourteen more; and with the assistance of the Cape Sable Indians, became so powerful and desperate, that at first they terrified all vessels that sailed along the eastern shore. They then went to St. Georges with a design to burn that garrison; in order whereto, they filled a couple of shallops with combustible matter, which they set on fire, but it was happily extinguished. They then offered terms on surrendering, which were rejected. And finding that neither force nor insinuation would prevail, they withdrew, and sailed to Annapolis, expecting to surprise the fort; but firing at a soldier in their march, gave an alarm, and a detachment issued forth, who, after a smart dispute, gave them a perfect rout, but not without loss to the whites.

At Rutland, they killed three men, wounded one, and took another Aug. 23rd, 1724; and at Oxford, beset a house that lay under a hill, but as one of the enemy attempted to break through the roof, he was shot by a woman of the house. At Oyster river, and Berwick, they killed one, wounded a second, and carried away a third.

Capts. Harmon, Moulton, Brown and Bean were now preparing for Norridgewock, with two hundred men in seventeen whale-boats. After they landed at Triconnick, they met with Bomaseen at Brunswick, (who had slain an Englishman some days before) whom they shot in the river, as he attempted to make an escape. They afterward killed his daughter, and took his wife captive; who gave an account of the state of the enemy, which encouraged them to march on briskly; and on August 12th, they got within two miles of the place. Capt. Harmon drew off with about sixty men to range their corn fields, in hopes of finding some there, imagining they saw some smoke. Capt. Moulton, with about a hundred men moved forward, and when he came within view of the town, artfully divided them into three squadrons, of thirty in each, having ordered ten to guard their baggage, and a squadron on each wing to lie in ambush, while he with the like number encountered them in the front. He went on with such resolution, that he got within pistol shot before he was discovered. The Indians were under amazing terror; yet in their surprise some of them snatched up their guns and fired: but their hands shook and they did no execution. They immediately betook themselves to flight, and in running fell on the muzzles of their pursuers' guns that lay in ambush. They were pursued so warmly, that several were slain on the spot; more got into their canoes, and others ran into the river, which was so rapid, and the falls in some places so great, that many of them were drowned. By this time Capt. Harmon came up, who was not so happy as to discover any of the enemy where he expected. The number of the dead which were scalped, were twenty-six, beside Monsieur Ralle, the Jesuit, who was a bloody incendiary, and instrumental to most of the mischiefs done the white people by preaching the doctrine of meriting salvation by the destruction of heretics. Some say that quarter was offered him, which he refused, and would neither give nor take any. After this, they burnt and destroyed the chapel, canoes, and all the cottages that lay round; they also took four Indians alive, and recovered three captives.

The number in all that were killed and drowned was supposed to be eighty, but some say more; the greatest victory we have obtained in the last three or four wars: and it may be as noble an exploit (all things considered) as ever happened in the time of King Philip. About seventy French Mohawks were now making a descent on the frontiers, who divided into several parties and killed a great number of cattle. Some of them fell on the house of John Hanson of Dover, who being a stiff Quaker, full of enthusiasm, and ridiculing the military power, would on no account be influenced to come into garrison; by which means his whole family (then at home) being eight in number, were all killed and taken. But some time after, his wife and two or three of his children were redeemed with considerable pains and expense.

September 4th, they fell on Dunstable, and took two in the evening; next morning, Lieut. French, with fourteen men, went in quest of them; but being waylaid, both he and one half of his company were destroyed. After that, as many more of a fresh company engaged them, but the enemy being much superior in number overpowered them, with the loss of one man and four wounded.

On the Monday after, they killed Jabez Coleman of Kingston, with his son, as they were gathering corn stalks. About the same time, Nathaniel Edwards of Northampton was killed;

and the next day, the same company of Indians went to Westfield, and fell on several people as they were coming out of the meadows with their carts loaded, and wounding one man had certainly taken him, but some of our men bravely faced about, and attempted a shot upon them. But their guns all missing fire except Mr. Noah Ashley's, his went off and shot down one of the enemy, which put a stop to their further pursuit of the English. Hereupon a company rallied, and went after the enemy, and quickly found the Indian whom Ashley had slain. And taking the scalp, said Ashley brought it to Boston, and received one hundred pounds reward for it.

CHAPTER X.

CAPTAIN JOHN LOVEWELL'S MEMORABLE BATTLE WITH THE INDIANS AT FRYEBURG.

The story of Lovewell's fight with the Indians was one of the nursery tales of New Hampshire for many years. It took place on the 18th of April, 1725, and was one of the fiercest and most obstinate battles on record. John Lovewell was a son of Zaccheus Lovewell, and an ensign in the army of Oliver Cromwell, who came to this country and settled at Dunstable, Mass., where he died at the great age of 120 years, the oldest white man it is said, who ever died in New Hampshire. With 34 men he fought the famous Indian chief Paugus, at the head of 70 savages, near the shores of a pond in Pequacket. Lovewell's men were determined to conquer or die, although outnumbered more than one-half. They fought till Lovewell and Pangus were killed, and all the Captain's men but nine were either killed or wounded dangerously. The savages having lost, as was supposed, 60 of their number, and being convinced of the fierce and determined resolution of their foes, at length retreated and left them masters of the ground. The scene of this desperate and bloody action was at the place where Fryeburg, Me., is now located.

Capt. Lovewell, who was endowed with a generous spirit and resolution of serving his country, and well acquainted with hunting the woods, raised a company of volunteers, and marched some miles beyond their common head-quarters. On the easterly side of Winnepiseogee ponds he crossed an Indian track, and soon after espied two of them, whose motions he watched all the day, and at night silently came upon them as they lay asleep round their fire. At his first firing, he killed seven, after that, two more, and wounded another, which was their whole company.

April 13th, 1725, there came two Indians to Maquoit, and took one Cockram, a soldier of about eighteen years of age, whom they carried thirty miles into the woods. The first night they pinioned him, but left him loose the second. He took an opportunity, as they were asleep, to knock them both on the head, scalp them, and take their guns. A vessel from Causo arrived about this time bringing an account of 70 Indians falling on an outhouse in view of the garrison, where they killed seven men, one woman and a child. This news animated Capt. Lovewell to make another attempt on Pigwacket. Before going they built a fort near Ossipee, to have resource unto in case of danger, as also for the relief of any that might be sick or wounded; and having one of his men at this time sick, he left the doctor with eight men more to guard him: with the rest of his company, he proceeded in quest of the enemy. On May the 8th, about ten in the morning, forty miles from said fort, near Saco pond, he saw an Indian on a point of land, upon which they immediately put off their blankets and knapsacks, and made toward him, concluding that the enemy were ahead and not in the rear. Yet they were not without some apprehensions of their being discovered two days before, and that the appearing of one Indian in so bold a manner, was on purpose to ensnare them. Wherefore, the Captain calling his men together, proposed whether it was best to engage them or not; who boldly replied, "that as they came out on purpose to meet the enemy, they would rather trust Providence with their lives and die for their country, than return without seeing them." Upon this, they proceeded and mortally wounded the Indian, who notwithstanding returned the fire, and wounded Capt. Lovewell in the belly. Upon which Mr. Wyman fired and killed him. But their dismantling themselves at this juncture, proved an unhappy snare; for the enemy taking their baggage, knew their strength by the number of their packs, where they lay in ambush till they returned, and made the first shot; which was answered with much bravery, killing nine. The encounter was smart and desperate, and the victory seemed assured till Capt. Lovewell with several more were slain and wounded, to the number of twelve: upon which the men were forced to retreat unto a pond, between which and the enemy was a ridge of ground that proved a barrier. The engagement continued ten hours, but although the shouts of the enemy were at first loud and terrible, yet after some time they became sensibly low and weak, and their appearance to lessen. Now whether it was through want of ammunition, or on the account of those that were slain and wounded, that the enemy retreated, certain it is, they first drew off and left the ground. And although many of our men were much enfeebled by reason of their wounds, yet none of the enemy pursued them in their return. Their number was uncertain, but by the advice which we afterward received, they were seventy in the whole, whereof forty were said to be killed upon the spot, eighteen more died of their wounds, and that twelve only returned. An unhappy instance at this time fell out respecting one of the men, who when the fight began, was so dreadfully terrified, that he ran away to the fort, telling those who were there, that Capt. Lovewell was killed with most of his men; which put them into such consternation that they all drew off, leaving a bag of bread and pork behind, in case any of their company might return and be in distress.

The whole lost in the engagement were fifteen, beside those that were wounded. Eleazar Davis of Concord was the last that got in, who first came to Berwick and then to Portsmouth, where he was carefully provided for, and had a skillful surgeon to attend him. The report he gave was, that after Capt. Lovewell was killed, and Lieut. Farwell and Mr. Robbins wounded, that ensign Wyman took upon him the command of the shattered company, who behaved himself with great prudence and courage, by animating the men and telling them, "that the day would yet be their own, if their spirits did not flag;" which enlivened them anew, and caused them to fire so briskly, that several discharged between twenty and thirty times apiece. He further added, that Lieut. Farwell, with Mr. Frye, their chaplain, Josiah Jones, and himself, who were all wounded, marched toward the fort; but Jones steered another way, and after a long fatigue and hardship, got safe into Saco. Mr. Frye three days after, through the extremity of his wounds, began to faint and languish, and died.

Mr. Jacob Fullam, who was an officer and an only son, distinguished himself with much bravery. One of the first that was killed was by his right hand; and when ready to encounter a second, it is said that he and his adversary fell at the very instant by each other's shot.

Lieut. Robbins, being sensible of his dying state, desired one of the company to charge his gun and leave it with him, being persuaded that the Indians, by morning, would come and scalp him, being desirous of killing one more before he died. Solomon Kies, wounded in three places, lost so much blood that he was unable to stand any longer; but in the heat of the battle, calling to Mr. Wyman said, he was a dead man; however, he said that if it was possible, he would endeavour to creep into some obscure hole, rather than be insulted by these bloody Indians: but by a strange providence, as he was creeping away, he saw a canoe in the pond, which he rolled himself into, and by a favorable wind (without any assistance of his own) was driven so many miles on, that he got safe to the fort.

Mr. Wyman, who distinguished himself in such a signal manner, was, on his return, presented with a silver-hilted sword, and a captain's commission. Edward Lingfield was made an ensign, and the general assembly (to show a grateful acknowledgment to the soldiers, and a compassionate sympathy to the widows and orphans,) ordered the sum of fifteen hundred pounds to be given them, and for further encouragement of volunteers, ordered four shillings a day to be paid every one that would enlist, beside a bounty of one hundred pounds a scalp. Upon which a great many brave men, under the command of Capt. White, Capt. Wyman, and others, went out, but the extremity of the heat prevented their marching far. Many of them sickened, and some died after their return; particularly, Capt. White and Capt. Wyman, whose deaths were very much lamented.

The following song was written at the time, to commemorate Lovewell's great fight, which is reproduced here as worthy of a place in this little volume. The tune is not designated:

Of worthy Captain LOVEWELL, I purpose now to sing,
How valiantly he served his country and his King;
He and his valiant soldiers, did range the woods full wide,
And hardships they endured to quell the Indians' pride.

'Twas nigh unto Pigwacket, on the eighth day of May,
They spied a rebel Indian soon after break of day;
He on a bank was walking, upon a neck of land,
Which leads into a pond as we're made to understand.

Our men resolved to have him, and travel'd two miles round,
Until they met the Indian, who boldly stood his ground;
Then speaks up Captain LOVEWELL, " take you good heed," says he,
" This rogue is to decoy us, I very plainly see.

INDIAN MASSACRES.

"The Indians lie in ambush, in some place nigh **at hand**,
In order to surround us upon this neck of land;
Therefore we'll march in order, and each man leave his pack,
That we may briskly fight them when they make their attack."

They came unto this Indian, who did them thus defy,
As soon as they came nigh him, two guns he did let fly,
Which wounded Captain LOVEWELL, and likewise one man **more**,
But when this rogue was running, they laid him in his gore.

Then having scalped **the Indian**, they went back to the spot,
Where they had laid their packs down, but there they found them not,
For the Indians having spied them, when they them down did lay,
Did seize them for their plunder, and carry them away.

These rebels lay in ambush, this very place hard by,
So that an English soldier did one of them espy,
And cried out, "here's an Indian," with that they started out,
As fiercely as old lions, and hideously did shout.

With that our valiant English, all gave a loud huzza,
To show the rebel Indians they feared them not a straw;
So now the fight began, and as fiercely as could be,
The Indians ran up to them, but soon were forced to flee.

Then spake up Captain LOVEWELL, when first the fight began
"Fight on my valiant heroes! you see they fall like rain."
For as we are inform'd, the Indians were so thick,
A man could scarcely fire **a gun** and not some of them hit.

Then did the rebels try their best our soldiers **to** surround,
But they could not accomplish it, because there was a pond,
To which our men retreated and covered all the rear,
The rogues were forc'd to flee them, although they skulked for fear.

Two logs there were behind them that close together lay,
Without being discovered, they could not get away;
Therefore our valiant English, they travel'd in a row,
And at a handsome distance as they were wont to go.

'Twas ten o'clock **in** the morning, when first the fight began,
And fiercely did continue until the setting sun;
Excepting that the Indians some hours before 'twas night,
Drew off into the bushes and ceas'd a while to fight.

But soon again returned, in fierce and **furious** mood,
Shouting as in the morning, but yet not **half so** loud;
For as we are informed, **so thick** and fast they fell,
Scarce twenty of their number, at night did get home well.

And that our valiant English, till midnight there did stay,
To see whether the rebels would have another fray;
But they no more returning, they made off toward their home,
And brought away their wounded as far as they could come.

Of all our valiant English, there were but thirty-four,
And of the rebel Indians, there were about fourscore.
And sixteen of our English did safely home return,
The rest were kill'd and wounded, for which we all must mourn.

Our worthy Captain LOVEWELL, among them there did die,
They killed Lieut. ROBBINS, and wounded good young FRYE,
Who was our English Chaplain; he many Indians slew,
And some of them he scalp'd when bullets round him flew.

Young FULLAM too I'll mention, because he **fought so well**,
Endeavoring **to save a** man, a sacrifice he **fell**;
But yet our valiant Englishmen in fight **were** ne'er dismayed,
But still they kept their **motion**, and WYMAN Captain **made**,

Who **shot the old** chief PANGUS, which did the foe defeat,
Then **set** his men in order, and brought off the retreat;
And braving many dangers and hardships in the way,
They **safe** arriv'd at Dunstable, the thirteenth day of May.

CHAPTER XI.

GENERAL HARRISON AND THE INDIANS—TECUMSEH—THE PROPHET ELSKWATAWA—INDIAN DEFEAT AT TIPPECANOE.

In 1770, a woman of one of the southern tribes, domesticated with the Shawanees, gave birth to triplets, who received the names of Tecumseh, Elskwatawa and Kumshaka. Their father was a Shawanee warrior who was killed in a battle at Point Pleasant. By the time Tecumseh had attained the age of manhood he had already become noted as a bold and sagacious warrior. Elskwatawa proclaimed himself a prophet, commissioned by the Great Spirit to foretell, and to hasten, by his own efforts, the destruction of intruders, and by various appeals to the vanity, the superstition, and the spirit of revenge, of his auditors, he acquired a strong and enduring influence. The chiefs who opposed or ridiculed his pretensions were denounced as wizards or sorcerers, and proofs, satisfactory to the minds of the Indians, being adduced in support of the accusation, numbers perished at the stake, leaving a clear field for the operations of the imposter. Kumshaka, the other brother, is unknown to fame.

In September, 1809, while Tecumseh was pushing his intrigues among various distant tribes, Governor Harrison obtained a cession, for certain stipulated annuities, of a large tract of land on the lower portion of the Wabash, from the tribes of the Miamis, Delawares, Pottawatomies, and Kickapoos. Tecumseh and his brother made vehement remonstrances against this proceeding, and a somewhat stormy interview took place between the great chief and Governor Harrison, each party being attended by a powerful armed force. Upon this occasion, Tecumseh first openly avowed his design of forming an universal coalition of the Indian nations, by which the progress of the whites westward should be arrested, but he still insisted that it was not his intention to make war. One great principle which he endeavored to enforce was that no Indian lands should be sold, except by consent of all the confederate tribes. Two days after this conference he started for the south, with a few attendant

INDIAN MASSACRES. 81

warriors, to spread disaffection among the Creeks, Cherokees and other tribes of the southern states.

In 1811, during the prolonged absence of Tecumseh, and contrary, as is supposed, to his express instructions, bold and audacious depredations and murders were committed by the horde of savages gathered at the Prophet's town. Representations were forwarded to Washington of the necessity for active measures in restraint of these outrages, and a regiment, under Colonel Boyd, was promptly marched from Pittsburg to Vincennes, and placed under command of Harrison. With this force, and a body of militia and volunteers, the whole amounting to about nine hundred men, the governor marched from Fort Harrison, on the Wabash, for the Prophet's town, on the 28th of October. The troops encamped near the town on the 5th of November. Before daybreak next morning the treacherous Indians had stealthily crept up near the sentries, with the intention of rushing upon them and killing them before they could give the alarm. But fortunately one of the sentries discovered an Indian creeping toward him through the grass, and fired at him. This was immediately followed by the Indian yell, and a furious charge upon the left flank.

The onset of the Indians, stimulated as they were by the assurances of their prophet, that certain success awaited them, was unprecedented for fury and determination. They numbered from five hundred to a thousand, and were led by White Loon, Stone-Eater, and a treacherous Pottawatomie chief named Winnemac. The Prophet took, personally, no share in the engagement. The struggle continued until daylight, when the assailants were driven off and dispersed. The Indians immediately abandoned their town, which the army proceeded to destroy, tearing down the fortifications and burning the buildings. The object of the expedition being thus fully accomplished, the troops were marched back to Vincennes.

In the battle at Tippecanoe, the loss of the victors was probably greater than that of the savages. Thirty-eight of the latter were left dead upon the field: of the whites, fifty were killed, and nearly one hundred wounded. It is not to be supposed that the Prophet's influence maintained its former hold upon his followers after this defeat. He takes

Indeed, from this time forward, a place in history entirely **subordinate** to his warlike and powerful brother. An interval of comparative quiet succeeded this over-throw of the Prophet's concentrated forces, a quiet destined to be broken by a far more extensive and disastrous war. When open hostilities commenced between England and the United States, in 1812, it was at **once** evident that the former country had pursued her old policy of rousing up the savages to ravage our defenseless frontier, with unprecedented success. Tecumseh proved a more valuable coadjutor, if possible, than Brant had been during the revolution, in uniting the different nations against the American interest.

A strong British fortress at Malden, on the eastern or Canada shore of Detroit river, proved a rendezvous for the hostile Indians, of the utmost danger to the inhabitants of the north-western frontier. The place was under the command of the British General Proctor; the officer whose infamous neglect or countenance led to the massacre of a body of wounded prisoners at Frenchtown, on the river Raisin, in January, 1813. This post was abandoned by the British and Indians, about the time of the invasion of Canada, in September, of the above year, by the American troops under Harrison.

General Harrison hastened in pursuit of the enemy up the Thames river, and, on the 4th of October, encamped a few miles above the forks of the river, and erected a slight fortification. On the 5th, the memorable battle of the Thames was fought. General Proctor awaited the approach of the American forces at a place chosen by himself, near Moravian town, as presenting a favorable position for a stand. His forces, in regulars and Indians, rather out-numbered those **of his** opponents, being set down at two thousand eight hundred; the Americans numbered twenty-five hundred, mostly militia and volunteers. The British army was flanked, on the left, by the river Thames, and supported by artillery, and on the right by two extensive swamps, running nearly parallel to the river, and occupied by a strong body of Indians, who were commanded by Tecumseh in person.

The British line was broken by the first charge of Colonel Johnson's mounted regiment, and being thrown into irretrievable disorder, the troops were unable to rally, or **oppose** any further effective resistance. Nearly the whole army surrendered at discretion. Proctor, with a few companions, effected his escape. The Indians, protected by the covert where they were posted, were not so easily dislodged. They maintained their position until after the defeat of their English associates and the death of their brave leader. By whose hand Tecumseh fell, does not appear to be decisively settled; but, according to the ordinarily received account, he was rushing upon Colonel Johnson, with his tomahawk, when the latter shot him dead with a pistol.

This battle was, in effect, the conclusion of the Northwestern Indian war. Deputations from various tribes appeared suing for peace; and during this and the ensuing year, when Generals Harrison and Cass, with Governor Shelby, were appointed commissioners to treat with the Northwestern tribes, important treaties were effected. Tecumseh was buried near the field of battle.

CHAPTER XII.

ACQUISITION OF INDIAN LANDS BY THE GOVERNMENT—GENERALS ATKINSON AND DODGE'S CAMPAIGN—BLACK-HAWK'S SURRENDER.

In July, 1830, a treaty was formed at Prairie du Chien, between United States commissioners and the tribes of the Iowas, Sioux, Omawhas, Sacs and Foxes, for the purpose of finally arranging the terms upon which the lands east of the Mississippi should be yielded up. The Sac chief, Keokuk, was present, and assenting to the arrangement in behalf of his people; but a strong party, headed by the celebrated Black-Hawk, utterly refused to abide by it. This chief was then between sixty and seventy years of age, and had been, from early youth, a noted warrior.

To enforce the removal of the Sacs from their villages, on Rock river, General Gaines visited that locality in June, 1831. He proceeded up the river in a steamer, with several pieces of artillery and two companies of infantry. Before the close of the month the forces of the United States and the state militia took possession of the settlement. The Indians made no attempt at resistance, and betook themselves to the western bank of the Mississippi. In the spring of the following year, the Sacs began to straggle back to their old towns in Illinois; and Black-Hawk, with a considerable force of his warriors, marched up Rock river, with the avowed intent of spending the summer, and raising a supply of corn among the Pottawatomies, in accordance with an invitation from that tribe. He proceeded quietly and peaceably up the river offering no violence to either the persons or property of the white inhabitants. A body of mounted militia, under Major Stillman, set out in pursuit of the Indians about the middle of May. On their approach to his temporary quarters, Black-Hawk sent a number of his followers to meet and confer with the commanding officer; but it so happened, either through mistake as to their intentions, or from a reckless depravity on the part of certain of the whites, that several of these emissaries were killed.

Roused by this injurious treatment, the Indian chief prepared to fall upon his pursuers at a point where an ambuscade could be rendered most effective. It is said that when the militia came up, he had but about forty warriors with him, (the rest of his men being off in pursuit of game,) while the whites numbered no less than two hundred and seventy! As these undisciplined troops were crossing Sycamore creek, in entire disorder, and without any precaution against a surprise, they were fiercely attacked by the Indians. The route was complete: unable to form, or to offer any effectual resistance, the whites were driven off, leaving eleven of their number dead upon the field. Great excitement was produced by this skirmish, and a large army of militia was called into service by Governor Reynolds. Agents were sent to confirm the good-will of the Winnebagos, and other tribes, and the services of several hundred of the Menomonies and Sioux were enlisted against the dangerous intruders.

Black-Hawk and his party, feeling themselves now fully committed, were not slow in following up the advantage gained by the terror inspired by the engagement at Sycamore Creek. Between the breaking out of the war and the beginning of the month of August the Indians committed many murders, and various skirmishes took place between them and the troops sent in pursuit. A little settlement on Indian Creek was plundered. Fifteen of the inhabitants were killed, and two young girls, by the name of Hall, one sixteen and the other eighteen years of age, were carried into captivity. According to the almost universal custom of the North American Indians, these female prisoners were not exposed to the slightest insult or outrage, but were as well cared for as circumstances would allow. They were afterward ransomed, at a large price, and returned to their friends.

Little mercy was shown to any of Black-Hawk's followers upon any occasion of success on the part of the whites. Five persons were killed near Galena on the 14th of June, and, shortly after, twelve Indians, supposed to be connected with the attacking party, were pursued and driven into a neighboring swamp. When overtaken, although they made no resistance, they were every one killed and scalped by the whites.

The condition of Black-Hawk and his band grew daily more miserable, from destitution, exposure, and starvation. An

and would speedily have been put to their operations, but for that terrible disease, the cholera, by which the United States troops, on their route from the east to the scene of action, where almost wholly disabled. Driven from his encampment at the Four Lakes by the approach of General Atkinson, Black-Hawk retreated down the Wisconsin, expecting to find provisions and assistance among the Indians in that direction. General Dodge, with a strong force of militia, followed close on his trail. He came up with the fugitives on the 21st of July. The Indians were about crossing the river when they were attacked, and, but for the coming on of night, could hardly have escaped entire destruction or capture. They lost in the encounter not far from forty men. The discomfited savages continued their flight down the river in their boats, beset on every side by enemies, and with an overwhelming force—Dodge's army having been joined by Atkinson and his troops in hot pursuit. Some of the boats, conveying these poor wretches, were upset, and many of those in them drowned; the greater number, however, fell into the hands of their enemies in their passage. Many of the children were found to be in such a famished state that they could not be revived.

Having reached the mouth of the river, on the first of August, Black-Hawk prepared to cross the Mississippi, but was prevented by a force on board the steamboat Warrior. He did not wish to fight, but to escape; and when the steamboat fell in with him, he used every means to give the captain of her to understand that he desired to surrender. He displayed two white flags, and about one hundred and fifty of his men approached the river without arms, and made signs of submission. The only reply was a discharge of canister and musketry from the boat, which was returned from the shore. After about an hour's firing, which resulted in the destruction of more than twenty of the Indians, the boat moved off to procure a supply of wood.

Next morning General Atkinson, with the whole force in pursuit, (sixteen hundred men) came up with the remnant of the enemy. Retreat was cut off on every side, and the half-starved and dispirited savages were shot and cut down at the pleasure of the irresistible numbers who surrounded them. The following is extracted from an account published

DEATH OF AN INDIAN CHIEF.

shortly after this decisive and final engagement. "The battle lasted upwards of three hours. About fifty of the enemy's women and children were taken prisoners, and many, by accident, in the battle, were killed. When the Indians were driven to the bank of the Mississippi, some hundreds of men, women, and children, plunged into the river, and hoped, by diving, etc., to escape the bullets of our guns; very few, however, escaped our sharp-shooters."

Historians generally speak of an action in which the Indians prove successful as a "massacre," but the above-described proceeding is dignified by the name of a battle! Black-Hawk, who, with a few followers, managed to effect his escape, afterward declared that, upon the approach of the American army, he and his warriors made no attempt at resistance, offering to surrender themselves unconditionally, and that they only used their arms when it was apparent that the successful pursuers had not intention of showing quarter. It is hard to decide upon the true state of the case.

His cause now being palpably hopeless, and most of his remaining warriors having yielded themselves prisoners, or been taken by the various bands of Indians friendly to the whites, Black-Hawk surrendered himself at Prairie du Chien, on the 27th of August. With several other chiefs he was taken to Washington, and after holding conference with President Jackson, was confined, for a period, at Fort Monroe, on an island dear Old Point Comfort, on the Chesapeake. Here the captive warriors were well and kindly treated, and in June, 1833, there being no longer any necessity for detaining them as hostages, they were set at liberty.

Black-Hawk lived thenceforth in peace with the whites. He settled upon the Des Moines river, where he died in 1838. The body of the old warrior, in accordance with his own wishes, expressed shortly before his death, was disposed in Indian style. No grave was made; but his body was placed in a sitting position, with his cane between his knees and grasped in his hands; slabs or rails were then piled up about him. Such was the end of Black-Hawk. Here, however, his bones did not long rest in peace, but they were stolen from their place of deposit some time in the following winter; but about a year after, it was discovered that they were in possession of a surgeon, of Quincy, Illinois, to whom some person had sent them to be wired together. When Governor Lucas, of Iowa, became acquainted with the facts, they were, by his requisition, restored to his friends.

CHAPTER XIII.

FRENCH WAR WITH THE NATCHEZ AND CHICKASAWS—RAVAGES OF SMALL-POX AND RUM AMONG OTHER TRIBES.

The Catawbas, who dwelt between the Carolinas and the country of the Cherokees, by intercourse with the whites, they became very degraded and drunkenness, indolence, and poverty were obviously prevalent among them. They were a numerous and warlike people when South Carolina was first settled, mustering about fifteen hundred warriors; but small-pox and the use of ardent spirits had, about 1775, reduced them to less then one-tenth of their former numbers.

The Upper Cherokees inhabited the high and mountainous region of the Appalachian range, and that upon the upper portions of the Tennessee. The Lower tribe occupied the country around the head waters of the Savannah and Chatahoochee, to the northward of the Muscogees or Creeks proper. About the year 1735 they were computed by old traders to number six thousand fighting men. They had sixty-four populous towns. In 1738, nearly half of them perished by the small-pox. The strange remedies and enchantments used to stay its progress, were remarkable. One course was to plunge the patients into cold running water. The result of which operation was speedily fatal. A great many killed themselves; for, being naturally proud, they despaired of regaining their former beauty—some shot themselves, others cut their throats, some stabbed themselves with knives, and others with sharp-pointed canes; many threw themselves with sullen madness into the fire, and there slowly expired, as if they had been utterly divested of the native power of feeling pain. One of them, when his friends had restrained these frantic efforts, and deprived him of his weapons, went out, and taking a thick and round hoe-helve, fixed one end of it in the ground, and repeatedly threw himself on it till he forced it down his throat, when he immediately expired.

The Creeks were a nation formed by the union of a number of minor tribes with the Muscogees, who constituted the nucleus of the combination. About the middle of the eighteenth century, they were computed to number three thousand five hundred men capable of bearing arms. They had learned the necessity of secluding those infected with the small-pox, so as to avoid the spread of the contagion, and their general habits and usages were such that they were fast increasing, instead of diminishing, like all the surrounding tribes.

While the Floridas were in the possession of Spain, the Creeks were surrounded by belligerent powers, both native and European, and they appear to have adopted a very shrewd and artful policy in their intercourse with each. There was a French garrison in their country; the English settlements lay to the north and east, and those of the Spaniards to the south; and the old sages of the tribe " being long informed by the opposite parties of the different views and intrigues of those foreign powers, who paid them annual tribute under the vague appellation of presents, were become surprisingly crafty in every turn of low politics." The French were very successful in their efforts to conciliate the good-will of the Muscogees, and in alienating them from the English.

The country of the Choctaws extended from that of the Muscogees to the Mississippi, reaching northward to the boundaries of the Chickasaws: their lower towns on the river were about two hundred miles north of New Orleans.

The strange custom of flattening the head, prevalent among some other American tribes, obtained with the Choctaws. The operation was performed by the weight of a bag of sand kept upon the foreheads of the infants before the skull had hardened. This process not improbably affected the powers of the mind.

The French had acquired great influence over the Choctaws, and their masterly skill enabled them to do more with those savages, with trifles, than all our experienced managers of Indian affairs have been able to effect by the great quantities of valuable goods they gave them with a very profuse hand. The former bestowed their small favors with exquisite wisdom; and their value was exceedingly enhanced by the external kindly behavior and well-adapted smooth address of the giver.

The nation of the Chickasaws was settled near the sources of the Tombigbee, a few miles eastward of the head waters of the Tallahache. They numbered about four hundred and fifty warriors, and were ever inimical to the French and friendly to the English colonists. It was by their efforts that the neighboring tribe of the Natchez was stirred up to attack the French settlements, in 1729. The French had, unadvisedly, imposed a species of tax upon the Natchez, demanding a dressed buck-skin from each man of the tribe, without rendering any return. The Chickasaws were not slow to foment a disturbance upon intelligence of this proceeding, and sent messengers, with presents of pipes and tobacco, to counsel an attack upon the exercisers of such tyranny. Nothing so strongly excites an Indian's indignation as any attempt at taxation, and the Natchez were easily persuaded that the French had resolved to crush and enslave them. It took about a year to ripen the plot, as the Indians are slow in their councils on things of great importance, though equally close and intent.

In November, 1729, the Indians fell upon the French settlement. The commandant had received some intimation of the intended attack from a woman of the tribe, but did not place sufficient dependence upon it to take any efficient steps for the protection of his charge. The whole colony was massacred: men, women and children, to the number of over seven hundred perished by the weapons of the savages. The triumph of the Natchez was, however, but of short duration. The French came upon them the following summer with a large army, consisting of two thousand of their own soldiers and a great array of Choctaw allies. The Natchez were posted at a strong fort near a lake communicating with the Bayou D'Argent, and received the assailants with great resolution and courage. They made a vigorous sally, as the enemy approached, but were driven within their defences, and bombarded with three mortars, which forced them to fly. The Choctaws took many prisoners, some of whom were tortured to death, and the rest shipped to the West Indies as slaves.

The remnant of the Natchez fled for safety to the Chickasaws. This brought about a war between the French and the last mentioned tribe, in which, the Indians had decidedly the advantage. In one engagement, in which the French and their Indian allies had surrounded the Chickasaw settlements in the night, with the exception of one, which stood at some distance from the rest, the besiegers beset every house, and killed all who came out: but at the dawn of day, when they were capering and using those flourishes that are peculiar to that volatile nation, the other town drew round them, stark naked, and painted all over red and black; thus they attacked them, killed numbers on the spot, released their brethern, who joined them like enraged lions. The Indians belonging to the French party fled, but the whites were all killed except two, an officer, and a negro, who faithfully held his horse till he mounted, and then ran along side of him. A couple of swift runners overtook them, and told them to live and go home, and inform their people, that as the Chickasaw hogs had now plenty of ugly French carcases to feed on till next year, they hoped then to have another visit from them and their red friends; and that, as messengers, they wished them safe home.

On another occasion the French approached the Chickasaw stockade, strangely disguised, and protected from the balls of the enemy by paddings of wool. The Indians were astonished at their invulnerability, and were about to desist from active resistance, and resort to the skill of their own necromancers to oppose what they thought must be wizzards, or old Frenchmen carrying the ark of war against them. As the enemy approached, and began to throw hand-grenades into the fort, they were quickly undeceived, and set in earnest about the work of defence. They pulled the matches out of the grenades, or threw them back among the French; and, sallying forth, directed an effective fire at the legs of the enemy, who were speedily driven off.

CHAPTER XIV.

CHEROKEE WAR—INTRIGUES OF REV. THOMAS BOSOMWORTH—MURDER OF INDIAN HOSTAGES.

When James Edward Oglethorpe commenced the settlement of Georgia with his little colony of a 114 souls, in 1733, the Creek Indians laid claim to the territory southwest of the Savannah river. He secured the services of a half-breed woman, named Mary Musgrove, who could speak English, to bring about a conference with the chiefs of the tribe at Savannah, the seat of the new settlement.

Mary had formerly married a white trader from Carolina. Beside her usefulness as an interpreter, she had such influence over her tribe, that Oglethorpe thought it worth his while to purchase her services at the rate of one hundred pounds a year. She became afterward, a source of annoyance to the English.

Fifty chiefs of the Creek nation were assembled at the place of conference, and Tomochichi, the most noted among those then known to the settlers, made an amicable speech, proffering at the same time a present of a buffalo-skin, adorned with eagles' feathers. A treaty was concluded, subject to the ratification of the English crown, by virtue of which the Indians were to consider themselves the subjects of the king, and to live in peace and friendship with his white colonists. The lands lying between the Savannah and Altamaha, were made over to the English, with all the islands on that coast, except St. Catharine's and two others, which were reserved for the Indians as bathing and fishing stations.

In April, 1734, Oglethorpe took Tomochichi, his queen, and several other Indians with him to England. They were presented to the king, and every pains was taken to produce a strong impression upon their minds of the English power and magnificence. All the Indians with whom the first governor of Georgia held intercourse seem to have formed a great attachment for him, styling him their "beloved man." If others in authority among the English colonies had pursued as honest a course toward the natives, much bloodshed would doubtless have been averted.

When difficulties arose in 1738, connected with the conflicting claims of England and Spain to jurisdiction over the new country, Spanish agents were dispatched to win over the Creeks. They decoyed a body of them to Augustine, by pretenses that Oglethorpe was there, and that he was desirous of seeing them. On their arrival, the Indians were told that the English governor was sick on board one of the ships; but they had begun to suspect deception, and, refusing to go out to the vessel, left the town in great disgust. Their suspicions were confirmed when they reached home, and the transaction only strengthened their dislike to the Spaniards. In the following year, Tomochichi died, being nearly ninety-seven years of age.

The year 1749 was memorable for a most audacious attempt on the part of one Thomas Bosomworth to aggrandize himself by attaining a supremacy over the Creeks. He had been formerly a chaplain in Oglethorpe's regiment, and had married Mary Musgrove, his half-breed interpreter. In December, 1747, this man fell in with a company of chiefs, belonging to the nation, then on a visit to Frederica; and persuaded them to sign certain articles, acknowledging one of their number, named Malatche Opiya Meco, as rightful king over the whole Creek nation. Bosomworth then procured from Malatche a conveyance, for certain considerations—among other things, a large quantity of ammunition and clothing,—of the islands formerly reserved by the Indians, to himself and his wife Mary, their heirs and assigns. This deed was regularly witnessed, and recorded in due form. Bosomworth made some efforts to improve these islands, but, his ambition becoming aroused by success in his first intrigue, he entered upon one much more extensive. By his persuasions, his wife now made the extraordinary claim that she was Malatche's elder sister, and entitled to regal authority over the whole Creek territory.

A great meeting of the tribe was procured, and, whatever of truth Mary's claims might be founded upon, she succeeded in persuading large numbers of the Creeks to acknowledge her as an independent queen. Accompanied by a strong force of her adherents, she proceeded to Savannah, sending emissaries before her to demand a surrender of all lands south of the Savannah river, and to make known her intention of enforcing her claim by the entire destruction of the colony, should her demands be resisted.

The militia were called out by the president and council, and the Indians were kept quiet, by a display of confidence and firmness, that matters might be fully discussed by their leaders and the colonial authorities. Bosomworth, in his canonical robes, with his queen by his side, followed by the kings and chiefs, according to rank, marched into the town on the 20th of July, making a most formidable appearance.

Lengthy discussions ensued between Bosomworth and Mary on the one hand, and the president and council on the other. The savages leaned alternately to either opinion, according as they were harangued by their new leaders, or listened to the explanations of the other party. They were told that Mary's claims to royal descent were entirely false; that she was the daughter of a white man by a squaw of no note, and that the mad ambition of her reprobate husband had led to the whole movement. They expressed themselves convinced, but no sooner had Mary obtained another opportunity to communicate with them than she succeeded in inflaming their minds. It was found necessary to confine her and her husband before the savages could be quietly dispersed. Before this was accomplished, the town was in imminent danger, as the Indians vastly outnumbered the whites; and a very slight matter might have so roused their fury that the whole colony would have been annihilated. Bosomworth and his wife obtained a decision in their favor, in 1759, by virtue of which they took possession of St. Catherine's island, and resided upon it the remainder of their lives.

The breaking out of the Cherokee war, in the winter of 1759, was an event of special interest. Upon the evacuation of Fort Duquesne, numbers of Indian warriors, whose services were no longer required, set out upon their return home. Having been ill-supplied with provisions, and having lost their horses, some of them caught such animals as they found loose in the woods. In revenge for this theft, the German settlers of Virginia fell upon them, and murdered and scalped a considerable number. They even imitated, in several instances, the horrible cruelties of the savages in the manner of butchery. The Cherokees did not, for a long time, attempt any retaliation for this act, but made peaceable ap-

INDIAN MASSACRES. 97

plications to the authorities of Virginia and the Carolinas; but all was in vain, and fresh insults and injuries, received from certain officers at Fort St. George, finally excited the nation to fury.

The French, and, at their instance, the Muscogees, were not slow in availing themselves of the above circumstances to stir up a war against the English. The Cherokees determined upon direct retaliation for the massacres by the Germans. A party, bound on this errand, first killed two soldiers near Fort Loudon, on the south bank of Tennessee river, and afterward spread themselves among the western settlements of North Carolina, killing such of the whites as fell in their power.

William H. Lyttleton, governor of South Carolina, then set himself strenuously both to prepare for the defense of the colonies, and to bring about an adjustment of difficulties. At Fort St. George, on the Savannah, he held a conference with six Cherokee chiefs, on the 26th of December, 1759, and formed a treaty of peace, secured by the delivery of thirty-two Indian hostages. These were placed in close confinement in a small and miserable hut, and the governor returned to Charleston. According to the usual course of events, the Cherokees denied the authority of the chiefs who had concluded the above treaty, and hostilities broke out afresh. Captain Coytmore, commandant at Fort George, was an object of the bitterest hatred on the part of the Indians, and a large party of them, besieged the fort in February, 1760. The place was too strong to be taken by assault, but the Indian chief managed to entice Coytmore out of the defenses into an ambush, where he was shot dead, and lieutenants Bell and Foster, who accompanied him, were wounded. The hostages who were confined within the works, shouted to encourage their friends without, and when an attempt was made to put them in irons, resisted manfully, stabbing one soldier, and wounding two others. Upon this, a hole was cut in the roof over their heads, and the cowardly garrison butchered them by shooting down from above.

Colonel Montgomery reached Carolina in April, 1760, and hastened, in command of regulars and provincials, to make an effective inroad upon the Indians. His progress through the lower Cherokee country was marked by the destruction of Indian towns. Estatoe, containing two hundred houses, with great quantities of provisions, was entirely destroyed; but the inhabitants were saved by a timely flight. Every other settlement east of the Blue Ridge afterward shared the same fate.

The army made some stay at Fort Prince George, and useless endeavors were put forth to bring about a pacification with the upper portion of the Cherokees. In June the troops were again on their advance into the wilderness of the interior. Near Etchoe, the native warriors prepared a most skillful ambuscade to check the advancing forces. It was in a deep valley, through which ran a muddy stream, with steep banks; on either side of which the way was completely choked with brushwood. Some hard fighting took place at this spot, in which twenty of the whites were killed and seventy-six wounded. The loss on the side of the Indians was much less, and, although driven from the spot where the first stand was made, they intrenched themselves a little farther on. Under these circumstances, Montgomery determined to secure the safety of his troops, and to provide for the requisite attention to his wounded men, by a retreat. He soon after sailed for New York, leaving four companies of regulars, under Major Hamilton, for the protection of the frontier.

The garrison at Fort Loudon was now in peril. The provisions of the place were nearly exhausted, and Chief Occonostota was laying close siege to it with his fierce and enraged warriors. After suffering great extremes of privation, the two hundred men at this place were obliged to capitulate, and trust to the honor of their savage enemy. Captain Steuart, an officer greatly in favor with all the friendly Indians, arranged the terms upon which the fort should be evacuated. The troops were to be allowed a free and unmolested passage to Virginia, or Fort Prince George, and a detachment of Indians was to accompany them for the purpose of supplying provisions by hunting.

The garrison marched out on the 7th of August, 1760. Occonostota himself, with a number of other natives, kept company with the whites, during the first day's march of fifteen miles; but these all disappeared when they reached Taliquo. On the next morning, just before day, (the time generally selected by Indians for a surprise, as men sleep more soundly then than at any other hour,) a large body of armed savages, in war-paint, were seen by a sentinel, creeping through the bushes, and gathering about the camp. Hardly was the alarm given when the attack was made: twenty-six of the half-starved soldiers were killed outright, and the rest were pinioned and marched back to the fort.

Captain Steuart was among the prisoners, but his evil fortune was alleviated by the staunch friendship of the benevolent Atakullakulla. This chief, as soon as he heard of Steuart's situation, hastened to Fort Loudon, and purchased him of the Indian who took him, giving him his rifle, clothes, and all that he could command by way of ransom: he then took possession of Captain Demere's house, where he kept his prisoner as one of his family, and humanely shared with him the little provisions his table afforded, until an opportunity should offer of rescuing him.

A quantity of ammunition was discovered by the Indians, buried in the fort, and Occonostota determined to proceed at once to lay siege to Fort Prince George. Captain Steuart was informed that the assistance of himself and his men would be required in the management of the great guns, and that, furthermore, if the garrison should refuse to capitulate, all the prisoners now in the hands of the Indians should, one by one, be burned in sight of the fort. Perceiving the difficulty of his situation, the captain begged his kind old proprietor to assist him in effecting an escape, and Attakullakulla readily lent his aid. Upon pretence of taking his prisoner out for a hunt, he left Fort Loudon, with his wife and brother, and two English soldiers, and took a direct course for the Virginia frontier. After a most toilsome and dangerous march, they fell in with a party of three hundred men, sent out for the relief of such of the garrison at Fort Loudon as might have effected their escape. Being now in safety, Captain Steuart dismissed his Indian friends with handsome rewards, to return and attend to the welfare of his former fellow-prisoners. Such of them as had survived were afterward ransomed and delivered up at Fort Prince George.

In the following spring, Colonel James Grant, who had succeeded to the command of the Highlanders employed in British service in America, commenced active operations against the belligerent nation. What with the aid of the provincials and friendly Indians, he was at the head of about twenty-six hundred men. The army reached Fort Prince George on the 27th of May, 1761, and there old Attakullakulla made his appearance, deprecating the proposed vengeance of the whites upon his people. He was told that the English still felt the strongest regard for him individually, but that the ill-will and misconduct of the majority of the nation were too palpable and gross to be suffered to go longer unpunished. Colonel Grant marched from the fort in the month of June, and advanced nearly to the spot where Montgomery's progress had been arrested, before coming to an engagement. Here the Cherokees, on the 10th, made a desperate but unavailing stand; they were routed and dispersed, leaving their towns and villages of the interior to be destroyed by the invaders. Etchoe was burned, and other towns, fourteen in number, shared the same fate: the corn, cattle, and other stores of the enemy, were likewise destroyed, and those miserable savages, with their families, were driven to seek shelter and subsistence among the barren mountains.

Upon the return of the army to Fort Prince George, after this campaign, Attakullakulla again visited the camp, bringing with him a number of other Cherokee chiefs. Broken down by their disastrous losses, and disgusted with the deceitful promises of the French, they gladly acceded to such terms as Colonel Grant thought fit to impose, and a treaty of peace was formally concluded.

CHAPTER XV.

WAR OF 1813-14—GENERAL JACKSON DEFEATS THE INDIANS AT HORSE-SHOE BEND—END OF THE CONFLICT.

AFTER the termination of the revolutionary war, and the establishment of the independence of the United States, the intrigues of foreign opposing parties no longer operated to foment disturbance, or to tempt the unfortunate savages to engage in quarrels where they had nothing to gain, and which ever resulted in their final discomfiture. By a steady increase of numbers, and the adventurous spirit of pioneers, the white settlers every where made advances upon Indian territory. Sometimes large acquisitions would be made by a government purchase; but, to no small extent, the opinion that the occupation of a few roving savages could give no natural title to lands, as opposed to the claims of those who had reclaimed, inclosed, and improved the wilderness, satisfied the consciences of the encroachers. The argument in favor of this conclusion is by no means without force; but who can take upon himself to draw the line of demarkation which shall decide, upon any principle of universal application, the bounds of so artificial a right as the ownership of land?

At the time of the declaration of war with England, (June 18th, 1812,) the whole western border of the United States was in a position of the greatest danger and insecurity. Many minor forays took place, but the destruction of Fort Mimms in Mississippi, in 1813, and subsequent battles of that year were the most important in the early part of the century. A party of about 1,000 warriors, led by Chief Weatherford, fell upon this fort August 30. The post was garrisoned by one hundred and sixty efficient soldiers; the rest of its occupants, to the number of one hundred and fifteen, consisted of old men, women and children. The forces were under the command of Major Beasly. No regular preparations had been made for the reception of so powerful an enemy, and although the soldiers did their duty manfully, they were overpowered, and all slain except seventeen. The women and children having ensconced themselves in several block houses, met with a more terrible fate. The savages set fire to the buildings, and consumed them, together with their inmates.

The settlers inhabiting exposed districts were now obliged to fly for safety to places of protection, and the hostile hordes of Indians were collecting their warriors, for further inroads upon the frontier. To resist them, a large force was called into requisition in Tennessee, and the command bestowed upon General Andrew Jackson, who determined to take the field in person, and pushed on the necessary preparations with all that zeal and energy which marked his character through life.

While encamped at Ten Islands the general ascertained the rendezvous of the enemy to be about 13 miles below. Colonel Coffee, with nine hundred men, was promptly ordered to engage them. He approached the Indian camp, and so disposed his forces as to partially surround it, while several companies, were marched in to beat up the enemies' quarters. The savages fought boldly and desperately, but were overpowered and driven into their buildings, where one hundred and eighty-six of their number perished, fighting hand to hand. Eighty-four women and children were taken prisoners, and a number were killed. This battle was fought on the 3rd of November.

A species of fortification was now prepared at the islands, and named Fort Strother. On the 7th of the month, information was received that the enemy was collecting in force to attack Talladega,—a post about thirty miles below, occupied by friendly Indians,—and General Jackson, with nearly his whole army, consisting of twelve hundred infantry and eight hundred mounted men, hastened to its relief. It was about midnight when the march commenced, and on the evening of the ensuing day, a spot only six miles from Talladega was reached. By four o'clock, on the following morning, the troops were again in motion; and, acting upon intelligence obtained by reconnoitering during the night, General Jackson was enabled so to dispose his troops as partially to surround the camp before the action commenced. The Indians displayed both courage and firmness, and by the impetuosity of their attack, broke through the line of the advancing forces and made their escape to the mountains, three miles distant. The force of the enemy was one thou-

Kireben*uit* 103

Warraeensitt

Bomaseen

Wadacanaquin

Æneas

Iteansis

Jackoid

Joseph

Sauguaaram

Arexus

Francois Xavier

Meganumba

sand and eighty, of whom two **hundred** and ninety-nine were **left dead** on the ground; and **it is believed** that many were **killed** in the flight, who **were not found** when the estimate was made. Their loss, on this occasion, was not less than six hundred: that of the Americans was fifteen killed **and** eighty wounded, several **of** whom afterward died.

After the battle at Talladega, the Hallibee Indians, who were largely concerned in that transaction, sued for peace. They were told by the American general that this should be accorded, upon condition **of** the restoration of plundered property, and the delivering up of those who had taken part in the massacre at Fort Mimms. Unfortunately, while these negotiations were pending, General White, acting **under** orders independent of General Jackson, attacked the towns **of** these Indians, destroyed many of their warriors, and carried off several hundred captives. Supposing that this was **by** Jackson's orders, they expected no further favor, and fought thereafter **with** the desperation of men to whom **no** quarter was to be given.

The result of this Indian campaign was the entire reduction of the hostile nations. In various battles they were defeated and destroyed. The most noted of these were at Autossee, where some two hundred were massacred, on the 29th of November, and that of the great bend in the Tallapoosie, known as Horse Shoe Bend. At this latter point, **the** Indians fortified themselves for a last and desperate stand.

They were supposed to be about one thousand in number, and had been, for some time, strengthening their position by every means within their reach. This **was in** March, 1814. On the 27th, General Jackson, with a **force of** whites and friendly Indians, three times the **number of** the enemy, **commenced** operations against the **fort**. General Coffee, with most of the cavalry and Indian allies, was directed to surround the bend, in order to cut off all retreat across the river. The place was then carried **by storm**, under a **heavy** fire from within. More than half the Indians were killed at the fort, and **an** unknown number perished in their endeavors to escape by crossing the river, beset as it was by the assailants. Not more than twenty ever **reached a** place of safety. At a time when **it** was evident that the fortune **of the day** was decided, **General Jackson sent a** messenger, with a flag of truce, to invite a surrender, but, from ignorance or desperation, the savages fired upon the bearer of the flag. After this, no mercy was shown: until night put an end to the work of destruction, they were shot or cut down wherever they could be found, and even on the following morning a considerable number were ferreted out from the "caves and reeds," where they had sought concealment, and were remorselessly put to death. Several hundred women and children were made captives. The loss of the attacking army, in this battle, was fifty-five killed, and one hundred and forty-six wounded.

In April, General Jackson, having effected a junction with the troops from Georgia, under Colonel Milton, received a deputation from the principal hostile tribes, expressing a wish for peace. The general demanded, as one condition upon which he would treat, and as a test of the sincerity of the proposal, that the great but notorious Weatherford should be delivered up for punishment. This chief, hearing of the requisition, and hopeless of further success in resistance, came voluntarily to the American camp, and presenting himself before the commander, with characteristic dignity and composure, requested peace for his people, and announced his own submission to his fate, whatever it might be.

This was the last important incident of the campaign. The Indians submitted to the dictation of the whites, and retired to the districts assigned them, eastward of the Coosa.

CHAPTER XVI.

THE MINNESOTA, FETTERMAN, PIEGAN, CUSTER AND UTE MASSACRES.
GENS. SHERIDAN, CUSTER AND MILES AMONG THE INDIANS.

In July, 1862, while the War of the Rebellion was being carried on, Sioux and other Indians belonging to the Upper Agency in Minnesota came down to the Government buildings by the Yellow Medicine river and encamped there in order to secure then annuities, as they were suffering from hunger. On Aug. 4th they broke into the Government storehouse, in presence of soldiers, and took out provisions. Four Indians shortly after this went to the houses of Robinson Jones and Howard Baker and shot those gentlemen, their wives, Miss Clara Wilson and Mr. and Mrs. Webster A general uprising of the Indians took place after this taste of blood, and the inhabitants of the place were entirely helpless, as many men had gone to enlist for the Southern war. James Lynde, a clerk in a store, was shot and instantly killed, as were two other persons in the store. As the Indians entered another store a clerk rushed through their midst and succeeded in getting 200 yards away, when he received two shots. He was stripped and had logs piled upon him to prevent his escape. When all were butchered at the agency the savages scattered over the country.

At the river the heroic ferryman continued to carrry over all who came, and was killed just as he had taken the last man across. He was disemboweled and his hands, feet and head cut off and thrust into the cavity.

The atrocities committed in this massacre almost surpass belief. Seven hundred people perished under the most heartrending cruelty. Neither age nor sex was regarded. Their great ambition seemed to be to outvie each other in new forms of torture. Girls of a tender age were violated by ruffians until death from exhaustion ended their sufferings. A father returned home to find his entire family killed, except a little boy, who was left for dead.

The Indians, about 400 in number, attacked New Ulm. The inhabitants were mostly German. They huddled together in the centre of the town and made a barricade of wagons, barrels, etc. The Indians were repelled, but ten whites were killed and fifty wounded. Four reds went to Mr. Anderson's house and asked for milk; after drinking it and returning the pan, they shot him dead and also killed his son who went to get them some potatoes. A boy, to escape detection, had covered himself with pulled grass by the roadside; but he was discovered and had his head cut off.

It was feared the Chippewas and Winnebagoes might join the Sioux. This would have meant annihilation to the people of Minnesota. There were 4,000 warriors within two days' march of St. Paul. The fact that there were several thousand volunteers in the state enlisted to fight the Southern Confederates probably was the salvation of the whites from wholesale butchery. Gov. Ramsey requested Col. Sibley to take charge of these troops and move up the Minnesota river. They came across a white woman who had traveled 70 miles without tasting food, carrying her babe on her pack. The savages had shot her through the shoulder. The same bullet cut off the baby's finger.

A company of 150 men under Major J. R. Brown came near being cut to pieces when detailed to bury the dead. Twenty-three men were killed and forty-five **wounded**. Ninety horses were killed. The soldiers had fallen **asleep** after a hard day's work, with no suspicion of danger. They were 31 hours fighting without food or water, **before** help arrived from the main body.

On the day after the battle, Little Crow and his braves took flight. Col. Sibley took possession of their camp of 100 tepees, furnished with carpets and stolen furniture. Here he found 250 captives. It was thought that if Col. Sibley had marched immediately to the camp after the battle, all the prisoners would have been killed. The Indian prisoners taken in these combats were tried by a military commission of five officers and a recorder, and on Feb. 26th, 1863, thirty-eight of them were hung, by order of the president of the United States.

* * * * * * * *

In 1866, the Government sent an invading expedition of whites to open a new route from Fort Laramie to Montana. Col. H. B. Carrington was in command of the force numbering 220 men. Fort Laramie was reached in June. There was a current of opposition noticeable among the Indians to the entrance of the whites upon their territory.

From July 26th to Dec. 21st the hostiles had killed 91 enlisted men, 5 officers, 58 citizens, and wounded 20 citizens and driven away 700 head of stock. On Dec. 21st the wood train was attacked about two miles from Fort Phil Kearney. Col. Carrington sent Col. Fetterman with 50 infantry and 26 cavalry men to defend the train, with orders not to engage or follow the Indians. Orders, for some reason that will never be known, were disregarded. Not a soldier returned. While the firing was progressing Capt. Ten Eyck, with 76 men, (all there were in the fort), went to the rescue. They found the dead naked bodies of Col. Fetterman, Captain Brown and 65 soldiers. They were all in a space of about 35 feet in diameter. A mile further on the bodies of Lieut. Grumond, three citizens and four or five soldiers were found. Only six men of the whole command lost their lives by balls, and two of these, Lieutenant-Colonel Fetterman and Captain Brown, no doubt inflicted this death upon themselves or each other, both being shot through the left temple, the powder being burnt into the skin and flesh about the wound Both officers had been heard to assert that they would not be taken alive by Indians.

The United States Senate committee, appointed to investigate the Fetterman massacre, reported that they found no living officer deserving of censure, but that the fault was traced to the Government itself in not sending reinforcements of men and ammunition to these new forts in Wyoming, where all was war, instead of permitting them to remain at such places as Fort Laramie, where all was peace.

* * * * * * * *

In 1868, Gen. Sheridan made a winter campaign against the Camanches and other Indians who did most of their fighting in summer. Through lack of provender many ponies died of starvation in winter. The expedition started from Fort Dodge November 12th. The 7th Cavalry consisted of 800 or 900 men. "California Joe" and a few half-civilized Osage Indians acted as scouts. Gen. Custer was in command. After arriving at the level of the valley of the Washita, white lodges were discovered among the trees. Soon a rifle shot rang out on the other side of the village, demonstrating that the other detachments had arrived at their posts, according to agreement. A grand charge was made upon the surprised warriors, but they seized their weapons and fought with desperate valor. Some of the savages ran in the direction of Major Elliot's attacking party and met with a warm reception. Many cavalry men dismounted and fought on foot. A squaw was seen trying to escape with a little white boy captive. Upon finding escape impossible, she drew a knife from her blanket and killed the child, and was immediately shot by a soldier. The Indians were routed and all of the lodges were burned. News of the victory was sent by courier to Gen. Sheridan, and in due season the army reached Camp Supply. Over 800 ponies were captured in this fight and all had to be shot. One hundred Indians were killed and a large number of prisoners captured. Among the whites killed were Major Elliot, Captain Hamilton and 19 soldiers. When the command got back to headquarters, Gen. Sheridan was so well pleased with the work done that he honored it with a review. The General continued operations against the Indians also in 1869 and 1870.

GEN. SHERIDAN.

Fabulous stories about mineral discoveries in Montana attracted a great number of whites to that territory, who wholly disregarded the rights of Indians, and of course there were conflicts and depredations of all kinds. In 1869, the settlers having been much injured by the murders and assaults of a small band of Piegan Indians, the authorities determined to punish them, and, after considerable discussion and consultation as to the extent and character of the chastisement, General Sheridan sent word to Colonel Baker, who was then moving against them, to "strike them hard."

On the morning of the 23rd of January, 1870, Colonel Baker came upon a village of these Piegans on the Marais river, who had not been implicated in the atrocities of the rest of their tribe. But the colonel deemed it advisable to regard the instructions of Sheridan, and accordingly attacked them, killing one hundred and seventy-three (fifty-three of whom were women and children), and capturing one hundred women and children, beside over three hundred horses.

* * * * * * * *

The rush to the Black Hills by miners and speculators when gold was discovered there, and the presence of troops under Gen. Custer, made the Sioux Indians, under Sitting Bull, very angry. In 1876, it became necessary to take measures to quiet the hostiles. On May 29th, Gen. Crook started north from Fort Fetterman with 47 officers, 1,000 men, and the necessary scouts and wagon train. On May 17th, General Terry marched westward with 600 cavalry and 400 infantry from Fort Lincoln. Col. Gibbon moved eastward from Fort Ellis with 450 men, cavalry and infantry. At the mouth of the Rosebud river the three columns met, and their three leaders decided on a plan of action. Failure to carry out this plan at the right time resulted in the sacrifice of Gen. Custer and his noble band. His command first discovered the Indian village in the valley of the Little Big Horn—the largest number of Indian huts ever seen in the West, and it was estimated that there were about 4,000 Indians.

The only knowledge the Government could get of this terrible massacre was through Curly, the Upsaroka scout, from Kill Eagle (an Indian who was in Sitting Bull's camp, but afterward surrendered), and from Ridgely, a white prisoner in the Sioux camp, all of whom were eye witnesses of the conflict. Curly's testimony was taken by Gen. Terry's staff officers through an interpreter. Custer and every man of his five companies were killed. The battle began at 2 o'clock and continued till sundown. Curly stated that Custer lived until nearly all his men were killed or wounded. When he saw Custer hopelessly surrounded, he watched his opportunity, washed the paint from his face, let down his hair like a Sioux, put on a Sioux blanket and worked his way up a ravine. When the savages charged he mingled with them and was not known from one of their own number. Seeing one of the mounted warriors fall, Curly ran and got on his pony, galloped down as if going toward the white men, but instead passed up a ravine and made his escape. He said he offered to show Custer a way of escape, which his thoroughbred horse could easily have aided him to accomplish, but he mo-

INDIAN MASSACRES. 111

tioned him away with his hand and stayed to die with his comrades. At last the General received a shot in his left side, and sat down; another shot struck him and he fell over. This battle occurred on Sunday, June 25th, 1876. On Monday, Col. Gibbon's column reached the bloody scene. They found that Custer's body was the only one not mutilated. Around him were **seven** of his officers, **among** whom were his two brothers, Boston and Thomas, and his brother-in-law, Lieut. Calhoun. Almost at his feet lay his nephew, Autie Reed, only 19 years old. The body of Mr. Kellogg, the correspondent of the *New York Herald*, was also among the dead.

Ridgely said that after the massacre the Indians took six of the prisoners and tied them to stakes and burned them to death, while the Indian boys were allowed to fire red-hot arrows into the in flesh. At night the squaws went to the battle-field and robbed and mutilated the bodies of the dead soldiers.

GEN. MILES.

As soon as possible after the Custer massacre, Gen. Sheridan concentrated his forces. Generals Cook and Terry were reinforced under Lieut.-Col. Curr, Lieut. Otis and Col. Miles, so that by Aug. 5th the united forces of the two generals numbered 4,000 men. All their hard marches were fruitless in engagements with the savages, until Oct. 21st, when Col. Miles overtook Sitting Bull, and held a two days' consultation with him, which was ended by a renewal of hostilities. He pursued the Indians for 42 miles, but they soon sued for peace. The campaign of 1877 was almost continuous with that of the preceding year, until April, when the Sioux became anxious to surrender. Spotted Tail brought 1,100 to the agency, which virtually ended the Sioux war.

On May 5th, Col. Miles (who afterward became General) engaged Tame Deer's forces on a branch of the Rosebud river, and captured 450 ponies and destroyed much property, **but he came** near losing his life while holding a conference **with Iron Star,** who, after shaking hands with him, picked up **his** gun and fired, but the bullet struck and killed a soldier behind the Colonel.

On July 25th, Gen. Sherman wrote, in one of his official reports from Fort Custer, that "there are no Indians hereabouts."

* * * * * * * *

The Ute Indians up to 1879 were peaceable with the whites. In 1868, a tract on Southern Colorado was set apart for their exclusive use; but soon immigrants began to encroach upon their lands. In 1873, they relinquished claim to their mining property for a consideration from the United States Government. They were the wards of Indian Agent Meeker, who was at one time agricultural editor of the *New York Tribune*. When he left its employ he formed a colony to settle in Colorado, and he called the place selected Greeley, after Horace Greeley, his former employer.

In the spring of 1879, Ute hunting parties went north beyond the limits of their reservation. Mr. Meeker wrote to the commander at Fort Steele to arrest the trespassers, and either retain them or send them back to their own reservation. Sept. 8th, of 1879, serious difficulty arose at Mr. Meeker's White River Agency. He was ploughing some of their land on which were some tents and corrals, and some of the Indians objected to the work. Equally as good ground was offered them in exchange, but they wouldn't listen to his proposal, so he ploughed away until stopped by armed men. Sept. 10th Mr. Meeker telegraphed to Washington for help, saying he had been forced out of his own house and badly injured. The War Department ordered Major Thornburgh, commandant at Fort Steele, to go to White River Agency to arrest the insubordinate Indians and enforce obedience. When the knowledge of the approaching troops was known, there was an uprising in which Agent Meeker and all his male assistants were killed, the agency building sacked and fired, and the women and children carried off to the south.

On the morning of the same day Major Thornburgh's command was attacked by a body of Utes when 15 miles distant, and the Major himself was killed. The captive women and children were rescued soon afterward by General Adams, who had been a former guardian of the Utes on their reservation.

INDIAN MASSACRES.

* * * * * * * *

In the *Commercial Advertiser* of Feb. 24th, 1895, Mr. John A. Cockerill gave his version of the Custer massacre. He holds that injustice was done the noble General by some critics, who claimed that he aimed at self destruction.

For nearly 20 years, he **says**, the "affair" at the **Little Big Horn** has been misunderstood, and a grave injustice has been done, first to General Custer, and secondly to the officers and soldiers **under** his command, who died with him that day. There are to day, probably, thousands of people in the United States who believe that General Custer engaged with the Indians on that occasion with a recklessness and a purpose which **in point** of fact aimed at self-destruction. This most unjust and cruel belief grows out of the fact that General Custer, **having** been but a few weeks before **summoned** to Washington to testify concerning the management in the West of army affairs, and especially with reference **to** the "sutler" or "post-trader" system, as well as the methods of awarding and fulfilling army contracts, had given testimony not only wholly unexpected and surprising, but most embarrassing and doubtless incredible to certain high government officials. He was, therefore, made very uncomfortable. He was brought to feel that he **was in** disgrace. **Never** before had his cards been returned to him when he **called at** the homes of distinguished men and influential officers **of** the government. His brilliant career during the war, wherein he rose from the rank of a just graduated second lieutenant to that of a major-general of volunteers, his proven courage and his wonderful success in all his daring, dashing forages upon the enemy or charges in battle—all these had made him a favorite hero in Washington, and up to this time he had been accustomed to be warmly welcomed and made much of wherever he went. When **all this was** changed he was cut to the heart, and refused to be comforted.

He undoubtedly left Washington feeling most keenly the injustice with which he had been treated; but to assume that **he went** determined to find death on the first occasion, is to cast a shadow of shame upon his name—a thing intolerable! Doubtless he went inspired by the purpose to demonstrate anew his value as **a** soldier; **but** those who knew him knew

well that there was not a drop in his **veins** of the cowardly **blood** which would lead a man to seek **to escape** by death unfairly accomplished those annoyances which had grown grievous to him.

Aside from this there is the testimony of the battlefield itself to show that Custer did not make a headlong plunge from a precipice from motives of pique, dragging down with him as brave a battalion of soldiers as the June sun ever shone upon. The "Custer massacre" was not a "massacre" in the sense in which it has been understood. It was a scene of carnage—that is true. It was an awful slaughter. But the popular notion that Custer and his men were driven **or** led into a trap and, huddled together like sheep, were slain **as** a band **of** men made helpless and delivered over to their **fate** by the folly of their leader, is a baseless invention.

For some days Custer had been hastening to overtake a band of Indians, which, from the trail they left, he knew did not exceed 1,200 or 1,500, at the most, who were, in turn, hastening to join Sitting Bull, to assist in that satanic schemer's uprising. He was deceived as to the numbers of those whom he was destined to meet, even after he had "located" their village and had made his attack accordingly. Was it poor scouting or was he deceived by treachery, pure and simple? Nobody lives to tell. We only know that the chivalric soul of General Custer would have never permitted him to sacrifice other lives than **his** own, even if he were determined upon deliberate suicide.

Dividing his command, Custer sent Major **Reno**, with four companies, to the left of **his** route, while Captain Benteen, with two **companies**, was to assail the Indian right more directly **and** perhaps turn it, while he, himself, with five companies, after giving Reno and Benteen time to reach their positions, moved boldly and swiftly around the point of the "hog-back," behind which he knew the enemy lay, forded the creek and advanced upon the village. At once, he was antagonized and with such force, determination and **confidence** as must have greatly surprised him. Here was his first opportunity to learn that he had more than 1,200 or 1,500 Pawnee Indians to engage with—and it is fairly a question whether he lived long enough to realize that he was sur**rounded** by an army numbering not less than 5,000 of **the** most savage and bloodthirsty of the Sioux and Cheyenne warriors.

Whatever he may have comprehended, **he fought like** the accomplished soldier that he was. After the battle the poor, defaced and mutilated bodies of his brave followers were buried where they fell, and where they were found—and through this circumstance we are afforded ample proof that neither he nor his followers suffered in the slightest from panic or demoralization. A long and mathematically accurate array of marble headstones dotting the front of the line of his main force shows where his skirmishers fell, each dead on his post; for the field has now become a national cemetery, and the cheap and simple boards which once marked the last resting place of these brave men have been succeeded by more lasting monuments.

No white man, as has been said, lives to tell the details of this battle; but there is a direct and pathetic story in the battle field itself which speaks with a clearness which cannot be misunderstood.

As he rushed forward with the major part of his five companies, the serried ranks of Sitting Bull's warriors rose **up about** and enclosed him in a wall of ferocious human devilishness—right, left, front and rear. He made his dispositions with rapidity, but with skillful coolness. Two troops of sixty men were thrown out upon the left to advance in parallel lines with his own movement.

With every step the slaughter became more terrible, but every landmark, every indication, shows that he fought his men with a presence of mind he could not have exceeded on parade. But the end was inevitable and in the length of time, as one Indian witness estimates, that it would take "a hungry Indian to eat his dinner," or as another said that would allow a candle "to burn a quarter of an inch,"—in, **say from 20 to** 25 minutes—all that was left of Custer and his men were their torn, mutilated and bleeding bodies lying on the spot where they had fought.

Instinctively, but according to military drill and discipline, as the mute but convincing testimony of the field itself demonstrates, the doomed soldiers gathered in groups of twos and fours; and here and there one **fell** fighting single-handed, without the "elbow touch" which gives courage to even the bravest. And there are sixty headstones which mark the graves of the men sent to the left—none are unaccounted for.

Around **Custer himself was**, of course, the greatest number of those under his **immediate** command—of the five companies—and on them the fiercest, hottest anger of his assailants was spent. Every white man was slain without mercy, and under the lead of the red **demon**, Rain-in-the-Face, who commanded a thousand Cheyennes, each and every body, save that of Custer alone, was shamefully mutilated. That chief himself tore the heart, hot and reeking, from the **body of** Lieutenant Tom Custer, the general's brother, and ate **it**, amid the diabolical applause of the fiends whom he led. This was in pursuance of a vow which he had made, and as revenge for a fancied wrong done him by the Lieutenant. Custer's body was saved from insult and mutilation. The wonderful career of the fearless leader was known to the savages, and secured this **immunity.**

Further than this it is **not** necessary to rehearse the story. It is true that Reno failed to come to the relief of his commander, and has been most severely criticised for that failure. Whether he ought to be or not, I cannot pretend to say. The "hog-backs" offered such resistance to the transmission of sound that I can readily understand how it might happen that Reno heard nothing and suspected nothing of the terrible conflict in which his comrades were engaged. But I do not understand why, under the circumstances, he did not at least try to keep in touch with his commander.

Still, I do not undertake to decide. It is too grave a matter.

History may and does show instances where men have bravely "died for men," but history cannot show an instance of greater devotion to duty than that of the men who fought and died in the battle of the Little Big Horn.

CHAPTER XVII.

PHYSICAL ENDURANCE BY YOUNG WARRIORS—INDIAN FIGHTING COURAGE—SUFFERINGS OF CAPTIVES, AND VARIOUS INDIAN MATTERS OF INTEREST.

The college athletes of the present day, who undergo many hardships on the football field, would collapse if they were called upon to undergo such ordeals as young Indian "bucks" were subjected to in being initiated into the order of warriors. Mr. Catlin, in his book on Indians tells what he saw enacted among the Mandan tribe.

The young warriors, preparatory to undergoing torture, were obliged, until the fourth day from their entry into the lodge, to abstain from food, drink, or sleep! On the fourth day commenced the more horrible portion of the exercises. Coming forward, in turn, the victims allowed the flesh of their breasts or backs to be pierced with a rough two-edged knife, and splinters of wood to be thrust through the holes. Enough of the skin and flesh were taken up to be more than sufficient for the support of the weight of the body. To these splints cords let down from the roof were attached, and the subject of these inflictions was hoisted from the ground. Similar splints were then thrust through the arms and legs, to which the warrior's arms, and, in some cases, as additional weights, several heavy buffalo heads, were hung.

Thus far the fortitude of the Indian sufficed to restrain all exhibition of pain; while the flesh was torn with the rude knife, and the wooden skewers were thrust in, a pleasant smile was frequently observable on the young warrior's countenance; but when in the horrible position above described, with his flesh stretched by the splints till it appeared about to give way, a number of attendants commenced turning him round and round with poles, he would burst out in the most lamentable and heart-rending cries that the human voice is capable of producing, crying forth to the Great Spirit to support and protect him in the dreadful trial.

After hanging until total insensibility brought a temporary relief to his sufferings, he was lowered to the floor, the main supporting skewers were withdrawn, and he was left to crawl off, dragging the weights after him. The first movement, with returning consciousness, was to sacrifice to the Great Spirit one or more of the fingers of the left hand, after which the miserable wretch was taken out of the lodge. Within the court a new trial awaited him; the last, but most terrible of all. An active man took his position on each side of the weak and mutilated sufferer, and, passing a thong about his wrist, urged him forward at the top of his speed in a circle round the arena. When, faint and weary, he sank on the ground, the tormentors dragged him furiously around the ring until the splints were torn out by the weights attached, and he lay motionless and apparently lifeless. If the splint should have been so deeply inserted that no force—even that of the weight of individuals in the crowd, thrown upon the trailing skulls—could break the integuments, nothing remained but to crawl off to the prairie and wait until it should give way by suppuration. To draw the skewer out would be unpardonable sacrilege.

It is told of one man that he suspended himself from the precipitous river bank by two of these skewers, thrust through his arms, until, at the end of several days, he dropped into the water, and swam ashore. Throughout the whole ordeal, the chiefs and sages of the tribe critically observed the comparative fortitude and endurance of the candidates, and formed their conclusions thereupon as to which would be the worthiest to command in after time.

"It takes a special kind of courage to fight Indians," said Major Ragsdale, in Topeka. "They're pretty sure to surprise you and as hard to catch. Their yelling and whooping alone are enough to stampede men not trained to their style of fighting. Sometimes they fight under cover, and you catch a fire from an enemy you can't get a sight of, and again, where there hasn't been one to be seen, they seem all to spring out of the ground at once and charge you as though nothing could stand their onset. Then there's the knowledge that if they catch you alive you'll be skinned alive, or burned, or your life tortured out of you by slow degrees in a thousand other ways they can think of to make you suffer. There's many a stout-hearted desperado, a terror in white settlements and not afraid to have a pistol or shotgun scrap any hour of the day or night with a man of his own color,

RETURN FROM BATTLE.

who doesn't count for a row of pins in an Indian fight.

"Take Sam Brown of Nevada for a case in point. He wasn't afraid of any man that wore boots, and he was the terror of the mining camps everywhere he went. The Piute Indians got bad one time and a party was organized in the camps to go out against them. Sam joined the volunteers, and everybody in the party and all that stayed behind were talking about the big deeds Sam Brown would do, and chuckling to think of the way those redskins would be wiped out when they run up against him.

"Well, when they came upon the Indians, things didn't turn out quite as they had expected. It was the whites that got licked out in short order, and those that weren't left on the ground stampeded for safety. Sam Brown was one of the first ones to run, and the pace he set his horse at to get away from those red-skins was something that beat quarter racing in the way of reckless riding. As they stampeded down a canyon, every man trying to be the foremost to get away. Sam hailed Joe McMurtie, who was riding a better horse than his:

"'Oh, Mac! Pull your horse a little so I can come up. We'll ride safer together.'

"McMurtie's answer to that friendly invitation was to bend down to his horse's neck, set in the spurs, and get out of that canyon ahead of Sam and back to Bodie as fast as hoofs could carry him. He knew Sam Brown, and that if that worthy once got alongside of him he wouldn't hesitate to shoot him off his horse so as to get a better mount for himself. After they all got back to the settlement he didn't go round to places where he was likely to meet Sam, lest it might stir him up to unpleasant recollections of their Indian campaign."

A few personal recitals of persons in captivity about their sufferings while with the Indians will be read with interest.

John Gyles said that one winter, as he and his captives were moving from place to place in the wilds of Maine, a moose was killed, and he and a young Indian were ordered to carry home the best parts of it. It being late in the evening when they came to where the moose lay, they had not time to collect materials for a fire. At the same time a heavy snowstorm set in and continued all night. They made what fire they could and sat by it until morning, when they set out on the return march. Their clothes were soaked with the melted snow, and they had not traveled far before the mooseskin coat of Gyles (which was about his only apparel) was frozen stiff around his knees like a hoop, while his snow-shoes and snow-moccasins were frozen fast to his feet. During the entire day he continued the weary march, without food or fire, sick, drowsy and disheartened. The young Indian, who was better clad, soon left him behind. At length he reached the wigwam. When the Indians removed his pack they found that the place where it had lain on his back was the only part of his body not frozen. His snow-shoes were cut off from his numbed feet, and after sitting by the fire a short time the blood began to circulate, his feet and ankles turned black and swelled with bloody blisters, painful to the last degree. Soon afterward the skin came off his feet entire, like a shoe, as high as the ankles, leaving his naked toes without nails and the ends of his great-toe bones bare, which shortly turned black, so that he was forced to cut off the first joint with his knife. The Indians furnished him rags and fir balsam for a dressing, but told him at the same time he would undoubtedly die. By careful nursing, however, he got so he could walk on his heels with the aid of a cane. In fifteen days the Indians again moved. They made two little hooplike shoes for Gyles, so that he was able to follow them, though often in the most excrutiating torture from the snow and water. He was eventually sold to a Frenchman in Canada.

Robert Rogers was caught in a hollow tree where he had hidden from the Indians. They pulled him out, stripped him, and spurred him forward at the points of their knives until they reached camp. He was tied to a tree, and after a dance around him a fire was kindled and thrust upon him with much laughter and shouting. They then cut scollops of flesh from his body and threw them in his face. After he was dead, his body was set down upon the glowing coals, and left tied to the stake.

Peter Williamson, who lived near the forks of the Delaware river, with several others, were captured and had bitter experiences. At their halting places the Indians stripped him and painted his body in various colors. At other times they would pluck the white hairs from his head and mockingly tell him he had lived too long; again, tying him to a tree they would whip him and scorch his cheeks with red-hot coals and burn his legs with fire-brands. Williamson saw the bellies of three other captives ripped open and their bowels burned before their eyes. Another victim was buried in the ground, with only his head left in view. After scalping him, he was thus left in agony for several hours; a fire was then kindled near him and his brains were literally roasted. Then they cut off his head and buried it with the other bodies. Williamson was compelled to dig the graves. He finally escaped one night when the Indians were asleep and reached his home in Pennsylvania.

On the 23rd of July, 1836, John Thompson, the keeper of the Cape Florida Lighthouse, discovered a large body of Indians behind the kitchen as he was passing from that place to the lighthouse. Calling to an old negro, they ran for the tower, reaching the door amid a shower of bullets, and just in time to lock it before the savages reached them. Thompson stationed the negro at the door, and, taking his three muskets, which were loaded with ball and buckshot, went to the second window, and by firing from this and other windows succeeded in keeping them at bay until dark. The savages continued pouring in a heavy fire of balls, and at length set fire to the lighthouse. The balls of the enemy had penetrated the tin tanks containing two hundred and twenty-five gallons of oil, which, escaping, saturated everything —woodwork, clothes and bedding. The flames, fed by this unctuous fluid and by the yellow-pine lumber, spread fast and fiercely. When driven away by the fire, the heroic keeper took a musket, balls and keg of gunpowder to the top of the house; then, going below again, began to cut away the stairs halfway from the bottom. The negro now coming up, he with difficulty drew him up over the space already cut; in a short time both were driven by the flames to the top of the building. Covering the scuttle that led up to the lantern, they succeeded in keeping the fire from them for some time. At length the dreadful moment came; the flames burst through, and at the same time the savages began their fiendish yells. The poor old negro looked at his master with tears in his eyes, but could not speak. They went out of the lantern, which was now full of flames, the lamps and side glasses bursting and flying in all directions. With their clothes on fire and their flesh roasting they lay down on the edge of the platform, which was two feet in width; to move now from this spot would be almost certain death from the balls of the Indians. To more quickly end his excruciating sufferings, the keeper then threw the **keg of gunpowder** down the scuttle, hoping to be instantly blown into eternity; but in this he was disappointed; the explosion indeed shook the tower from top to bottom, and for a moment checked the progress of the fire by throwing down the staircase and all the woodwork near the top of the lighthouse. But soon the fierce element again raged relentlessly. At this point the old negro died. Thompson had received six balls, three in each foot, and, finding **that** he was roasting alive, he resolved to **jump** off. Going outside of the iron railing and recommending his soul to God, he was on the **point of** precipitating himself on the rocks below, when something whispered to him to return and lie down. He did so, **and in two** minutes the fire fell to the bottom of the house, **and in a very** short time died out.

The Indians, thinking him dead, next set fire to **the dwelling**-house, kitchen and other outbuildings; and **began** to carry their plunder down to the little sloop belonging **to** the keeper. **About** ten o'clock the next morning they departed. Thompson's position was **now** almost as desperate as before. A burning fever was **on him**; his feet **were** shot to pieces; his clothes burned from **his** body; he had nothing to eat or drink; a hot sun was overhead, a dead man by his side, with **no** friend near **or** likely **to** be; and between seventy and eighty feet from the ground, with **no** prospect of getting down. About twelve o'clock he thought **he** perceived a vessel not far off. **His e**yesight had suffered from the fire, but served him **well upon** this occasion. Taking a piece of the negro's trousers, that had escaped the flames from bei**ng** saturated with blood, he **made** a signal. In the afternoon, seeing **his** sloop coming **in** tow of two boats, he felt sure that the Indians had noticed his sign and were returning to murder him. But it proved to be boats of the United States schooner, Motto, Captain Armstrong, with a detachment of seamen **and** marines. They had retaken

Thompson's sloop after it had been divested of everything. They told him that they had heard his explosion twelve miles away, and had at once sailed to his assistance, although scarcely expecting to find him alive. Night coming on, **they were forced to return on board, but assured him of their prompt assistance in the morning; at which time they tried to send a line to him by means of a kite** which they had made during the night. But this not succeeding, they **next fired twine from their muskets, tying it to the ramrods. This effort proved successful.** Thompson hauled up a tail-block, made it fast to an iron stanchion and dropped the twine through the pulley, by which means those below hoisted a strong rope. Two men were then raised, by this means, to the wounded man, whom they soon had on the ground. He stated that after being received aboard the Motto, **every** man, from the captain to the cook, endeavored to alleviate his sufferings. He was taken to the military hospital in Charleston, S. C., where he eventually recovered, although he remained a cripple all his life.

INDIANS AS EQUESTRIANS.

As bold **and skilful riders** Indians **have no superiors; some** of their **feats of horsemanship** appear **almost supernatural to** a stranger. One of the most singular of these is that of throwing the whole **body upon one side of the horse, so as to** be entirely shielded **from the missile of an enemy,** with the exception **of the heel, by which** they still **maintain** their hold, and are enabled **to regain their** seat in an instant. **The manner in which** this seemingly impossible **position is retained is as follows:** A short hair halter is passed around **under the neck of** the horse, and **both ends tightly braided into the** mane, on the withers, **leaving a loop to hang** under the neck, and against the **breast, which, being caught** up in the hand, makes a sling **into which the elbow falls, taking** the weight **of the body on the middle of the upper arm.** Into this **loop** the rider drops **suddenly and** fearlessly, leaving his **heel to hang over the back of the horse, to steady** him, and also to restore him when he **wishes to** regain his **upright** position on **the horse's back.**

The Indian rider, as he sweeps, at full speed, past his enemy, in this unnatural attitude, is said to manage his long lance, and his bow and arrow, with nearly the same facility as if fairly mounted. He will discharge his arrow over the back of the horse, or even his neck! Indians are awkward and ungainly in their movements when on foot, but when mounted upon the animals that have become almost a part of themselves, nothing can exceed the lightness and freedom of their posture and movements. Their wild horses were taken by the lasso, and were at first disabled by being "choked down," as it is termed. When the hunter had thus conquered and enfeebled his prize, he proceeded to tie his fore feet together, and, loosening the noose about his neck, took a turn with it about the lower jaw, and completed the subjection of the animal by closing his eyes with his hand and breathing in his nostrils. After this, little difficulty was experienced; the horse submitted to be mounted, and was soon entirely under the control of his tormentor. The Indians are severe and cruel riders, and the ease of supplying the loss of a horse on the plains created disregard for the animal's safety or welfare.

BUFFALO HUNTING.

The bison, or North American buffalo, was the staple food of the wild Indians in their palmy days. The extension of civilization and the wanton destruction of these noble beasts have nearly caused their extinction. During certain seasons of the year, they congregated in immense herds, but were generally distributed over the country in search of the best pastorage. They had no certain routine of migration, although those whose occupation led to a study of their movements could in some localities point out the general course of their trail; and this uncertainty rendered the mode of subsistence depended upon by extensive western tribes of Indians exceedingly precarious. Upon the open prairie the bison was generally pursued upon horseback, with the lance and bow and arrow. The short stiff bow was little calculated for accurate marksmanship, or for a distant shot; riding at full speed, the Indian generally waited till he had overtaken his prey, and discharged his arrow from the distance of **a few feet.** The admirable training of the horse, to whom the rider was obliged to give loose rein as he approached his object and prepared to inflict the deadly wound, was no less noticeable than the spirit and energy of the rider. Such was the force with which the arrow was thrown, that repeated instances are related of its complete passage through the huge body of the buffalo, and its exit upon the opposite side. This near approach to the powerful and infuriated animal was by no means without danger. Although the horse, from instinctive fear of the buffalo's horns, sheered off immediately **upon** passing him, it was not always done with sufficient quickness to avoid his stroke. The hunter was so carried away by the excitement and exhilaration of pursuit, as to be apparently perfectly reckless of his own safety; trusting entirely to the sagacity and quickness of his horse to take him out of the danger into which he was rushing. The noose, or lasso, used in catching wild horses, was often left trailing upon the ground during the chase, to afford the hunter an easy means of securing and remounting his horse **in** case he should be dismounted, by the attack of the buffalo **or** otherwise. In the winter season it **was** common for the Indians **of the** northern latitudes **to drive** the buffalo herds from the bare **ridges,** where they collected to feed upon **the** exposed herbage, into the snow-covered valleys. The unwieldy beasts, as they floundered through the drifts, were easily overtaken by the hunters, supported by their snow-shoes, and were killed with the lance or bow. Another method, adopted by the **Indians,** was **to put on the disguise** of a white wolfskin, **and** steal unsuspected among the herd, where they **could select** their prey at leisure. Packs of wolves frequently followed the herds, **to feed** upon the carcasses of those that perished, or the remains left by the hunters. They dare **not** attack them **in a body,** and were consequently no objects of terror to **the buffaloes;** but, should **an** old or wounded animal be **separated from** the company, they collected around him, and gradually wearied him out and devoured him. When buffaloes were plenty, and the Indians had fair opportunity, the most astonishing and wasteful slaughter ensued. Beside the ordinary methods of destruction, the custom of driving immense herds over some precipitous ledge, where those behind trample down and thrust over the foremost, until hundreds and thousands were destroyed, has been often described. Even at seasons in which the fur was valueless, and little beside a present supply of food could be obtained by destroying the animal which constituted **their sole** resource, no spirit of forethought or providence restrained the wild hunters of the prairie. A party of Sioux returned from a hunt in 1832 bringing **four**teen hundred buffalo tongues, all that they had secured of their booty. One **hundred** and fifty or two hundred thousand of their robes were supplied annually, the greater part **of** which were taken from animals killed expressly for the robe, at a season when the meat was not cured and preserved, **and for** each of which skins the **Indian** received but a pint **of** whisky!

THE BUFFALO DANCE AND RAIN MAKING.

In times of scarcity of provisions, when the buffalo herds had wandered away from the vicinity, so far that the hunters dared not pursue them, for fear of enemies, the "buffalo dance" was performed in the central court of the village. Every man of the tribe possessed a mask made from the skin of a buffalo's head, including the horns, and dried as nearly as possible in the natural shape, to be worn on these occasions. When the wise men of the nation determined upon their invocations to attract the buffalo herds, watchers were stationed upon the eminences surrounding the village, and the dance commenced. With extravagant action, and strange ejaculations, the crowd performed the prescribed manœuvres: as fast as those engaged became weary, they would signify it by crouching down, when those without the circle would go through the pantomine of severally shooting, flaying **and dressing** them, while new performers took their place. Night and day the mad scene was kept up, sometimes for weeks together! until the signal was given of the approach of buffalo, when all prepared with joy and hilarity for a grand hunt, fully convinced that their own exertions had secured the prize.

No less singular was the ceremonial restored to when the crops were suffering for want of rain. A knot of the wisest medicine-men would collect in a hut, where they held their session with closed doors burning aromatic herbs and going through with an unknown series of incantations. Some tyro was then sent up to take his stand on the roof, in sight of the people, and spend the day in invocations for a shower. If the sky continued clear, he retired in disgrace, as one who need not hope ever to arrive at the dignity of a medicine-man. Day after day the performance continued, until a cloud overspread the skies, when the young Indian on the lodge discharged an arrow toward it, to let out the rain.

CATCHING BEAVERS AND BEARS.

The Indian method of taking beaver was as follows: Before the waters were frozen they caught them in wooden and steel traps; after that they hunted them on the ice. When the animals were in their houses, and not in subterranean lodgings in the banks, the Indians, taking mauls and handspikes, broke all the hollow ice to prevent them from getting their heads above the water under it. They then forced open the houses, and the beavers, escaping, would run to the open places to breathe, where the savages would either catch them by the hind legs, throw them out on the ice and tomahawk them, or else shoot them when their heads appeared above the water. Tecaughretanego (adopted brother of Tontileango) told Smith that the dams made by the beavers served them in a variety of ways; for example, in raising the water over the mouths of their lodging-places in the bank, and also by enabling them to cut down saplings without going out much upon the land; for, as they live chiefly upon the bark of trees, and are extremely slow and awkward when out of the water, they would be killed by their enemies if found far from the banks.

To kill bears in winter they searched about until they found a tree that had been scratched by the bear in climbing, and discovered if the hole were large enough to admit him. Then, when it was possible, they would fell a sapling in such a way that it would fall against or near the opening, when one of them would climb up and drive Bruin from his retreat. If the saplings or trees near at hand leaned the wrong way, they gathered some rotten wood and tied it in bunches with bark; then, making a wooden hook and taking a long pole, one of them would ascend a neighboring tree, draw up the pole by means of a hook which he reached from limb to limb as he climbed, and igniting his spunk-wood, place it into the cavity. Presently the bear would come forth and be shot by the one below.

FUNERAL RITES OF SOME TRIBES.

Long years ago the body of the dead Indian was tightly wrapped and bound up in fresh or soaked buffalo skins, together with the arms and accoutrements used in life, and the usual provision of tobacco, flint and steel, knife and food. A slight scaffold was then prepared, of sufficient height to serve as protection from the wolves and dogs, and there the body was deposited to decay in the open air. Day after day those who had lost friends would come out from the village to this strange cemetery, to weep and bewail over their loss. Such genuine and long-continued grief as was exhibited by the afflicted relatives puts to shame the cold heartedness of too many among the cultivated and enlightened. When, after the lapse of years, the scaffolds had fallen, and nothing was left but bleached and mouldering bones, the remains were buried, with the exception of the skulls. These were placed in circles upon the plain, with the faces turned inward, each resting upon a bunch of wild sage; and in the centre, upon two slight mounds, "medicine-poles" were erected, at the foot of which were the heads and horns of a male and female buffalo. To these new places of deposit, each of which contained not far from one hundred skulls, would the mourners again resort, to evince their further affection for the dead—not in groans and lamentations, however, for several years had cured the anguish; but fond affections and endearments were renewed, and conversations were here held, and cherished, with the dead. The wife or mother would sit for hours by the side of the white relic of the loved and lost, addressing the skull with the most affectionate and loving tones, or, perchance lying down and falling asleep with her arms around it. Food would be nightly set before many of these skulls, and, with the most tender care, the aromatic bed upon which they reposed would be renewed as it withered and decayed.

MATERNAL AFFECTION AND CARE OF INFANTS.

One of the most remarkable and touching traits of character observable among the Sioux, is the strength of maternal affection. Infant children, according to the common custom of western Indians, are carried, for the first six or seven months of their existence, strapped immoveably to a board, the hands and arms being generally left at liberty. A hoop protects the child's face from injury in case of a fall, and the whole apparatus is often highly ornamented with fringe and embroidery. This pack or cradle is provided with a broad band, which is passed round the forehead of the mother sustaining the weight of the child pendant at her back. Those who have been most familiar with this mode of treatment generally approve of it as best suited to the life led by the Indian, and as in no way cruel to the child. After the infant has in some degree acquired the use of its limbs, it is freed from these incumbrances, and borne in the fold of the mother's blanket. If the infant dies during the time that is allotted to it to be carried in this cradle, it is buried, and the disconsolate mother fills the cradle with black quills and feathers, in the parts which the child's body had occupied, and in this way carries it around with her wherever she goes for a year or more, with as much care as if her infant were alive and in it; and she often lays or stands it against the side of the wigwam, where she is all day engaged with her needle-work, and chatting and talking to it as familiarly and affectionate as if it were her loved infant, instead of its shell, that she was talking to. So lasting and so strong is the affection of these women for the lost child, that it matters not how heavy or cruel their load, or how rugged the route they have to pass over, they will faithfully carry this, and carefully, from day to day, and even more strictly perform their duties to it, than if the child were alive and in it.

PORTRAIT OF A MANDAN WARRIOR.

The dress of the Mandan warriors, although in its general fashion similar to that of the neighboring tribes, was singularly rich and elaborate. It was formed entirely of skins: a coat or hunting-shirt of buck-skin; leggins and moccasins of the same material, beautifully fringed, and embroidered with porcupine quills; and an outer mantle of the fur of a young buffalo, formed the principal equipment. The covering for the head was more elaborate, and was constructed, by all who could obtain the materials, of ermine skins and feathers of the war-eagle. So high a value was set upon these head-dresses, that Mr. Catlin, after having bargained for the entire suit of a chief, whose portrait he had just painted, was obliged to give two horses, of the value of twenty-five dollars each, for the crowning ornament. Some few chiefs had attained a height of authority and renown which entitled them to add to their head dress a pair of buffalo-horns, reduced in size and weight, and arranged as they grew upon the animal. The custom was not confined to the Mandans, but a similar ornament is widely considered as symbolic of power and warlike achievements among the western Indians. Nothing could exceed the pride and delight of the chiefs of the tribe, after their first apprehensions at the novelty of the proceeding were allayed, at the sight of their own portraits, for which they were induced to sit. Mr. Catlin was constituted and proclaimed from the moment of the first exhibition, a "great medicine man," and old and young thronged to see and to touch the worker of such a miracle. All declared that the pictures were, at least partially, alive, for from whatsoever side they were beheld, still the eyes were seen fixed upon the beholder. An idea was started, and obtained a temporary credence, that some portion of the life of the person represented must have been abstracted by the painter, and that consequently his term of existence must be shortened. It was moreover feared lest, by the picture's living after the death of the original, the quiet rest of the grave should be troubled. By a most ingenious and judicious policy in adopting a mode of explanation, suited to the capacity of his hearers, and by wisely ingratiating himself with the chiefs and medicine-men, Mr. Catlin succeeded in stilling the commotion excited by such suggestions and suspicions. He was held in high estimation, and feasted by the principal men of the tribe, whose portraits he obtained for his invaluable collection.

TWO STAR SEES THE KINETOSCOPE AND HEARS THE PHONOGRAPH.

Probably no Indian who ever visited Washington to counsel with the Great Father returned to his tribe better satisfied with the results of his trip than the Sisseton Sioux, Two Star. He not only accomplished the object of his mission, but he was entertained in a style that falls to the lot of few of the nation's wards. Agent Keller was with him, as well as the interpreter, Joe Brown. The latter, by the way, is a somewhat notable figure himself. He is a son of that Major Brown who commanded the troops at the battle of Birch Cooley during the Sioux outbreak. He has lived all his life among these Indians, and now keeps a large store on the reservation.

Two Star was sent by his tribe to ask the immediate payment to them of $199,000 of their principal now in the custody of the United States. This sum amounted to $1,699,000. The Indians were in destitute circumstances, owing to an almost complete failure of their crops in 1894, and the interest due them was not sufficient to tide them over another year. The impairment of the principal is a matter which by law rests entirely with the President. In this case he promised to follow the recommendation of the Commissioner of Indian Affairs, which was to the effect that the grant be made.

It is a somewhat singular fact that although Two Star was one of Gen. Silbey's scouts and had always associated with the whites upon terms of the friendliest intimacy, he cannot speak a word of English. His enjoyment of the white man's amusements is, however, none the less keen. Senator Kyle's clerk, Duncan McFarland, took him in to see the kinetoscope. As he looked in upon the picture in motion a look of amazement, not unmixed with a degree of consternation, crept over his face. He stepped back and looked around, above, and below the case to find out what caused the exhibition. It was some time before he could be persuaded to again apply the eye to the aperture, and when the machine stopped with a click the noble red man **jumped** as if he had heard the war-whoop of some of his tribal enemies.

He was equally amazed, but none the less pleased, **with the** phonograph, and **insisted** upon having a selection by the Marine Band repeated. **He** was taken to an amateur athletic and gymnastic performance at the Columbia Athletic Club, and witnessed the exhibition of skill and prowess with a delight that was almost childlike. Just before his departure for the West, Two Star said to a correspondent:

"I was here in 1867, **but** no one paid any attention to **me then.** I think Washington is a much **ricer** place now. It will be no use **for me to** tell my people about the things I have seen and heard (referring to the kinetoscope and **pho**-nograph), for no one would believe me. **They would** say I was not speaking the truth."

SOLDIERS' LETTERS ABOUT INDIANS.

The following letter was received by a member **of the** Philadelphia police force from his son on the frontier:

"Dear **Parents:**—We have had some hard times **since I** wrote you last. We left Pine Ridge on the 28th day of **De**-cember and marched all night, and on the morning of the 29th we went to disarm Big Foot's band, and it caused a hard fight in which **thirty** soldiers were killed and about eighty-five wounded. **One** officer was killed and one wounded. It was a very poor plan, the way they laid out the fight. They had four troops dismounted and formed a square around the Indians, and they were **so** close **together** that they could touch the Indians with their guns; then **the** other four troops were mounted **in rear of the** camp. They thought that the Indians were going **to lay down** their arms without a word. All the men were full of fun, but they soon changed their tune. After they had the tents searched they went to take the arms from the bucks. They were all in a bunch, and when they least expected it they made a break and started to shoot and cut at every one; and the way the soldiers were fixed they could not shoot for fear of killing one another, but they soon got straightened out, and then we got in our fine work. At the first volley we fired there were about twenty or thirty Indians dropped, and we kept it up until we cleaned out the whole band; all over the field you could see an Indian running and a soldier after him. There was a canon close by, and some of the Indians took refuge there, and it took us about two hours to get them out. They killed two men out of our troop and wounded two or three before we got them out. After it was all over it was an awful sight to see. It made me sick to look at it. There were about one hundred and fifteen bucks and about seventy-five women and children killed. I did not like to see the squaws killed, but they were as bad as the bucks after the fight started. Some of the men went wild; they would shoot men or women. The officers tried to stop them, but it was of no use; they would shoot any one they saw with a gun; and it was right, I think, as the women could kill as well as the men. Even after the Indians were wounded and lying on the ground, they would wait until they got a chance, and then would shoot a soldier in the back. There was one Indian who was lying in a tent. He killed about four men before they found out where he was, but after they found him they shot him, and then they burned him up in the tent. Then some of the men went around and shot every Indian that was able to do any damage. I don't think there were any more than five or six who got away out of the whole band. If our commanding officer had done what was right, we would not have lost one-fifth of the men that we did. After the fight was all over we moved back to the agency, and were on the road all that night, but we got a little sleep before morning; and it was a good thing that we did, for we had to pull out early in the morning of the 30th to help the Ninth Cavalry wagon-train, which the Indians had tried to take; but when we arrived they took to the hills. We then pulled back to the camp, but we did not have long to stay, for the Indians set fire to some buildings a few miles from the agency, and we were ordered out again. We then got lots of real Indian fighting. They led us up in the hills, and then they turned on us and kept us busy all day; we only lost one man and about six wounded. We do not know how many Indians were killed, because we had to get back to camp before it got dark. We had to stay up almost all night, so as to keep the

INDIAN MASSACRES.

Indians away from the agency, but none came near."

The following letter was written by a private in the Seventh Cavalry:

"Of course you read in the newspapers that we are in trouble here. Beside my own regiment, the Seventh Cavalry, the Ninth Infantry came in two days ago. But there seems to be no head anywhere. Some of our officers would make better clerks than soldiers. The government employes are merely a set of useless, mischief-making loafers. Thank fortune, most of them are badly scared and are packing to leave. The fact is, until the reservations are cleared of all civilians and turned over to military authority there will be no change for the better. Of course the Indians are robbed—we see it every day. All the fat cattle out of the government herd go to the settlements, and the greyhounds go to the Indians. Of course they are lazy and idle, but before we get through it will be plain that it's cheaper to feed than to fight them. One thing should be done: all preachers and philanthropists should be warned off. They do more harm than good. The competition between the half a dozen denominations which have their headquarters here to make converts leads to a regular system of purchase, and the preacher who pays the best rounds up the most Injuns. Sitting-Bull worked the philanthropists for all there was in it, and laughed at them when their backs were turned. As to making these savages self-supporting, the idea is regarded as absurd by those who know them best, and if the government would close the reservations against the whites, drive away the half-breeds and squaw-men, put the Indians under the rule of army officers, and, above all, feed them, I believe that henceforth there would be no trouble. Yesterday, the 29th of December, we had a stand-up fight at Porcupine Creek, about fifteen miles north of the agency. Just after midnight we were ordered to turn out, and at daybreak the bugles sounded "Boots and saddles," and about eight o'clock we came to Little Wound's camp, near Porcupine Creek. There were about fifty tepees set up. The squaws were packing in wood from the ravines. But very few bucks were to be seen. Everything seemed peaceful enough. After sitting two hours in our saddles, half frozen, as the weather was mighty cold, we found out that our business was to disarm the Indians. Of course the whole thing was bungled. About a dozen bucks came forward with two old blunderbusses, and then Colonel Forsyth ordered a detail of five men from each company to search the tepees. I was crawling into one when I got a kick from behind that fairly drove my head through the cover on the opposite side, and landed me on a pile of dogs and babies. I got outside, mad as a hatter, and there stood a squaw grinning with delight. I made a grab at her bangs, when down both of us went, and this saved my life. Suddenly there was a crash and the air was full of bullets. I heard them racing past. The poor squaw had got on her feet first, and went down, shot through the head. Her blood flew over the cape of my coat. I scrambled up. Every one was shouting and shooting, and there was no more order than in a bar-room scrimmage. I ran for my horse; it was kicking on the ground, and my file-leader, Murphy, was under the animal's heels, dead. Half a dozen others lay around wounded and dead. In front a crowd of blanketed forms was making for the coolies, when crash went the rifle-volley, and they were gone. No orders were given, either by voice or bugle, that I heard. I shot one buck running, and when I examined him he had neither gun nor cartridge-belt. The women lay thick. One girl about eighteen was supporting herself on her hand, the blood spurting from her mouth as from a pump. Near her lay two others, and all around, like patches on the snow, were dead squaws, each in a pool of blood. The howitzers were at work firing grape into the brushwood that filled the ravines, but the Indians were gone, and I had time to draw my breath. From beginning to end I don't think I saw two dozen bucks, and it is a mystery to all where the bullets came from that killed and wounded one-third of my regiment. My left arm felt sore, and I found that a bullet had cut my sleeve and grazed the flesh. It was bleeding freely, and I have no doubt that I was shot by one of my comrades—the rip in my coat showed this. The bugles sounded "Cease firing," but many of the men were up in the hills, and now and then a shot was heard. Colonel Forsyth looked very white as he gave orders to see if any of the women who lay thick around were alive. From the blanket of one we took a boy five years old and a baby about as many months—both unhurt, but the mother was dead. She must have been **shot with** a revolver held not five feet away, as her hair was **burned** and **the skin** blackened with powder. But we had got it "in the neck." My captain, Wallace, was dead and eight of **my** company, and when we mustered in it looked as if half the regiment was gone. I had my arm dressed, and we returned **to** Pine Ridge next day. Of course the camp-liar was in **his** glory, but **who** shot the squaws was not known, at least **no** one boasted of it."

INDIAN TELEGRAPHY.

It is wonderful to what **a** state of perfection Indians had carried a simple mode **of** signaling **by** smoke. Scattered over a great portion of the plains are isolated peaks that can be seen 20 to 50 miles. These were selected for telegraphic stations. By varying the number of columns of smoke different meanings were conveyed. A simple and easily varied mode, resembling somewhat the ordinary alphabet of the magnetic telegraph, was arranged by building a small fire which was not allowed to blaze; then, by placing an armful of partially green grass or weeds over **the** fire, as if to smother it, a dense white smoke was created, ordinarily ascending in a vertical column hundreds of feet. **This** column of smoke is to the Indian mode of telegraphing what the current of electricity is to the system employed by white men; the alphabet, as far as it goes, is almost identical, **consisting** of long and short lines and dots. Having this current of smoke established, the Indian operator simply took his blanket, and by spreading it over the small pile of weeds **or grass from** which the column of smoke took its source, **and properly controlling** the edges and corners of the blanket, he **confined** the smoke, and in this way was able to retain it several movements. By rapidly displacing the blanket, the operator was enabled to cause a dense volume of smoke to rise, the length or shortness of which, as well as the number and frequency of the column, he could regulate perfectly, simply by the proper use of **the** blanket. For the transmission of brief messages, previously determined upon, no more simple m**eth**od could easily be adopted.

INDIANS THAT WORK.

For the benefit of people who imagine Indians too lazy to work, Commissioner Morgan says that in one year $642,000 were paid them for services rendered. This money was paid to agency and school employes, to farmers, interpreters, police, judges of Indian courts, for hauling supplies purchased from them, for breaking land on government property and for logs cut and banked by them. This is a very good showing for Indian labor, and the sum paid would be ten times as large as it is if there were work enough to give employment to all who wish it.

The Umatilla Indians of Oregon have been under care of the government for many years and are practically self-supporting, and would long ago have been entirely independent had their lands been allotted to them in severalty. With population of only one thousand, in one year they harvested three hundred and fifty thousand bushels of wheat, cut two thousand tons of hay, and other crops in proportion. In a short time, this tribe, as well as others which have rich lands and fair opportunities, such as the white settlers select for themselves, will be able to stand alone. The Utes, who a few years ago were leading the life of nomad savages, have six hundred acres under cultivation, and raise goodly quantities of wheat, corn and oats. They have learned the art of irrigation by means of ditches. The Jicarilla Apaches show an inborn thrift. Though the white settlers have all the best lands, and the Indians have no water for irrigation purposes, they cultivated in one year three hundred and fifty acres with fair results, and cut four hundred tons of hay.

INDIAN SCHOOLS AND WHAT IS TAUGHT.

There are schools established to teach young Indians "how to shoot" with their brains instead of the old-time bow and arrow. They are located at Carlisle in Pennsylvania, Salem in Oregon, Genoa in Nebraska, Haskell in Kansas, Chilocco in Oklahoma, Grand Junction in Colorado, and Albuquerque in New Mexico. In round numbers they cost the government $300,000 during the fiscal year of 1890, and on an enrollment of about 2,100 pupils **had an** average attendance of about 1,800, with 288 employes. Four other such schools—those of Carson, Santa Fe, Pierre, and Fort Totten—will increase the capacity by over 600 pupils. The Lincoln, Hampton and St. Ignatius, conducted by private enterprise, although with government appropriations, fall into this list.

In such schools the Indian lads may learn something of blacksmithing, broom-making, carpentering, farming, fruit-culture, harness-making, printing, tailoring, shoemaking and wheelwrighting, while the girls are instructed in the various duties of housekeeping. The outing system at **some** of these schools allows Indian boys and girls to find homes, at wages, during a part of each year with farmers and others. They have the great advantage also of being removed from the drawbacks of reservation life. These schools form one of the most promising portions of our system of Indian management. The chief trouble is that they can only accommodate about half the children of school age, so that their number should be increased. In many ways the pupils learn the new life in store for their race. The very holidays are instructive, as well the school-time. These holidays, beginning with New Year's Day, then taking in Franchise Day on February 8th, Washington's Birthday, Decoration Day, Arbor Day, Fourth of July, Thanksgiving and Christmas, **are** celebrated in a way that makes them a part of the general education.

IMPROVIDENCE OF THE NASCAPEE INDIANS.

Distressing intelligence was sent out by missionaries early **this** year (1895) of the misery and privation among the Nas-**capee Indians** along the Labrador coast. Though industrious, these aborigines **are** fearfully improvident, **and** it **is** largely owing to their **wilful** destruction of game and fur-bearing animals in the summer that they are reduced to dire **extremity in the winter.** Hitherto these Indians have been allowed **to kill** whatever they like, irrespective of game laws, **and the result is** such a falling off in late years in the number **of furs** coming from their country that there is a general **outcry against the exemptions** in favor of these improvident people, and a demand that they be made amenable to law and reason like everybody else. They might make a comfortable living in summer without killing game and fur-bearing animals out of season, for the waters of the north shore swarm with codfish and salmon, and sea trout are to be had in great abundance in nearly all the streams. But these Nascapees have a great aversion to both fish and fishing, and would rather want than take fish. When taken ill they generally blame fish for causing the trouble and wrap up their throats in a piece of fish net, to propitiate the spirit of the fish. Only when no game or fur-bearing animals can be killed in the summer do they resort to fishing in order to sustain life, and then only after their nets have been propitiated by having been married to two young girls of the tribe, with a ceremony far more formal than that observed in the case of mere human wedlock. The fish, too, are propitiated, being addressed from the fishing camp by one of the party chosen for the function, who exhorts them to take courage and be caught, assuring them that the utmost respect will be shown to their bones. These Indians decline to believe themselves responsible for the present dearth of game and fur bearing animals, and affect to believe that either some evil-disposed sorcerer has kept the game from them or that the spirits of the animals themselves have taken affront, probably because dogs have been allowed to feed upon some of their bones, or because some wounded representative of their species has not been properly addressed and propitiated by his slayer. Since reason, therefore, is of no avail in inducing a more prudential line of action among these people, it is pretty certain that a few more years will find the tribe extinct. Even the eider duck, which was formerly so plentiful in Labrador, is fast disappearing before the steady killing of the birds and robbery of the nests in hatching time by the Nascapees.

SATANTA'S FAMILY REUNION.

Satanta and Lone Wolf, chiefs of the Kiowas, held as prisoners by Gen. Sheridan at Fort Cobb, to insure the peaceable surrender of their people, who were encamped within a day's journey from there, were given to understand that unless they sent messages to have their villages come in by sundown of the next day they would be hung the day following. This peremptory order had the desired effect and the tribe came marching in on time. Next morning the family or families of Satanta appeared in front of headquarters and expressed a wish to see the "head of the house." No objection was made and the guards passed them through the lines. Satanta's home circle was organized somewhat on the quadrilateral plan; that is, he had four wives. They all came together, and apparently constituted a happy family. They were all young and buxom, and so near alike that they might have passed as sisters. It is customary among Indians for one man to marry an entire family of daughters as rapidly as they reach the proper age, thus avoiding the evil of a multiplicity of mothers-in-law. To add to the striking similarity in appearance of these dusky spouses, each bore on her back, encased in the folds of a scarlet blanket, a pledge of affection in the shape of a papoose, the difference in the extreme ages of the four miniature warriors, or warriors' sisters, being too slight to be perceptible. In single file the four partners of Satanta's joys approached his lodge, and in the same order gained admittance. The chief was seated on a buffalo robe when they entered. He did not rise, but each of the squaws advanced to him, when instead of going through the ordinary form of embracing, with its usual accompaniments, on such occasions considered proper, the papoose was unslung and placed in the outstretched arms of the father, who kissed it repeatedly, with every exhibition of paternal affection, scarcely deigning to bestow a single glance on the mother, who stood by meekly, contenting herself with stroking Satanta's face and shoulders gently, at the same time muttering almost inaudible expressions of Indian endearment. This touching little scene lasted for a few moments, when a kiss was bestowed on the rosy lips of the child and it was handed back to the mother, who quietly took a seat by the side of the chief. The second wife then approached, when precisely the same exhibition was gone through with, not being varied from the first in the slightest particular. This being ended, the third took the place of the second, the latter passing along with her babe, and seating herself next to the first, and so on until the fourth wife had presented her baby, received it back and taken her seat by the side of the third. Not a word was spoken by Satanta from beginning to end of this strange meeting.

LITTLE ROCK'S CHARMING DAUGHTER.

Mo-nah-se-tah, the daughter of Little Rock, **was an exceedingly** comely squaw, possessing **a** bright, **cheery face and a** countenance beaming with intelligence, **and a disposition** more inclined to be merry than one usually **finds among** Indians. She was probably under 20 years of **age. She** had laughing eyes, pearly teeth, a rich complexion and beautiful silken tresses rivaling in color the blackness of the raven, and extending, when allowed to fall loosely over her **shoulders**, below her waist. She had been traded in marriage. An Indian maiden who should be so unfortunate as **to** be " given away" would not be looked upon as a very desirable match. Being the daughter of a chief high in rank, Mo-nah-se-tah was justly considered as belonging to the cream of the aristocracy, if not to royalty itself; consequently the suitor who hoped to gain her hand must be prepared, according to custom, to pay handsomely for an alliance **so** noble. Among the young braves who aspired to her **possession** was one who, so far as worldly wealth **was concerned,** was eligible. Unfortunately, however, he had **placed too** much reliance upon this fact, and had not thought **that** while obtaining the consent of paterfamilias it would be **well** also to win the heart of the maiden. The consent **of a maiden** to a proposed marriage, while desirable, was not **deemed** essential in a "swap." If the bridegroom was acceptable to the father of the bride, and had the " wherewith" in ponies, that **settled it.** From two to four ponies was the average market price for a squaw; but Mo-nah-se tah came high, and Little Rock held the price at eleven ponies. The young warrior raised the stock and the transfer was made. It turned out an unsatisfactory investment. The bride was taken **to his** lodge, but refused to acknowledge him as her husband, or to render him that obedience and menial service which the Indian **exacts** from his wife, and time failed to soften her heart. The **patience** of the young husband became exhausted. Having failed to win love by kindness, he determined to have recourse to harsh measures. He mistook the character of her upon whose obdurate heart threats nor promises produced the desired effect. Mo-nah-se-tah, like most squaws, was as skilful in the use of weapons as warriors are, and reminded her husband that she would not submit to any dignities, and that she would resist even to the taking of his life, and suiting the action to the word, she leveled a small pistol which she had carried concealed beneath her blanket and fired, wounding him in the knee and disabling him for life. Little Rock, learning of what occurred, and finding upon investigation that his daughter had not been to blame, concluded to cancel the marriage, or grant a divorce, which was accomplished simply by returning to the unfortunate husband the eleven ponies which had been paid for **his wife**. What an improvement upon the method prescribed **in the** civilized world! No lawyers fees, no publicity nor scandal, and tedious delays avoided.

THE EDITOR OF "TEXAS SIFTINGS" ATTEMPTS TO RIDE A MUSTANG.

The majority of Texas ponies buck, or pitch, as it is sometimes termed, whenever circumstances seem to demand an exhibition of this facetious freak, or the condition of things seems to justify the sportive caprice. In fact, some ponies will buck for hours, only stopping to get breath for a fresh start. This kind is recommended for the use of dyspeptics and invalids suffering from torpidity of liver. A pitching mustang, when working on full time and strictly devoting his attention to business, is the most moving sight I ever beheld. His spine seems to be of whalebone, and he appears to possess all the elements of a steamboat explosion, a high-pressure pile-driver, an earthquake, in addition to the enthusiasm of a county convention. We were glad to find that ours were not bucking ponies, and we congratulated each other on the fortunate circumstance. Of course, as we argued, if there had been any buck in them it would have developed itself at an early stage in the journey. Understand, we were not afraid. I named my pony " Deliberation;" the name seemed so appropriate—no pomp or circumstance about him—and he was so gentle and tranquil; nothing seemed to flurry him. You could throw the reins on his neck and strike a match on the pommel of **the saddle.** I say you coul l do this, but the after **fate of that** match would be of no moment to you; **you would be otherwise** engaged. I regret to say that I **tried** the experiment. I lighted a match—at least I think **I did**—but there was a haziness about the **subsequent proceedings that** prevents accuracy **of** statement. I distinctly remember striking the match. At that moment, however, I was fluently propelled upward; a tornado caught me—whirled me around eleven times. As I came down a pile-driver drove me in **the** stomach, and I came to earth **with that** sensation (only intensified) that **a** man feels **who** sits down in what he imagines to be a high chair, and which he afterward thinks was about seven feet lower than his estimate. I saw whole milky ways of constellations that never before existed. I realized for the first time the dense solidity of the earth, and **made** the astonishing discovery that under certain circumstances **our** planet, instead of revolving on **its** own axis once **in every twenty-four** hours, can rush **around** at the rate of at least **one** hundred revolutions a minute. There is not **in** the whole range of languages, ancient, modern, or profane, terms sufficiently expressive to describe the state of my fellings, the amount of mud on my person, or the chaotic condition of my brain. As soon as the earth settled down to the usual speed of her diurnal motion, I came to the conclusion that it was not always best to judge by appearances. I had been hasty in bestowing a distinctive cognomen on **my** erratic steed. **He** had no more deliberation in him than has a fugitive flea under the searching scrutiny of **a determi**ned woman. I re-named him. This time I called him "De ay," because delay is—but it does not matter.

Come to think of it since, the reason was weak. If, however, the reader shou d pierce the intricate labyrinth of mental ingenuity that constitutes the conundrum, I trust **he will** be charitable enough to consider the circumstances **connected** with its perpetration.

There are times that try men's souls. There are seasons in every good man's life when he wishes he was not a church member for just about five minutes, that he might have a chance to do justice to the surroundings. Such to me was the trying moment when I gathered my bruised remains together and, looking around, saw the festive "Delay" quietly eating grass, while a little distance off sat the doctor on his pony complacently whistling, "Earth hath no sorrow that Heaven cannot heal."

COW-BOYS, AND SOME OF THE DIFFICULTIES OF HERDING.

To overlook the mention of the closest neighbors of the red-skins—the cow-boys—in this volume would appear like a misdemeanor. No better description of the men and their dangerous work can be given than that found in *Wilkes' Spirit*, written by one of them, Mr. J. B. Omohundoo (Texas Jack:

The cow-boy! How often spoken of, how falsely imagined, how greatly despised (where not known), how little understood! How sneeringly referred to, and how little appreciated, although his title has been gained by the possession of many of the noblest qualities that form the romantic hero of the poet, novelist, and historian; the plainsman and the scout. What a school it has been for the latter! As "tall oaks from little acorns grow," the cow boy serves a purpose, and often develops into the most celebrated ranchman, guide, cattle-king, Indian-fighter, and dashing ranger. How old Sam Houston loved them, how the Mexicans hated them, how Davy Crockett admired them, how the Camanches feared them, and how much you 'beef-eaters' of the rest of the country owe to them, is a large-sized conundrum.

As the rebellious kid of olden times filled a handkerchief (always a handkerchief, I believe) with his all, and followed the trail of his idol, Columbus, and became a sailor bold, the more ambitious and adventurous youngster of later days freezes on to a double barreled pistol and steers for the bald prairie to seek fortune and experience. If he don't get his system full it s only because the young man weakens, takes a back seat, or fails to become a Texas cow-boy. As there are generally openings, likely young fellows can enter, and not fail to be put through. If he is a stayer, youth and size will be no disadvantage for his start in, as certain lines of the business are peculiarly adapted to the light young horsemen, and such are highly esteemed when they become thoroughbreds, and fully possessed of "cow sense."

Now "cow sense" in Texas implies a thorough knowledge of the business, and a natural instinct to divine every thought, trick, intention, want, habit, or desire of his drove, under any and all circumstances. A man might be brought up in the states swinging to a cow's tail, yet, taken to Texas, would be as useless as a last year's bird's nest with the bottom punched out. The boys grow old soon, and the old cattle men seem to grow young; thus it is that the name is applied to all who follow the trade. The boys are divided into range-workers and branders, road drivers and herders, trail-guides and bosses.

As the railroads have now put an end to the old-time trips, I will have to go back a few years to give a proper estimate of the duties and dangers, delights and joys, trials and troubles, when off the ranch. The ranch itself and the cattle trade in the state still flourish in their old-time glory, but are being slowly encroached upon by the modern improvements that will, in course of time, wipe out the necessity of his day, the typical subject of this sketch. Before being counted in and fully indorsed, the candidate has had to become an expert horseman, and test the many eccentricities of the stubborn mustang; enjoy the beauties, learn to catch, throw and ride the "docile" little Spanish American plug, an amusing experience in itself, in which you are taught all the mysteries of rear and tear, stop and drop, lay and roll, kick and bite, on and off, under and over, heads and tails, hand springs, triple somersaults, standing on your head, diving, flip-flaps, getting left (horse leaving you 15 miles from camp—Indians in the neighborhood, etc.), and all the funny business included in the familiar term of "bucking," then learn to handle a rope, catch a calf, stop a crazy cow, throw a beef steer, play with a wild bull, lasso an untamed mustang, and daily endure the dangers of a Spanish matador, with a little Indian scrape thrown in, and if there is anything left of you they'll christen it a first-class cow-boy. Now his troubles begin.

I will simply give a few incidents of a trip over the plains to the cattle markets of the North, through the wild and unsettled portions of the Territories, varying in distance from fifteen hundred to two thousand miles—time, three to six months - extending through the Indian Territory and Kansas to Nebraska, Colorado, Dakota, Montana, Idaho, Nevada and sometimes as far as California. Immense herds, as high as thirty thousand or more in number, are moved by single owners, but are driven in bands of from one to three thousand, which, when under way, are designated "herds." Each of these has from ten to fifteen men, with a wagon driver and cook, and the "kingpin of the outfit," the boss, with a supply of two or three ponies to a man, an ox-team, and blankets; also jerked beef and corn meal—the staple food. They are also furnished with mavericks or "doubtless-owned" yearlings for the fresh-meat supply. After getting fully under way, and the cattle broken in, from ten to fifteen miles a day is the average, and everything is plain sailing in fair weather. As night comes on, the cattle are rounded up in a small compass, and held until they lie down, when two men are left on watch, riding round and round them in opposite directions, singing or whistling all the time, for two hours, that being the length of each watch. The singing is absolutely necessary, as it seems to soothe the fears of the cattle, scares away the wolves or other varmints that may be prowling around, and prevents them from hearing any other accidental sound, or dreaming of their old homes, and if stopped, would, in all probability, be the signal for a stampede. So the cow-boy bawls out lines of his own composition:

> Lay nicely now, cattle, don't heed any rattle,
> But quietly rest until morn;
> For if you skedaddle, we'll jump in the saddle,
> And head you as sure as you're born.

But on nights when "Old Prob" goes on a spree, leaves the bung out of his water-barrel above, prowls around with his hash-box, raising a breeze, whispering in tones of thunder, and the cow-boy's voice, like the rest of the outfit, is drowned out—steer clear, and prepare for action. If the quadrupeds don't go insane, turn tail to the storm, and strike out for civil and religious liberty, then I don't know what "strike out" means. Ordinarily so clumsy and stupid-looking, a thousand beef steers can rise like a flock of quail on the roof of an exploding powder mill, and will scud away like a tumble weed before a high wind, with a noise like a receding earthquake. Then come fun and frolic for the boys!

CHAPTER XVIII.

A RESCUE BY CUSTER'S MEN—BRETTA VAN NESS' NARROW ESCAPE FROM DEATH.

The summer of 1872 was a season of fearful peril to the scattered settlers of Dakota and Montana. A large proportion of them were immigrants, ignorant of the dangers that surrounded them on the border, and knowing nothing of the horrors of Indian warfare till awakened from their dreams of peace and plenty by the blood-curdling war-whoops resounding around their cabins.

The powerful and warlike Sioux, jealous of the encroachments of the whites, angered by the cheating of Government agents, and urged on by their own fierce tempers, donned their war-paint, many of the young braves going to join Sitting Bull's camp, while others roamed the country in bands, committing fearful depredations on defenseless ranchmen and outlying settlements.

GEN. CUSTER.

General Custer, commanding the Seventh Regiment of Regular Cavalry, stationed at Fort Lincoln on the Missouri, taking six companies of cavalry supported by three of infantry, made a rapid march into the Indian country, to punish the marauders and drive them back to their reservations.

An unclouded June sun smiled down upon this fine array of blue-and-yellow, halted for their mid-day rest and refreshment in the midst of a vast prairie that, on three sides, stretched to the horizon. In the northwest, a range of low hills broke its dull monotony. The summer's heat had not yet curled and shriveled every green thing as it does later; but the broad plain was waving with grass and gay with brilliant flowers.

General Custer had ridden to the rear, to inspect, with his usual care, the wagon and mule trains—for nothing was too insignificant for his notice that concerned the comfort of his men. Close behind him, almost as well mounted as himself, pressed the orderly who had just dashed down to him from the head of the column.

Reining-in his fiery steed at the head of his command, the general was quickly surrounded by a mingled mass of officers and orderlies.

"Runners in our front," said Captain Custer, handing him a powerful field-glass.

"Yes," replied the general, after a long and earnest survey, "they are scouts, and the running of the first is like the running of Bloody Knife. He comes, no doubt, with important information."

"What horsemen are those just rising the crest of the divide?" eagerly inquired the captain. "A pursuit?"

"I think not," replied the general, after a searching gaze. "There are but two riders, and one looks more like a squaw than a warrior."

"Possibly it's a decoy," suggested an officer, "and a larger body of the enemy may be on the other side of the divide."

"They ride," replied Custer, "as though they themselves were pursued. I do not think the enemy would dare attack us on the open plain, even with greatly superior numbers; however, it will do no harm to be ready either to march or to fight." And, in a clear ringing tone, he shouted: "Bugler, sound 'boots and saddles'!"

With the first notes of that stirring call, the men sprang to their feet, thrusting half-eaten rations into their haversacks, and, almost as quickly as one can tell it, were in their saddles, presenting, to the quick eye of the general, long lines of erect soldierly figures curbing their restive horses with steady hands. Nearer and nearer came the Indian runners. With characteristic impatience, he galloped forward to meet them, followed by his orderly and a few officers.

"How!" said the general, as his favorite scout reached his side; "what news, Bloody Knife?"

In terse Indian language, the scout told him that he had crossed the trails of numerous hostile bands of Sioux; and that, after many successful attacks upon the whites, they were concentrating on the Tongue river, loaded with plunder and bringing scores of captives.

"Who are those that follow you?" asked the general,

pointing toward the mysterious travelers, now at the foot of the hills and just entering upon the plain.

Waving the proffered glass aside, the Indian fixed his keen eyes, shaded by one brown hand, on the advancing party.

"Palefaces," said he, sententiously: "one squaw, two papoose; white man, **arm** hurt; carries gun across horse's neck; looks **back** every step—thinks Sioux on every side."

"That is **true**," said the **captain**, who had been studying them closely. "They are escaped prisoners or refugees, in momentary danger of being scalped."

"Go back," said the general, turning to an **orderly**, "and order the troops forward. Send an ambulance with all speed. Take horses, and don't spare them."

Away flew the orderly, and the party rode forward to meet the approaching strangers.

On dashed the cavalcade, and now they could plainly see what the Indian had described at a much greater distance that the foremost rider **was** a woman mounted on a large gray horse. In her arms, she bore an infant; astride the horse's neck rode a boy of five; while, at her back, a girl of ten clung trembling to her mother. Behind them, on a black horse, came the father, one arm in a sling and his rifle across his horse's neck, as the scout had said.

All were fair-haired and blue-eyed—unmistakably German. Tears of joy ran down their pale faces at the sight of their deliverers, and thanksgivings, fell from their lips.

Tenderly the kind-hearted officers lifted the mother and her tired children to the ground, while the general warmly extended his hand to the father, who, as he approached, respectfully gave the military salute.

At his side, the man wore an old cavalry sabre; his shirt was soaked with blood from his wounded shoulder; about his head was tied a handkerchief, also blood-stained; and a rivulet of blood coursing down his sunburned cheek showed the wound was severe. Under his shaggy eyebrows shone wide-open fearless blue eyes—while, in spite of his wounds and fatigue, he bore himself with a soldierly air that at once took the eye of the general.

"You have been attacked by Indians," said Custer. "When did it happen—and **where**?"

"Ve haf lifed," replied the man, "at Bald Butte—how var

from here, I cannot tell. Ve haf tree neighbors—all German. The night before last, mine leetle girl Bretta had gone to spend der ebening mit dem, ven, all at vonce, ve hear dreadful yells und screams—our neighbors' houses all one blaze. We haf no light—trees all around; dey no see us at first. Ve saddle our horses in der dark, und shtart to run avay; ve not go var vhen a big Indian rose up before us und fire upon me.

"See," he said, pushing back his gray flannel shirt and showing his shoulder, closely bound with bloody cloths evidently torn from their clothing. "Den he dhry pull me off mine horse; ve fight; mine horse shy vone side. Den I hit him mit mine old sabre dot I carry in der vhars long ago; he lay down in der road und not vant to fight any more."

"You have been a soldier, then?" said Custer, with interest.

"Yaw; ich vas at Sadowa, und ich von dis," replied he, showing, on his broad sunburnt breast, a small steel cross suspended from his neck by a silver chain. "Our goot emperor gif it me mit his own hand. Ich tired of vhars; I dake mine leetle vamily und come here. I know notting about Indians. Agent say: 'All right; soldiers all around—dey take care ob you.' But ah! Gott in Himmel! mine leetle Bretta—mine leetle girl!" and the father's grief burst forth afresh.

"What is your name?" asked a young orderly, riding close to the German and gazing eagerly in his face.

"Van Ness, sir."

"And is Bretta Van Ness your daughter?"

"She is, sir—mine own dear leetle girl."

"What of her? Where is she?" asked the young man, the blood receding from his cheek, and his eye growing dark and stern.

"I haf every reason to believe she is a prisoner in der hands of der savages," replied the striken father.

"How do you know that she is a prisoner?" again questioned the young soldier.

"I vhas shtandin' in mine door, vhen I hear her cry 'Fader! fader!' und scream. I hid mine schildren in der bush, und, vhen der Indians gone, I creep back to vind her. All mine neighbors dead—every one—Bretta not dere."

Leaning his head on his hand, supported by his gun-barrel, he sobbed as only a man overwhelmed by sorrow can, while the low weeping of the mother mingled with the wails of her infant, as she in vain tried to soothe it.

"General," said the orderly, turning to that officer, "with your permission, I will go in search of this man's daughter, and snatch her from her captors, or perish in so doing."

A look of wonder overspread the faces of that circle, as they noted the deep intensity of his tones, the tight-drawn lips, and the pallor of his face, that showed even through its deep bronzing.

"Where had he seen Bretta Van Ness, and why did her fate move him so deeply?" was the wondering comment of his fellow-soldiers.

"It would be madness," said Custer, after a prolonged pause, during which time he keenly eyed the young soldier; "sheer madness! Why, man, your life would not be worth a straw, a mile from the column; the creeping savages would pick you off in no time. Better leave it to the movements of the regiment to bring them to terms. Beside, this band have probably retreated to their village or joined the main body of the enemy, and pursuit would be worse than useless!"

"The greater need, then," replied the brave fellow, "that Bretta's friends stir themselves in her behalf. If they cannot save her a bullet through her heart will put her beyond the reach of those incarnate fiends."

The brave and generous Custer strongly felt the force of these words. He shuddered at the horrors confronting this fair young girl, but keenly alive to the perils incurred by her would be deliverer.

"I will go with him, general, if I can be spared from the service," said a young man who now stepped forward. "I know this country very well—was through here when looking for the hostile camp. I think I know where those German families lived, and believe I can strike the trail of this band within twelve hours."

"But, Reynolds," said Custer, "it is extremely perilous!"

"I know all the chances for and against," returned the scout, "and am willing to take them."

"Thank you, and God bless you!" exclaimed Harland.

warmly clasping the hand of this bravest of brave men.

"Well," said the general, springing lightly to the ground, "since you are bound to go, I wish you to have every advantage that can be given you. I cannot spare a detachment—but here, Harland, you must take my horse. Vic'll bring you through if any horse can. She's a Kentucky thoroughbred, and there's not her match on the plains for speed or endurance."

"Unless it is mine," said Captain Custer, "and Reynolds can have him."

Both men protested against taking their officers' horses, saying they would be needed in the coming campaign; but the general declared "they had good enough horses in reserve, as they did not anticipate the necessity of running away from the Indians, and, if Reynolds' theory was correct, they would be back before a blow could be struck at the enemy."

Still urged by their commander to lose no more time in vain protests, they sprang into their saddles, and, bidding the German mother—who, with her children and wounded husband, had been tenderly placed in an ambulance—a hasty farewell, dashed off across the plain.

"Go back, Blucher! go back!" shouted Harland, as the general's great stag-hound bounded along by his side. But Blucher had no idea of returning to headquarters for his conge, and kept steadily on, only falling far enough to the rear to be out of reach of any missile that might be thrown at him.

"Let him go," at length said the scout. "There is a great affection between him and the horse you ride; he goes where she goes, and sleeps by her side at night. He has a keen nose for the trail, too, and never gives tongue following it."

"If we're lucky enough to find the redskins, he might help us out in a 'hand to hand,' you know; he has scars enough to prove him a good fighter. Come on, old dog!"

In his delight at being permitted to go, the dog fairly bounded over the horse, and jumped barking at her nose, while she whinnied and playfully struck at him with her forefeet.

On the crest of the divide, the soldiers paused, waved a last adieu to their comrades, took a last look at the old flag they might never see again, and then plunged down **through** chaparral and cactus to the plain below.

It was an easy matter to follow the broad **trail** made by the flying family, and, no signs of Indians appearing, they traveled at a good rate of speed, and, **late in** the afternoon, drew rein on the top of the next divide **and** looked down on another vast plain, through which a sluggish stream crept **to** mingle its **waters with** the far distant Missouri.

To the west lay the great butte country, which, the scout said, " was filled with narrow and deep gulches, where **the** Indians could find a hundred secure hiding-places; and beyond, where the mountains were purpling in **the setting sun,** Sitting Bull was thought to have his camp."

" Do you see that film of gray smoke rising against the dark line of trees far in our front? That," said Reynolds, " probably marks the scene of one of their last attacks; now, by diverging from this trail and striking diagonally across the prairie to where **those** cottonwoods outline the river's banks, we shall probably find their trail. I only hope there'll be daylight enough left to see it before we camp."

An hour's hard riding, and they reached the first of the sentinel-like cottonwood-trees, and, as they plunged deeper and **dee**per into their shade, they began to look carefully for Indian signs. Both men had dismounted and were closely scrutinizing each leaf and blade of grass, when a deep growl from the dog caused them to look up. A short distance ahead of them stood **an** Indian, his gun reversed and his hand raised in token of peace.

With a savage snarl, Blucher sprang at his throat. By a dextrous movement, the Indian caught him under the jaw, and, the next moment, the dog crouched at his feet, licking his moccasins and whining softly.

" Bloody Knife, by all that's good! " cried the scout. And, springing forward, each grasped a hand of the friendly savage.

" Ouches tell-a-me come," said Bloody Knife, and then, in his own tongue, which Reynolds understood, informed them he had taken an Indian pony recently captured, and, following a **more** direct route where he found good traveling, he had reached the river before **them.** " And here," said he, " is the trail."

THE RESCUE.

A few feet from where they were standing, the earth showed unmistakable signs of a **party of about** twenty having passed, but no trace of the **captive girl.** In one place, the trail dipped down to the **river, showing the** Indians had stopped for water; and their **own** horses, being sadly in need of similar refreshment, **were** led by the scout to the river's edge and drank deeply **of** its yellow tide. Meanwhile, Harland and the Indian followed along the trail, unwilling to lose a moment of daylight. A few rods brought them to a large sycamore-tree with wide-spreading branches. Here **the** short grass was much trampled, and the remains of **a fire** showed food **had been** prepared.

Bloody Knife next turned **his** keen eyes on the massive trunk.

"See," whispered he; "paleface stand here."

On one side, the grass was much trodden, and, following the movement of the dusky finger, Harland saw the bark was broken and worn, as by a rope or lariat bound tightly around it.

"And see," he cried: "here are gashes made by hatchets! My God! the red devils have amused themselves by throwing their tomahawks at her golden head! What has she not suffered?"

He turned away, to hide the emotion that almost overpowered him at this proof of their barbarous treatment.

A guttural ejaculation from the Indian caused him to turn back quickly, to see him deftly untangling from the rough bark a thread of long yellow hair.

"Thank God for that!" said Reynolds, **coming** up at that moment with the horses. "We will yet **save her.**"

"God willing!" added Harland, **with a** deep-drawn breath.

The last gleam of daylight had now faded from the western sky, and the shadows of the great buttes, falling across their path, deepened and intensified the gloom till the keen eyes of the Indian could no longer see **the** trail. Still he pressed on with stealthy steps, his attentive **ear** analyzing even the cries of the night-birds and the far-off howls of some wild animal, pausing till he made sure it was what it seemed to be.

For a mile or more, **they pushed on in this** manner, when suddenly the Indian, rising from a listening posture—his ear to the ground—drew his pony one side and directed the others to do the same.

To a whispered "What is it?" he simply answered: "Sioux—sh!"

They had barely quieted their horses, when their strained ears caught the click of a pony's hoof striking against a stone. Each scout, taking his horse firmly by the bits, patted and smoothed his nose to keep him from neighing at the presence of other horses.

Presently, a bulky shape showed in the darkness, then another and another, till seven warriors had filed along past them, so near that they could have touched them with their rifles. Blucher's body trembled with rage, and the first note of a deep growl rumbled in his capacious throat; but a vigorous kick in the side from the scout's foot stopped his growl, and breath too, for a time. After the file of warriors came their ponies, bearing heavy loads that crashed through the bushes on either hand—game, it was afterward known to have been. Silent as statues stood horses and men, till the last footfall had died away—then the Indian, dropping on the ground, remained long in a listening attitude. Starting to his feet, he pushed rapidly forward, followed by the others. They had covered another mile in this way, when, turning sharply to their left, he led them deep into the bushes and halted at the foot of a huge rock. With the muttered word "Reconnoitre," he was gone.

Long they waited, till dark thoughts of possible treachery began to fill their minds—waited till the tired horses noisily champed their bits and stepped about on the uneven ground. They had drawn close together, in order to consult in regard to the advisability of going on without him, when, like a shadow of the night, he rose at their side.

"Come," he whispered; "leave horses and come."

The animals were tethered, and the dog ordered to stay and watch them. After a sharp scramble up what seemed a rough mountain side, they found themselves at the top of a high bluff overlooking a long narrow valley. Carefully parting the bushes that fringed its edge, a wild scene burst upon their startled vision: At the farther end of the glade, a large fire was burning, lighting up with fitful gleams and flashes the rugged faces of the rocks that hemmed in the little valley on three sides, and bringing into red relief the trunks of forest-trees that, on its farther edge, seemed crowding upon the plain like the ranks of an advancing army. Around the fire, several squaws were grouped, broiling venison for their masters' suppers. A few rods away and nearer the center of the opening, a tall post had been set in the ground, and to it, bound hand and foot, was their prisoner, the girl they were seeking.

Around her circled in a wild dance twenty or more warriors, singing a monotonous chant, to which they stamped and gestured, occasionally breaking into a whoop, and brandishing their tomahawks and knives close to her head. So still she stood—or rather hung, for she drooped heavily on the thongs that bound her arms—that the scouts thought her already dead. But suddenly a squaw, becoming excited by their wild dancing, seized a burning fagot from the fire and, rushing into the circle of warriors, applied it to her bare shoulders. A piercing scream rose on the air, and the whoops and yells of the fiendish crew were redoubled, while the squaw circled round and round in the dance, touching the shrinking flesh of the poor girl as long as the brand continued burning.

When they ceased their gyrations, two warriors stepped forward and began to untie the hard knotted thongs that bound her to the stake. Again a scream of mortal terror pierced the night. Instantly the scouts brought their rifles to their shoulders, and two locks simultaneously clicked.

"Not yet," said Reynolds; "when we do fire, you aim at her head, and I at her heart."

A deep groan answered him.

Released from her bonds, she dropped helplessly at their feet, for she neither moved nor stirred. To their intense relief, the squaws now left the fire, mingled with the men, and proceeded to tie her hands and feet, while her body was again securely bound to the stake. The men, gathering around the fire, greedily devoured the food prepared for them, washing it down with copious draughts of "fire-water," of which they seemed to have a plentiful supply. Their meal finished, they rolled themselves in their blankets and lay down about the fire, their heads to the blaze and their feet outward. One big warrior, striding to the edge of the woods, sat down, his back to a tree, his gun across his lap, as sentinel, while the squaws, bringing two long poles, laid them across the body of their prisoner and lay down in a circle around her, disposing themselves in such a manner that a squaw lay on each end of the poles.

"That is hopeful," whispered Reynolds; "if they thought there was the least danger of an attack, they would never leave the squaws to guard the prisoner, or go to sleep in that careless manner. It is evident they feel perfectly safe."

Long they waited for sleep to close every eye of the drunken crew. At length, Bloody Knife rose and motioned the others to follow. Silent as shadows, they descended the western slope of the bluff, the Indian in advance. Fortunately the wind was rising, and the swaying and creaking of branches greatly favored their movements. Once the sentinel rose, apparently listening intently, his strong features and figure making a huge silhouette against the light of the camp-fire. At length he sat down, drawing his blanket about him and holding his rifle in the hollow of his arm. Nearer and nearer to the watchful Sioux crept Bloody Knife, a long bright blade in his hand. The hearts of the scouts stood still when he was near enough to touch the robe of this living statue.

Suddenly, without a cry or groan, he fell forward on his face and never moved. The knife of his enemy had entered his heart.

For some moments, Bloody Knife lay in the shadow of the tree, then rising, motioned the scouts to approach.

"Go," he said, "kill squaw, take paleface; me stay here."

With cat-like tread, they crept around till they were exactly opposite the circle of squaws. Then Harland went boldly into the light and made an attempt to step within the narrow cordon, in order to cut the thongs that bound the prisoner. Instantly a squaw sprang up, but, before she could utter a warning cry, he struck her a tremendous blow between the eyes, that effectually silenced her. The motion given to the pole by this action awoke the squaw on the opposite side, who, in the act of springing to her feet, received an arrow in her throat from the bow of Bloody Knife, and fell back dead. Drawing the stunned squaw one side, he knelt beside the girl and placed the palm of his hand firmly over her mouth.

Her large blue eyes flew open with a great horror in them. "Be brave," he whispered; "we will save you." The eyes closed again, while tears rolled from under her long brown lashes.

With a sharp knife, he cut the thongs about her wrists and the lariat that bound her to the stake. To get her feet free without waking the squaws who lay on the ends of the second pole was the next task. Stepping softly between them, he had almost cut the cord that bound her, when a squaw sprang up, but was instantly brained by a blow from the butt of Reynolds' rifle. Harland lifted the girl from the ground and dashed with her into the forest shades. The remaining squaw sprang up, with a yell that caused every Indian around the fire to bound to his feet and rush for his weapons. Reynolds aimed a blow at her head, and an arrow flew out of the darkness; but it only pierced her shoulder, causing her to utter terrible cries.

The scouts placed the helpless and almost unconscious girl in the shelter of a tree-trunk, and, dropping on one knee, brought their rifles to their shoulders, to meet the rush of their infuriated enemies.

At that moment, the report of a rifle rang out from the other side of the valley, then another and another, and each time an Indian rolled on the ground. Dazed by their late potations and the suddenness of the attack, they appeared for a moment bewildered, and then, with fearful yells, rushed into the woods in search of their hidden foe and to gain the cover of the trees.

The howling and firing receded until it came faint and far from the depths of the forest, and the scouts, knowing that Bloody Knife, with his breech-loader, was making this diversion in their favor, lost no time in skirting the open with their precious charge, and were looking hurriedly for the path by which the Indians descended to the plain, when Bloody Knife appeared, and, swinging Bretta to his shoulder, sprang lightly up the rocks.

In a few moments, they had reached their horses, and the Indian resigned his burden to her lover.

Bloody Knife led the van of the little procession, while Reynolds, calm and cool as at the beginning of the fight, brought up the rear, pausing often to listen for sounds of pursuit. Soon the great tree was reached that was fraught with such terrors for Bretta; but they rode quickly past, and she was not allowed to see it.

They halted where the trail led down to the river, and the horses again drank their fill from the waters now sparkling in the light of the rising moon. Pursuit was certain in the morning, and, in order to confuse their foes, they determined to follow as nearly as practicable the trail made the preceding afternoon by Harland and the scout.

The keen eyes of the Indian soon found it, and in a single file they traversed it as rapidly as the nature of the ground and the condition of their horses would allow. They traveled in this manner till the moon set, when, feeling quite secure from pursuit until daybreak, they decided to camp and take a few hours of much needed rest. The horses were carefully picketed; two blankets, raised on sticks a little way from the ground, made a shelter for them all, the men taking turns as sentinel. Blucher was company for each in turn, and gave them a wonderful sense of security and companionship. At the first faint streak of daylight, the little camp was astir; a hasty breakfast from their haversacks eaten, a draught of river-water from their canteens drunk, and they were in their saddles, following closely the trail of the day before.

They had reached the divide, and the men, dismounted, were toiling up the steep ascent, when a cry from the Indian caused them to turn, and, to their horror and dismay, they beheld a large body of redskins, double the number they had fought the evening before, coming after them at the greatest speed their ponies were capable of making, and not more than a mile distant.

At the top of the ascent, they vaulted into their saddles and dashed down to the plain. The war-cries and howls of their enemies were plainly heard, and the horses, scenting the danger, flew with the winds. Over the hill swept the Indians with triumphant whoops, for they deemed their prey almost within their grasp. Under favorable conditions, the two thoroughbreds could have easily distanced the Indian ponies, fleet as they were; but Harland's noble animal was beginning to show the effect of her double weight in labored breathing and forced spurts of speed.

On came their pursuers, wilder than ever, elated by the

slight advantage gained. Reynolds and Bloody Knife turned, and, without checking the speed of their steeds, emptied two Indian saddles. The fire was instantly returned, and Bloody Knife's pony fell to the ground, while Reynolds' horse got a severe wound in the shoulder, but did not lessen his speed—the scout, placing his hand on his companion's saddle, easily kept alongside. From the first, they had kept in the rear of Harland and his terrified burden—who, in pitiful accents, begged him to kill her and save himself; but, with a tightened pressure of his arm, he told her he would live or die with her.

The object of the Sioux seemed to be to take them all alive, and, spreading out over the prairie, they were gradually flanking them on both sides. Almost in their course, the fugitives descried a rocky ridge rising above the level of the plain, with a few scattered bushes beyond. Thinking if they could but gain its shelter they might check for a time the advance of their foes, they strained every nerve to reach it. Their horses were reeking with foam, and bloody spume-flakes flew from their nostrils. They were within a few rods of this desired haven, the enemy close upon their heels, when a line of smoke and flame burst from this natural earthwork, and the report of a dozen carbines woke the echoes of the hills, emptying as many Indian saddles. Instantly a troop of cavalry poured out upon the plain, and, without stopping to form a line of battle, charged the flying Sioux with their war-cry of "Ouches! Ouches!" (Custer's Indian name.)

The tired ponies were no match for the fresh horses of the troopers, and their riders soon abandoned them and sought safety in the tall grass and sage-brush. The old dog took a lively interest in this fight, and, wherever the grass waved in snaky undulations, there he flew with tremendous leaps, his eyes glaring and foam dripping from his huge jaws; then a series of yells and fierce growls told the troopers where he had found an enemy, and many times the carbine finished the work the dog's fangs had begun. The fight was soon over; many ponies were captured, with rifles, blankets, and all sorts of Indian trappings.

The soldiers who had made so timely an appearance on the scene were a part of a company that Custer had sent out for the double purpose of securing supplies for his command

and looking after the absent scouts, about whom he felt the greatest anxiety. They had camped, the evening before, in the dry bed of a stream, and were in the act of preparing their breakfast when the rush of hoofs and the yells of the Indians burst upon their ears. Snatching their arms, they met them with the result already detailed.

What had appeared from a distance to be bushes proved to be the tops of trees having their roots in the bottom of the canon, and under their shade the fugitives found grateful rest, bringing splendid appetites to the ample breakfast of the soldiers.

By making short halts and long marches, they soon overtook the regiment. We will not dwell on Bretta's joyful reunion with her afflicted family, the general's delight at the safe return of the party, nor Blucher's triumphal entrance into the camp, his collar filled with eagle-feathers, and barking with all his might in response to the acclamations of the men. Custer received his old favorite with many caresses, and laughingly assured him that he should be breveted for his gallant conduct.

Two weeks later, and a merry party—consisting of Will Harland, his lovely bride, the Van Ness family, and several Eastern-bound officers—crossed the plains, and only separated in New York.

CHAPTER XIX.

WILD BILL'S TERRIBLE HAND-TO-HAND FIGHT—SEVEN MEN SHOT AND FOUR STABBED TO DEATH.

WILD BILL, one noon, in his wandering expeditions, found himself in a village of about a hundred houses. The one tavern of the place was made conspicuous by a huge sign as well as by a crowd congregated about its door. Bill rode directly up to it, leaping from his mare, and walked boldly into the bar-room, which was crowded with people. Of these he knew some, and some knew him, and he knew that most of them were Southerners. Among them was Dave Tutt, on whom Bill had sworn vengeance at sight for abducting his friend Buffalo Bill's sister. Tutt stood at the bar, raising a glass of whisky to his lips, as he saw Bill enter. The color left his face, and with trembling hand he set the liquor down untasted.

"Drink it, Dave, for you'll need it now more than you ever did in your life!" said Bill, sternly, as he strode up with in two feet of him, the crowd parting to right and left as he advanced. "Drink it, I say, and then go to the opposite side of the street with your revolver, and remember, it is *you* or *me!*"

David Tutt, reassured, when he found that work was not to commence instantly, swallowed the fiery liquid, and the color came back in his face. Seeing there was no chance of evading a combat, he at once put his hand on the butt of his revolver and slowly passed from the bar-room into the street, and on across it to the front of the court-house.

"A fight!" screamed all the men, and all got out of the way to arrange a free line of fire between the duelists. When all was ready and the signal given both men fired at the same time, and for an instant it seemed as if both had missed, for both stood erect, calm apparently, looking at each other. Only a second, and with a death-yell on his whitening lips, Dave Tutt essayed to fire again, but his pistol exploded harmlessly as he fell forward on his face, dead. Then Bill raised the hat from his head and looked at a hole in it where the ball had passed through, actually cutting away the hair on his head as it grazed the skull.

"There's one debt paid!" said Bill, as he glared fiercely on the crowd. "If any of you cared enough for him to stand in his place, I'll wait just one minute to see it done!"

Bill calmly waited the minute. Not a man stirred or spoke. He mounted his horse and rode away. The spectators, after Bill's disappearance, were sorry they hadn't hung him on the spot.

"I reckon the talking would have had to lead the swinging!" said a rough-looking customer.

"Are you a friend of his?" asked half a dozen men.

"Not if I know myself. But I know him, and the man that tackles Wild Bill single-handed has got his winter's work paid for in advance. I thought I'd see if you all would let him go before you'd speak or raise a hand—so I kept still and saw you do it. Now I'm going to fix him, or start them that will. I want a gal that's smart as lightning who can ride a race-horse and tell a smooth lie without blushing."

"Mister, I'm one that can do all of that if it will pay," said the landlord's daughter.

"It shall pay—Bill's purse and gold watch, the one is full, I reckon, and the other worth two hundred dollars, for 'twas a gift from General Harney," said the man.

The girl was given the man's own horse to follow out his directions. The man was Ben McCullough, the Texan ranger.

Bill had gone four or five miles, perhaps, when he saw a woman coming on behind him. She was soon alongside, and turning carelessly in his saddle, he glanced, first curiously, and then admiringly at her, for she sat that horse in a way to captivate the fancy of any one like Bill.

"That's a stunnin' animal you're on, miss," said he.

"It ought to be. Aunt Sally gave two hundred for him when he was a yearlin' colt," said the fair rider. "Uncle Jake M'Kandlas wants to buy him, but I don't mean to let Aunt Sally sell him, for he just suits *me*."

The girl spoke in a careless way, and did not *appear* to observe the sudden start which Wild Bill involuntarily gave as that last name left her lips.

"Who is Uncle Jake M'Kandlas? Is he Aunt Sally's husband?" asked Bill with assumed carelessness.

"Oh, no—we call him *Uncle* Jake because he's old. He

isn't well; he got hurt among the Indians not long ago, and he's stayin' at our house to get well," said the girl, speaking as easily and natural as if she had not learned a lesson.

A house in the distance, half hidden in a little grove of locusts, was pointed out as Aunt Sally's. They reached the place side by **side**, but when Bill turned to help the girl dismount, she **laughed and cried** out, "Jake M'Kandlas comes yonder, I'll go to tell him **Wild** Bill is here!" She pointed to **eleven men** who were coming that way, and she instantly rode toward them.

An **old** woman came to the door, who**m Bill knew, and** seeing the horsemen approaching, she cried: "Oh, merciful Heaven, Mr. Hitchcock (Bill's real name) what will become of you? Jake M'Kandlas and his gang will murder you under *my* roof! Oh, what brought you here?"

"Your precious niece there," said Bill.

"My niece? **I have** no niece—I do not know that girl," said the woman, looking in wonder to see the black mare speed away as **if** she flew.

"Then I'm sold and the money paid in," cried Bill. "She has told Jake M'Kandlas, and there he and his tigers come. Old woman, if you ever do any prayin', get into your cellar, out of the way, and pray your tallest, for there's going to be the toughest fight here that ever was fought. Go quick, I **want a** clear range and no squalling to bother me."

There was a cellar and a trap-door leading to it, and through this the weeping woman fled for safety, perhaps to pray, as Bill asked her to do. The next moment, throwing aside his hunting shirt and putting knife-hilt and revolver-butt where his hand would reach them easiest, Bill stood firm, fronting the door with his rifle cocked and ready.

A rush of horsemen, the sound of heavy feet leaping from the saddle to the ground, and then the burly form of Jake M'Kandlas loomed up before the door.

"Surrender, Yank!" shouted the renegade.

He never spoke again, for a ball from Bill's rifle tore away the very tongue that spoke, and took half the head with it, for he was on the threshold and the muzzle of the gun was in his face. As he fell back dead the gang rushed in on Bill, and firing as he backed to a corner—one, two, three, four, five, six successive shots sent a man down. Four more were left, and now knives in hand they were on him. One clutched him by the throat with a strangling grasp, while the others hewed and mangled him as he struggled to free himself. One fearful blow with his clenched fist sent one combatant stunned out of the way, then he clutched the arm which was extended to his throat, and and now his own knife was out. Like tigers mad for blood, with flashing, clashing knives, silent only that their breathing could be heard for rods, they sprang and leaped at each other, parrying and thrusting, until the last man of the crowd lay dead before the hero.* He, a mass of blood from head to foot, staggered out of the door, where the brunette yet sat on her horse to await the issue. She saw him, and with a wild scream gave her horse the rein and fled away in the thickening twilight. Bill staggered to the well, and bending his head down to a trough full of water, drank a few drops, and fell senseless. The widow came up from the cellar and soon got him in the house on a bed and dressed his wounds as well as she could—stanching them with cold water and lint hastily scraped from the bed linen. She had the joy presently to see his eyes open and hear the question, "Have I wiped them all out?"

"Yes, all but the girl, and she fled away. I do believe there's good in prayer!" said the old woman, "God must have heard me, for though you are hacked and slashed all over, there isn't a wound that has reached your vitals. Heaven be praised, you'll live!"

"Yes, it is to Him I owe it all!" said Bill, solemnly. "Nothing else could have saved me, for every man of 'em was a fighter! I reckon my old mother must have been prayin', too, for 'twould take a heap of it to carry me through such a scrape. Are you sure all them cusses are dead?"

"Yes—there is not a breath in any of 'em. I'll drag 'em out of the house—it's an awful job, but I can't bear to see 'em lie here after I light up."

All the long night the widow watched poor Bill. He was so weak that the fluttering breath, the low pulse, scarce told that he lived; but she prepared a mild stimulant and by noon of the next day he was able to take a little broth.

Friends soon discovered his predicament, and an impro

---

* A historical fact.

vised ambulance was made out of the widow's wagon and a feather bed, and she accompanied him on his journey, taking a course which Bill believed would soonest bring him to where Union forces were stationed.

It was a painful ride for the wounded man, but he was too much of a hero to show by any complaint what he suffered. In ten days, by slow and easy stages, carefully nursed by the widow, Wild Bill reached St. Louis. A regular surgeon attended to his wounds and soon he was convalescent and a happy man.

CHAPTER XX.

"BUFFALO BILL" AND "WILD BILL"—THEIR ADVENTURES ON THE BORDERS—TRIALS OF MR. CODY'S FAMILY.

No modern book about Indians would be complete without a little of the history and experience of Buffalo Bill (Mr. Cody) and Wild Bill (Mr. Hitchcock) was found in it. They were boon companions and side by side had many terrible struggles with the Red Men in the settling of our frontiers by the whites. Ned Buntline's true story of the tribulations of the Cody family enables us to ascertain something of a hero's early career.

On a little green spot on a Kansas prairie, in a log house, a white-haired man sits by a table, reading the Bible. On stools at his feet sit his beautiful twin daughters, while back of the mother's chair stands a noble boy. A cavalcade of horsemen halt before the door.

"What is wanted, and who are ye?" asked the good man, as he threw open the door.

"You are wanted, you nigger-worshipper, and I—Colonel M'Kandlas—have come to fetch you! And there's the warrant!"

BUFFALO BILL.

As the ruffian leader of the band shouted these words, a pistol in his hands was fired, and the father, fell dead before his horror-stricken family.

"You, Jake M'Kandlas, have murdered my father!" said the boy, "and you, base cowards, who saw him do this dark deed, spoke no word to restrain him. I am only little Bill, his son, but as God in heaven hears me now, I will kill every father's son of you before the beard grows on my face!"

The party soon dashed away, with their leader, and the heart-stricken family were alone with their dead.

In 1861 the old log house had given place to a white cottage, a lovely flower garden, fine grain fields, with barns, sheep, cattle and horses. The war of the Rebellion had begun. One day there came a letter from **Fort Kearney** to the little cottage stating that William Cody would arrive on the 25th of the month, and two friends would be with him—Wild Bill and Dave Tutt.

The trio came on time, and the strangers were thus introduced.

"This, mother," said William, is Bill **Hitchcock**, the best friend I ever had, or ever will have, outside of our own family. Three times has he saved me from being wiped out. Once by the Ogallalas, once when I was taken with the cramps in the ice-cold Platte, last winter, and once when old Jake M'Kandlas and his gang had a sure set on me. He and I will sink or swim in the same river, and that's a safe bet. And this other, is Dave Tutt. He is good on a hunt, death on the reds, and as smart as bordermen are made now-a-days. Now, boys, you're all acquainted, make yourselves at home. The darkey out there has got the horses, and he'll see them all right. I know that mother will soon have a good old supper for us."

Lillie, on whom Dave Tutt directed frequent glances, could scarcely conceal her aversion for him.

The sisters sang after supper to please their brother and his guests. The night was charming outside, and the moon shone brightly. Mrs. **Cody**, who was looking out of the window, suddenly screamed and became deathly pale.

"What is it, mother?" cried the son springing to her side. Being told that she had seen the face of his father's murderer at the window, he opened the casement, and as he did so a bullet whistled near his ear.

Wild Bill instantly blew out the lights, exclaiming: "Darkness here and moonlight out thar! We'll be all right in a shake. Jump for your tools, boys. Gals, lay down out o' range; we'll soon let the reds know old hands are here."

The three young men, reinforced by three negroes and one white man, the farm hands, were ready for work in less than a minute, and as the Indians did not seem disposed to make a rush for the inside of the house, crept quickly to points where from the doors and windows they could pick the fiends out among the trees around.

Buffalo Bill suggested getting out to the horses so as to come in on the Indians like fresh hands in the fight, and he told Dave Tutt and the men of their scheme, and to peg away at the foe meantime. The horses were soon secured and mounted without saddle or bridle, and both men dashed among the fiends, who were also after the farm stock. Wheeling and circling here and there in the rear of the astonished redskins, never missing a shot, the attacking party soon fled from the two fighters, but not before half their number had fallen. The search for a white man among the bodies of the slain was unsuccessful, so Bill decided that if M'Kandlas had been in the party he had escaped this time.

After breakfast the morning following the attack, while the negroes were burying the dead Indians, Buffalo Bill and his companions held a consultation in regard to what they had best do.

"They may have got enough last night to sicken them of coming again," said Buffalo Bill. "I believe I'll get on my insect, Powder Face, and follow their trail and see what they're about. You boys stay here on the watch, and mother and the girls can pack what they need for moving with, if I find that it will be best to move."

He was off at a gallop in a moment.

Bill, on his return, ordered preparations to be made for moving. What he discovered during his absence led him to believe that a second attack would be made on his home that night. The cottage home was soon deserted and the cavalcade of horsemen, wagons, and stock moved over the prairie. The first wagon, with the white laborer driving it, contained Mrs. Cody and the three girls, and Dave Tutt, without being specially told to take the post, rode near it. A negro was driving each of the other wagons, and the horses and cattle were driven up by Buffalo Bill and his mate. When night came on, they were just passing a low range of sandy hills not more than ten or twelve miles from the farm. Buffalo Bill looked back, and saw a bright light, which indicated the fate of their recent home.

"One more debt for Jake M'Kandlas to pay before I am done with him!" he muttered.

The wind now came sharp and spitefully in blasts, and the clouds rapidly overspread the sky, until at last the moon and stars were so nearly obscured that the travelers could see but little around them. The wagons were parked—that is, drawn into a square so as to leave a space in the quadrangle. Then the cattle were put inside, the harnessed horses hitched around outside and secured as well as they could be in the darkness. The three bordermen agreed to remain mounted so as to keep guard against any hostile approach.

Suddenly a fearful scream rose from one of the girls in the wagon—one wild cry for help, that fairly rent the air as well as the hearts and ears of those who heard it. The guards by the same lightning flash got a bare glimpse of a girl struggling in the arms of a man on horseback, and then all was darkness. Both dashed toward the spot where they had seen the man—another flash lit up their own forms and faces, but nothing else could they see.

"Lillie! Oh, Heaven, where is our Lillie?" screamed Mrs. Cody.

"Dave Tutt—where is he?" shrieked Lottie. "He was here and asked how we were, not a minute ago, and Lillie answered him."

"Dave Tutt!" shouted Buffalo Bill. "Dave Tutt, where are you?"

No answer came.

"The curse has carried Miss Lillie off!" cried Wild Bill. "It was him we saw with her in his arms."

"Oh, my child—my child!" moaned the unhappy mother. "You had indeed reason to hate and fear that man!"

"Do not try to move the wagons while we are gone," said Buffalo Bill, in a hoarse tone, to his mother. "Wild Bill and I must go after Lillie."

After a thunder shower the sky began to brighten, and the two horsemen neared the old farm, so that they could see men grouped close to timbers and rails that had been heaped on the fire for fuel.

"Let us creep up and see who is there," said Wild Bill.

"No—no! The murderer of my father is there! My poor sister, too. Ride on as I do, and let your revolver do your talking!"

Wild Bill saw that argument would be lost. Setting his teeth, his revolver in hand, and his eyes fixed on the group not now a hundred yards off, he urged Black Nell up to the side of Powder Face, and both horsemen at the same instant dashed into the circle of light.

Jake M'Kandlas sprang to his feet as a hoarse voice shouted his name, and fell the next instant with a bullet through his body, while dashing on and over them, firing as they came, the two riders swept, shooting down Indians and white men side by side as they passed on. In an instant, wheeling with fearful yells, back they came, but found few either of the white or red men waiting for the onslaught, for all but three or four had fled.

These fired only two or three random shots before the surer aim of the bordermen sent them to death, and then there were none to resist.

"Oh, Heaven, where is Lillie?" shouted Bill. "She is not here—back to the prairie, mate—the moon is coming out and we'll find her yet. Waste no time on the dead, but follow me!"

They returned to the wagons where the other dear ones had been left.

"Have you found Lillie?" was the cry of the mother, as her son rode up.

"Not yet, but I have slain the murderer of my father! His dead body lies roasting by the embers of our ruined home. Go on due east when day dawns—Bill and I will be scouting the prairie for the trail of Dave Tutt. We will not rest till our Lillie is found and his body left to sicken the howling wolves!"

When the two Bills had left the ruins of the cottage, Dave Tutt rode up, and on his saddle before him, lifeless in appearance, he held Lillie.

"Hallo—where are you all!" shouted Dave. "Some dead and the rest all run away from only two men. If I hadn't had the gal to bother with, I'd have fought 'em alone. They went by within twenty feet of me in the dark. Hallo—here! Jake M'Kandlas, or Frank Stark, where are you?"

"Who calls Jake M'Kandlas? Here's what's left of him and that's pretty much run out, I reckon!" said the ruffian himself.

"It is me, Dave Tutt, colonel—are you hurt bad?"

"Yes, I've got a heavy dose, Dave."

Dave laid his helpless burden down with her head on a saddle, and hurried to place the wounded man in a more comfortable position.

As this was done the eye of M'Kandlas fell on Lillie.

"Who have you got there, Dave!" he asked hastily. "Isn't it one of the twins?"

"Yes, it is Lillie, and her destiny is to be a robber's bride. She turned the cold shoulder on me, or I'd have been less rough in my courting—but the storm came up and I lifted her, and here she is."

"Then it was her them two, Wild Bill and her brother, were after when they charged on us here?"

"Of course it was, and as they found she was'nt here, they didn't wait to lift hair, but put out after me. They passed me twice within pistol shot, and if she hadn't been still in her faint, I would have had to still her. But where's all your men? There's not over half dozen, red and white, stretched here."

"No, there's more, but they've scattered. Blow this whistle, Dave, I'm too weak."

Tutt took a large whistle from the neck of the wounded man and blew a shrill call. It was answered by another whistle.

"That is Frank Stark," said the chief. "He will be here soon, and he carries what I need now, for I'm as weak as a sick chicken. There's a bad hole in my carcass. I've stuffed a bit of my hunting shirt in to stop the bleeding, but I'm afraid from the feeling, it bleeds inside."

Frank Stark came and stimulated the wounded man with whisky, which was also proffered Lillie, when she gained consciousness.

"Wretch! Take me back to my mother!" she said, as she pushed the flask away.

"Not yet—not before our honeymoon is over, my pretty wife that is to be!" said Dave.

"Your wife? Fiend! I will die a thousand deaths first. I hated you from the first moment I saw you! And now, coward, dog, I loathe and despise you!"

A consultation was held as to the next movements of the party. Frank Stark wanted to follow up the wagons. But Jake M'Kandlas could not, and Dave Tutt would not go. M'Kandlas could only be moved slowly and with care, so it took a part of the force to attend to him. Therefore a pursuit which would be attended with the certainty of a hard fight was given up, and as soon as day dawned the route for the Black Hills was taken up. Lillie was placed in a light wagon which had been saved from the flames, and the wounded colonel and his two injured men were laid on a heap of straw in the same vehicle. Before sunrise they were miles away, Dave Tutt now taking the leadership of the party and hurrying them on, for he dreaded pursuit from the two men whom he knew but too well, once on his track, would not leave it while he lived.

To and fro, rode the two bordermen, until day dawned, and yet they found no sign of the lost one.

"He has most likely made for the Black Hills. I've heard him tell how friendly him and the Ogallala Sioux were who live in that section," said Wild Bill.

"Then we will follow him there. If a hundred tribes, instead of one, were at his back, I'd have her from him and my knife in his heart! It maddens me to think she is in his power. If he wrongs her by an insulting word, much less a rude touch, I'll kill him by inches! Bill, let's bear for the Black Hills."

Wild Bill counseled going to the settlements first for help, and before the sun reached its meridian they were once more with the wagons.

"Have you given up the search for your sister?" asked Mrs. Cody, when she saw her son and his mate ride up.

"No, mother, nor will we until she is found. But we can strike no trail—the rain has washed it away. We know this, however, that Dave Tutt has friends among the fighting Sioux in the Black Hills, and he's most likely making for them. We must have more force than us two to go there with any chance to get her away—so our plan is to get you all in safety to the nearest post, then collect a party and start for the hills. Dead or alive we'll find her."

At sundown a settlement was reached and soon a volunteer company was organized for the expedition to rescue Lillie, who started next morning on their search.

Late on the afternoon of the same day on which Buffalo Bill left with his party, two smart-looking strangers, well mounted, but with no arms visible, arrived at the tavern where Mrs. Cody and daughter were staying. The presiding genius of the bar-room was Major Williams, the landlord—the presiding genius of the kitchen and boss of the whole house was Molly Williams, his young wife—that is, young compared with him, for she was only five-and-thirty, while he was eighty years old, if a day.

Most of the male population of the place found its way to the bar-room in the evening. To make themselves popular with these people, the strangers were liberal in treating, and it was not long before nearly all were more or less under the influence of the vile beverage vended at the bar. The strangers pretended to drink quite as freely as those whom they treated, but they poured out scarcely anything for themselves, and so diluted what they did take with water that they felt none of the effects which they were producing on others.

The old major hung out as long as he could, but at last sank down helpless in his chair behind the bar, and then the two strangers were alone. An eye was on them, however, for Mrs. Molly Williams, though perfectly willing to see the money come into the drawer, did not believe in its going out again, so when she saw her old husband sink down into helplessness, as she did through a crack, she went in to secure the money in the drawer, inform the strangers that it was bed-time, and drag her drunken old husband to his nest, when the tramp of horses' hoofs reached her ears.

"The boys are coming—we're all right now!" said the elder of the strangers, springing to his feet at this sound. "The plunder and the girls first, and a big blaze afterward!"

"Open the door, Hubert, and tell the boys that I, Alf Coye, am here!" cried the elder. "There's nothing to fear. Every man in the place is drunk or asleep. Surround the house—let no one leave or enter beside our own men, without my permission."

This order was given because, fully dressed and ready for departure, Mrs. Cody, her daughter Lottie, and Kittie Muldoon their servant, made their appearance in the back room.

"What does this mean?" asked the widow.

She addressed the question to Mrs. Williams, but was answered by Captain Alf Coye.

"It means, madam, that a part and parcel of the Southern

Confederacy has made a raid over the Kansas border, and as one Buffalo Bill is arrayed on the Union side, we shall deem it good policy to hold his mother and sister in our hands as hostages for his future good behavior. I am glad to see you are dressed, ready for traveling, for my men will only remain here long enough to collect what plunder they want and to make a bonfire of the rest. We will then head for Missouri, and you will accompany us."

"Hubert, find a good carriage or wagon to put these women in. I shall carry them over the border, and if Buffalo Bill comes after them I'll have a rope for his neck!" said the captain.

Buffalo Bill and his rescuers traced the kidnapper of Lillie to a stockade built by his friends. Frank Stark was a rival of Dave Tutt for the good graces of Lillie, and promised to aid her in escaping.

"Over the works, boys, and let your revolvers and knives tell the tale!" Buffalo Bill shouted, and sprang up the ladder. Amid the yells of the garrison some decisive work went on, by his followers.

"Mercy—we surrender!" shouted a huge villain already down with a bullet in his breast.

"Take the mercy your gang gave my father!" said Buffalo Bill, driving his knife into his skull.

Except a few wounded wretches on the earth not one of the Indians or robbers was left.

"Boys, it's a shame to butcher them that can't defend themselves," said Wild Bill.

"Excepting old Jake M'Kandlas, the rest may live for all me," cried Buffalo Bill. "As for him, he shall live until I can hang him over the grave of my murdered father, or roast him to ashes on the ground stained by his blood. But my sister—she is safe from here, but is Frank Stark to be trusted?"

"Yes, just as you could have trusted me, if I had got her off," said Dave Tutt, with a feeble voice; for, terribly hurt, he lay yet living among the wounded. "He is off for the Black Hills with her."

"That's a lie, for I saw him and her crossing the river by the light of the same flash which revealed you to us, and us to you, you mean sneak," cried Buffalo Bill. "If I wasn't sure you'd suffer more by being let alone, I'd cut your throat where your are, you infernal spy and deceiving cuss! Look out for him, men, and for old Jake M'Kandlas—I am going across the river to find Lillie."

"You need not cross the river to find her, for she is here," cried Frank Stark, coming toward them followed by the girl.

Lillie was soon in the arms of her brother, while Frank Stark was forgiven for the kindness shown his sister, who declared that he would thereafter fight under the stars and stripes.

A new-comer drove up after the above scene, whom Bill knew, and addressed thus: "You look as white as a ghost, man! What is the matter in Corrinne?"

"There's matter enough to drive us all mad. There's not a house left standing in town—all are in ashes. Worse yet, every man but myself, I think, is killed, with some of the women, too—and the youngest and fairest carried off. I crept away, ran miles on foot, then caught a loose horse, got on your trail, and am here."

"Who did this?" asked Bill.

"One Alf Coye, at the head of a hundred bush-whackers from Missouri."

"My mother and Lottie!" gasped Bill.

"I saw them in a wagon under guard as I crept away."

Said Buffalo Bill: "Now, men, we have work to do. Frank Stark, for the good heart you have shown, I am going to trust you as I'd trust no other man on such short acquaintance. I shall take all but five of my men and the best horses, and make after the party that have carried off my mother and sister, and we know not how many more. With those five and this man here, guard my sister Lillie and get her to St. Louis just as quickly as you can. I will meet you there if I live."

One brief embrace between brother and sister and our hero was off to rescue his mother and Lottie.

Lillie at once began to make preparations for her journey, while Stark went into the place where M'Kandlas and Dave Tutt were lying, and said: "I came in to see if you required any fixing up before we started."

"Started? What do you mean?" asked M Kandlas.

"That we start in a little while for the settlements. I am having mule-lifters fixed for you and Dave, and you'll swing when Buffalo Bill gets back from punishing Alf Coye."

"He'll never get back from that bit of business," said Dave Tutt. "Alf Coye is not the man to get away from, and Buffalo Bill will learn that if he crosses his path. Ah! your new sweetheart is in trouble, Mr. Frank Stark—and so are you! Here is Raven Feather—the Ogallala, and my friend."

Even as these last words passed the lips of Dave Tutt, caused as they were by a wild scream from Lillie, the opening in the brush house that served as a door was darkened by the presence of several Indians.

Frank Stark and Lillie were soon bound, and waiting upon the motion of the chief, who turned out to be Raven Feather who had his lodge in one of the fastnesses of the Black Hills, and thither the band, with the wounded and captives, marched.

For four days after having struck it, across the Missouri border, Buffalo Bill, with a force increased by volunteers to about fifty men, had followed the trail of Alf Coye, and he was again in Kansas, the route of pursued and pursuers tending toward the same section of the Hills to where Raven Feather was making his way. The one narrow passageway in and out of his chosen village could be defended by a few against the approach of thousands. For this reason had Raven Feather, the great war chief of the Ogallala Sioux, taken it for the home of his tribe. Their enemies would never risk their warriors in an attack on such a defensive spot as this.

One night, after sundown, Alf Coye rode into this valley at the head of his weary column. It was a long cavalcade, for beside his men, one hundred in number, he had nearly as many poor, unhappy women, mostly young and beautiful, including Mrs. Cody, Lottie and their servant, who had been dragged from desolate homes by the wretches whom he commanded. Raven Feather had given the friendly ruffians permission to come up into the village, and the night was passed in peace, until shouting and yelling announced the return of Raven Feather. He did not come alone. Clutched by the arm he led poor Lillie as if he feared that escaping from his grasp she might rush to destruction in the water of the river so near at hand. One wild, glad cry, and tearing herself from his grasp, she was in the arms of her mother and sister. Weeping and sobbing the four women clung together, while Raven Feather, who did not at first understand it, began to comprehend that he had brought a daughter to a mother and a sister to a sister in captivity,—that he had three of the nearest relatives of the dreaded Buffalo Bill in his power.

Arrangements were made to burn Frank Stark at the stake the following day.

When the sun sank behind the peaks of the mountains that same night, the hope of rescuing his mother and Lottie sank nearly in Buffalo Bill's breast. Little did he dream that Lillie was again in the hands of his enemies, much less than even then one twin was almost as near to him as the other. Though, by the exceeding freshness of the trail, he knew he was very close to the party of Alf Coye, for he saw that they must have gained the mountain range. There, with rocks, sheltering ravines, a thousand ramparts everywhere, the wretches could make easy defense. Only stratagem could dislodge them; only cunning could release their unhappy captives.

While he was musing, he heard the sound of a bugle, and recognized the well-known notes of the "Tattoo," or the turning-in call of the United States cavalry. And he knew to a mile almost in the gentle breeze of that evening how far away the bugler was who blew the notes that reached his ear; also, the precise direction. In this he rode swiftly for nearly half an hour, and came in sight of the encampment.

By a detour he passed the sentinels, and came close enough to recognize the Fifth cavalry, several officers in which he personally knew, especially Captain Brown. He at once made his presence known.

"Buffalo Bill, by the chances of war!" cried the captain. "I'm glad to see you."

"Not half so glad as I am to see you, cap, with all these boys about you, if so be you'll help me in a little matter of work that I've got close at hand."

"*Work*—what is it, Bill?"

"The whole story is too long to tell, cap, but the short of it is this. We are within two or three hours' ride of a hundred Missouri bush-whackers, who have got many helpless women prisoners, among them my own dear mother and one of my sisters. But if you'll help me, I know I can succeed. I have fifty as good men, regular rangers, as ever drew trigger—we can rid the earth of every rascal of the lot. Will you help me, sir?"

Orders were instantly sent out, and the next moment Wild Bill dashed into camp. "Bill, what have you seen?" asked Buffalo Bill.

"I've not seen your mother, nor Lottie," said Bill. "But they are in there, for Alf Coye has gone through the big canyon to the village. But I did see poor Lillie, riding behind old Raven Feather himself, and Jake M'Kandlas and Dave Tutt are in the party. So is poor Frank Stark, painted with black streaks, which means he is doomed to die at the stake."

Sim Geary, a scout with the cavalry, had been in Raven Feather's village twice, and so was capable of suggesting a plan of attack, one feature of which was to roll down rocks from the mountain into the village. Captain Brown was to make an open attack in front, keeping his men back far enough not to lose. A picked party of men was to get to the top of the hill overhanging the canyon before daylight, and not be seen when daylight came till it was time to roll rocks.

"While all this is goin' on, and it don't need any of us in front," said Sim, "we three old bordermen, with the party that Buffalo Bill bosses, will get behind 'em, come down on their rear after we've got their captives safe; and, if we don't finish 'em then, I'm willin' to eat dirt!"

When the sun next morning rose the preparations for torturing the chief victim, Frank Stark, were almost completed. In front of the lodge of Alf Coye a large post had been set, and near it dry fuel lay in a huge heap ready to ignite when all was arranged.

Jake M'Kandlas, Dave Tutt and all the warriors were present when Frank Stark was bound to the stake, when suddenly a piercing scream broke on every ear, and Lillie rushed through the yelling circle and with her own hands tore away the fagots from about the prisoner's form.

What Raven Feather or the rest would have done to her or those by her side for this interruption, may not be known, for suddenly, with no warning, a sound came rolling up the canyon which in a second changed everything. Not like the roll of pealing thunder, but sharp, quick and crashing, came the report of a cannon. It was the field-piece belonging to the cavalry train. For a few seconds every warrior was dumb. Alf Coye was first to break the spell of silence. And before he spoke the rattle of small arms and the yells of fighting men far down the gorge were heard.

"To the mouth of the canyon," he shouted. "Every man, red and white. There are regulars in that attack, or there wouldn't be cannon. If they get through the gorge we're whipped. Follow, men—follow!" And with his saber drawn he rushed to his horse picketed close by, mounted without waiting to saddle, and rode away. In less than a minute every white man and every warrior, except alone Dave Tutt and Jake M'Kandlas, was speeding off toward the sound of battle.

As if dropped from the sky, Buffalo Bill, his mate and Sim Geary, at the head of fifty riflemen, rushed into the lodge.

While Buffalo Bill was embracing his loved ones, Wild Bill cut the thongs which bound Frank Stark to the post of torture, and Sim Geary tied Jake M'Kandlas and Dave Tutt.

"We've no time to spend here!" cried Sim Geary. "There's a heap of warriors out there, beside Alf Coye's gang. Brown will have too much to do, if I don't close in on the enemy's rear. Not a rock will roll till we've opened fire. And we'll have time enough to attend to matters here when we've wiped them out that's in front."

"That is so—we must help our friends there. Mother, sisters, you are safe now. I will leave a half-dozen men, however. But I must go and help to exterminate the wretches. Boys, six of you release every prisoner here, and stay to keep the she-fiends of squaws quiet. The rest follow me!"

Buffalo Bill waited not to hear an objection, but, followed by his men, and Frank Stark also, who had armed himself from a lodge close at hand, bounded away toward the gorge.

Suddenly huge rocks came bounding down, noise louder than thunder, from the cliffs above. Down came ton after ton of rock, mangling men and horses in a dreadful mass. Nothing now reigned but confusion, despair—death. They threw down weapons which were of no avail, and rode over each other, trampled and even hewed each other down with their knives and hatchets in their mad endeavors to get out of the way of the terrible avalanche which rained down the mountain steeps.

"I surrender! In the name of mercy stop this butchery!" shouted Alf Coye to Buffalo Bill.

"Mercy is a name not fit for your lips, you woman-killing fiend!" shouted Bill.

"There is the mercy shown my gray-haired father in Kansas!" as he raised his rifle and sent a ball through the heart of the murderous man.

A dozen more shots and not one of Alf Coye's party was left in sight alive. Wild Bill slew Raven Feather with his knife.

When the battle was over the troops discovered the strategy of Raven Feather's squaw.

On a great rock, inaccessible except by a narrow path, but where one could ascend at a time, and this path overhung with a rock which her women stood ready to hurl down if the ascent was attempted, stood all the prisoners, also the Indian women of the village, the widow of Raven Feather, and the two wounded white renegades. The rock overhung the torrent of the river where it was roughest, and where no hope for life could exist if one were cast into its terrible foam. Foremost of all was this terrible tableau.

Holding poor Lillie, who was bound and helpless, as were all the captives, so before him that her form shielded his body, stood Dave Tutt, with a keen knife pointing to her heart, requiring but a motion to sink it there. And Jake M'Kandlas stood in the same position, holding Mrs. Cody as his shield and at his mercy. Lottie was in the hands of the Indian queen, and each of the other captives was in a similar position, at the mercy of the squaws who held them.

Dave Tutt was spokesman, and made the following terms of surrender and gave five minutes for their acceptance:

"Swear on your oath that you will allow every one on this rock, red and white, their free, unrestrained liberty to leave this plain, with provisions and stock to carry them away; that you will not harm them in anyway, or check their departure, nor follow them when they depart. On this condition, and this alone, we will surrender these captives unharmed into your hands. Speak quick, for if your answer is not yes, so help me high Heaven, I strike the first blow *here!*" And the broad blade of his knife quivered over the heart of Lillie.

"Yes,—in Heaven's name, *yes!*" cried Captain Brown.

"Let Buffalo Bill, Wild Bill, Frank Stark—let all say yes, and swear it!" cried Dave, his hand still upheld.

"Yes!" gasped all the men.

"*Swear* it, and we ask no more."

"We swear it!" came solemnly from every lip.

In an instant every prisoner stood free—their bonds were cut at a signal with the knives that threatened their existence. And those who would have slain them, even the widowed squaws, now helped them in the perilous descent to rejoin their friends.

The Cody women reached St. Louis in safety after their terrible experience in captivity.

CHAPTER XXI.

HOW "BUFFALO BILL" OBTAINED HIS SOBRIQUET—HIS DUEL WITH CHIEF YELLOW HAND.

Hon. William F. Cody, while passing through New York city for his ranch in the West, told a reporter of the *Mail and Express* how he came to be called "Buffalo Bill," about his duel with Yellow Hand, and other deadly combats with Indians:

"I earned the title of Buffalo Bill by killing buffaloes on the plains. The Kansas Pacific railroad was being built through the heart of the buffalo country in 1867. Some 1,500 hands were employed at that end of the route. The Indians were constantly on the war path, and fresh meat was difficult to obtain. Hunters were engaged to kill buffaloes for the firm who had the contract for boarding the employes of the road. I had some little reputation as a good shot, especially at live cattle, so I was engaged at a salary of **$500** per month to kill buffaloes. Twelve of these huge animals were required each day. Nothing but the hams and humps was eaten. I knew the work would be very dangerous, because the Indians were riding all over the country, indulging in their favorite sport of killing a white man when they caught one alone on the prairie. But I agreed to furnish the meat, Indians or no Indians.

"I knew I would often be five or ten miles from the road, and was liable to attack by the redskins. My success as a meat provider was so great that the road hands began to call me Buffalo Bill, and the name has remained with me. Many stirring adventures occurred to me during the seventeen months I hunted buffaloes for the Kansas Pacific road. I killed 4,280 buffaloes, beside some Indians. My favorite hunting horse was Brigham, who was trained to dash into a herd of wild buffaloes and chase them until I had slain almost as many as I desired for the day. In the spring of 1868 I was riding Brigham in a gallop trying to reach Smoky Hill river. I never shall forget that day. After twenty miles of fast riding I reached the top of a hill, and gazed down upon the smiling valley and the beautiful river in the distance. My attention was attracted toward some moving objects in the distance. They were half a mile distant, and as soon as they began to mount their horses I saw that they were Indians, and intended to capture me if possible.

"My horse was somewhat fatigued from the rapid pace I had been traveling and I doubted whether he would be able to keep ahead of the fresh horses of my pursuers. I resolved to run and fight. The horse seemed to know my life depended upon his speed. We sprung away at a brisk rate. The Indians followed. After crossing a ravine I halted a few seconds and sized up, as it were, the crowd after me. They were Indian braves well mounted and armed with rifles. If Brigham had been fresh I would have had no fears whatever about escaping, but how it would result after my long morning ride I had no idea. After five miles of fast riding, I discovered that nine or ten Indians were only two hundred yards behind, strung out for a distance of two miles. My horse made a spurt and for two or three miles did the finest running of that kind on record. The Indians had good horses, and one who rode a spotted horse gained on me far ahead of the rest. He had a rifle and sent several bullets around me that gave warning that my time had come to make a stand, or get shot in the back. I think Brigham knew the time had arrived to face about and fight. Suddenly I wheeled my horse and quickly raising my rifle to my shoulder, I sent a bullet into the head of the spotted animal. At the crack of my rifle, horse and Indian fell in a heap. I suppose they were some eighty yards distant. I did not wait, but dashed away with the speed of the wind. My short stop to shoot gave the other Indians time to gain on me, and soon they began popping away at me. I turned in my saddle and fired back occasionally and succeeded in breaking a horse's leg. This left only seven or eight Indians to continue the chase. Brigham got his second wind, and I rode rapidly ahead of them until I reached two companies of soldiers, three miles from the railroad track. They were stationed there to protect the workmen. They heard the firing, and came forward to give my pursuers a warm reception. The Indians had the tables turned and beat a hasty retreat. I jumped off my faithful horse and told the soldiers of his wonderful feat. We was quite a hero from that date. The cavalry gave chase to the Indians, and I soon **joined them** with a fresh horse. In a distance of five miles we overtook and killed eight of them. The rest escaped. When we **got** back to camp Brigham was quietly grazing, and looked **at me as** if to ask if we had made any happy dead Indians. **I think** really that horse **read** in my eyes the answer.

"During these same buffalo hunts, I got into a tighter place than being chased on a tired horse. The road had **been** pushed near the Saline river. I had **a man,** 'Scotty,' to go along in a light wagon to cut up the buffalo meat and haul it to camp. One day I had killed fifteen buffaloes, and we started for home with a wagon load of fine **meat.** We were eight miles from camp when we suddenly came upon a party of thirty Indians, who rode out of the head **of** a ravine. It happened this day that I was on an excellent horse that belonged to the railroad company, and could easily have **made** my escape. But I had no idea of deserting Scotty, who **was** driving a pair of mules to the wagon. Of course Scotty and I had often planned how we would defend ourselves if suddenly attacked by Indians. In a few minutes we unhitched **the** mules and tied them and my horse to the rear of the wagon. We then threw the large buffalo hams on the ground and built a breastwork around the wheels. We **had** an extra box of ammunition and four extra revolvers, **the** emergency battery we were forced always to carry along. Behind our hastily built breastwork we were prepared to give a warm reception. We didn't have long to wait. They rushed at us with all the noise and yelling enthusiasam of which the red man is capable. We opened such a lively fire that they stopped a direct attack and began to circle around us. Then of a sudden they made a concentrated attack. It was no more successful than the first, but they killed both of the mules and the horse. They charged back and forth several times, and Scotty and I killed three within a few yards of our breastworks. It was a scorching hot place for a time. The three braves dead and others wounded dispirited the Indians as to direct attacks, and they adopted other tactics.

"They got off at some distance, behind little knolls, and tried long range warfare. We were besieged, and our only chance for escape was a rescue from the railroad camp, where troops were stationed. We had been expecting, sooner or later, to be caught up by Indians in such a manner while buffalo hunting. I had an understanding with the officer who commanded the troops, that whenever their pickets saw a smoke in the direction of our hunting grounds, they were to know we were attacked by Indians. Scotty and I kept very close in our breastwork, subject to a raking fire from the little army around us. We held a council of war, and concluded we could not fight our way out, but must get relief. Scotty kept up a diversion by concentrating his fire in a certain locality. In a few minutes I struck a match, and quicker than I can tell you reached over and set the grass on fire to the leeward of our fort. The red warriors began a war dance at what they considered a piece of folly. None of them suspected that I had given a signal for aid. While the thick volumes of smoke rolled upward and the flames spread rapidly over the prairie, the Indians made another attack, but were repulsed. It began to look as if we were cut off, and would have to fight there for hours. Scotty was plucky, and we resolved to end our existence in making a gallant fight, rescue or no rescue. In an hour or so after the prairie was fired, I heard the neighing of steeds, and soon saw a company of soldiers riding rapidly toward us. The Indians saw them too, and began a hasty retreat down the canyons of the creek. We shouted to the advancing troops that we were alive, but our mules and horses were dead. Five dead Indians were discovered on the battlefield around our little breastwork. Scotty and I didn't do such bad work after all. How many were wounded and carried off we had no means of ascertaining."

The circumstances of his duel with Yellow Hand, Mr. Cody gave as follows:

The Sioux war broke out in 1873. Gen. Custer was slain on the 25th of June, when I was acting as scout for the Fifth Cavalry, under Gen Merritt. We were on our way to Fort Laramie when the news reached us that Custer and his gallant troops had been massacred on the Little Big Horn. We started back to join Gen. Crook in the Big Horn country, when we received word that 800 Cheyenne warriors had that day left the Red Cloud Agency to join Sitting Bull's forces. Gen. Merritt resolved to intercept the Cheyennes. He selected 500 men and horses, and pushed rapidly to War Bonnet Creek. On July 17th, 1876, I discovered the Cheyennes. They did not see our troops. Gen Merritt, several aids and I went ahead, and saw the Indians advancing directly toward us. Suddenly twenty or thirty of them dashed off in a western direction With our field glasses we discovered two mounted soldiers, perhaps bringing dispatches to us, riding rapidly forward on our trail. The Indians were endeavoring to intercept them. The general did not deem it wise to send soldiers to the aid of the couriers, because it would discover to the Indians that troops were in the vicinity waiting to attack them. I was commissioned to go back to the command, pick out fifteen scouts, and rescue the couriers. Just as the Indians began to charge the two soldiers I dashed with my scouts to intercept them. A sharp running fight took place, and we killed three of their number. The main body of Indians appeared in sight, and the skirmishers—the Indians we were chasing—took courage and charged us. A lively little fight occurred, and we checked their advance. We were perhaps half a mile from Gen. Merritt, who kept an eye on our movements. A big chief, gorgeously attired with top plumes and royal paraphernalia, rode out in front on a magnificent horse, and, in his own language, challenged me to mortal combat. He said:

"'I know you, Pa-he-haska; if you want to fight, come ahead and fight me.'

"I accepted and galloped forward to meet him. I advanced fifty yards and he about the same distance. We were at full speed when we came within thirty yards of each other. I raised my rifle and shot his horse dead in his tracks. At the same instant my horse stepped into a hole and fell. I was not injured by my horse's fall and sprang upon my feet The Indian arose as quickly as I did and faced me not twenty steps distant. We both raised our rifles and fired at the same time. He missed me and my bullet pierced his breast. In a second I was on him and drove my knife to the hilt in his heart. Then I pulled off his war bonnet and scalped him in the most approved Indian style. The Indians seeing their chief slain, charged upon me. Col. Mason, with Company K, came to my assistance and drove the enemy back. As the soldiers galloped up I held up the scalp and the war bonnet and shouted: 'The first scalp for Custer!' The chief killed was Yellow Hand, son of old Cut-nose. The latter offered me four mules to deliver up his son's scalp, war bonnet, and arms. I haven't complied with old Cut-nose's desire yet, and still keep the dead chieftain's war outfit."

CHAPTER XXII.

EXPLOITS OF OUTLAWS IN THE INDIAN TERRITORY—THE STARR AND WADE GANGS—BILL PIGEON.

A FEW reminiscences of the old time outlaws in the Indian Territory will be interesting to everybody. They were nearly all of mixed Indian and white blood, but so much more daring were their exploits, so much more desperate their character, that the exploits of the Cook gang appear as mere boys' play when compared to their deeds of outlawry. The most notorious of these old-time outlaws, says the St. Louis *Globe-Democrat*, was Henry Starr, long since dead. Much of the story of his life is shrouded in obscurity, but it is known positively that he alone killed over seventy men, fully a dozen of his victims having been felled with a single blow of his mighty fist. He was a Cherokee, with a tinge of Seminole blood, nearly seven feet tall, massively built, and with an arm and fist like a sledge-hammer. He terrorized the whole Cherokee Nation for years, and so great became his power that the Cherokee Council finally entered into a regular treaty of peace with him, granting him amnesty from all past deeds if he would cease his outlawry—the only instance on record of a nation entering into a treaty of peace with a single individual.

At one time $10,000 reward was offered for Starr's head and $5,000 for the head of one of his lieutenants. One day the lieutenant was killed by the accidental discharge of a gun at the outlaw camp, and Starr cut off his head, and putting it in a sack, went to Tahlequah, the Cherokee capital, and walking boldly into the office of the national treasurer, covered the officer with a revolver, took the gory head from the sack, and laying it on the table compelled the officer to pay over the $5,000 offered for the head, then walked out, mounted his horse and escaped.

After the treaty of peace the old man lived quietly for a number of years and died a natural death.

In later years one of the most cunning of outlaws was Bill Starr, a grandnephew of Henry, and father of the notorious Belle Starr. He did not turn outlaw until well along in years, but in a short time became the leader of one of the most adroit gangs of thieves that has ever infested the Indian country. He was not a common thief, and in one sense was not actively in the business, being rather a superintendent or general manager. His gang was large in numbers, and he had spies in every town, trading post and community in the territory and adjoining states. He did not make a practice of stealing for fun or excitement, but was in it for business, and would take only the best and when he was sure of a large return for the work, but once making up his mind to steal a thing, there was nothing at which he would hesitate. There was not much ready cash in the territory to steal in those days, and they confined their work mostly to stealing horses. A member of the gang in a neighborhood would take a fine horse, ride it a few miles and turn it over to a confederate, who would do the same, which procedure would be repeated in turn by a dozen different men, and as each one would be at home the next morning detection was almost impossible.

The gang had a cipher language whereby they could converse intelligently among themselves about their work, and an outsider listening would think them conversing about some ordinary topic. Occasionly, when there was some particularly valuable horse to be stolen, Starr himself would do the work. He was an expert blacksmith, would carry shoeing tools along with him, and after riding the horse a half day would take the shoes off and put them on backward. Thus those in pursuit were fooled, and it was a long time before they discovered his strategy. They would be on the trail all right following the horse's tracks, when suddenly the footprints would be reversed, indicating that the animal had been traveling in the very opposite direction. Had they followed the trail sufficiently long they would have come to a place where the tracks again changed, but they seldom went far enough, and gave up the chase in disgust.

Belle Starr was a fit successor to her father, and led a gang equally as daring. The narration of a single one of their exploits will serve to show the character of the work they did. While Major Neal was agent of the Sac and Fox Indians, Belle Starr and her brother Frank and Bill and John Wade drove up to the agency with a barrel of whisky, and in plain view of the agent's quarters and the officers of the Indian police, began selling the fiery liquid to the Indians, two of the gang keeping up a constant firing into the agency buildings with Winchesters. They sold as long as any of the Indians had money to buy, and then drove leisurely away. The Wades were captured soon after, and bought their freedom by turning traitor and delivering Frank Starr to the officers, who turned him over to the Texas authorities, where he was given a life sentence for murder.

The last of the old school of outlaws was Ned Christy and Bill Pigeon, both Cherokees. Christy led many a daring raid years ago, in a stone fort in the mountains of the Creek country, defying the deputies and repulsing attack after attack, only to at last fall a victim of treachery. He was shot down by a traitorous member of his gang, who agreed to deliver him to the officers for a monetary consideration.

In the mountain fastnesses forty miles northwest of Muldrow, in the Cherokee Nation, in 1894, lived Bill Pigeon, over 80 years of age, the only surviving member of the old-time outlaw bands. For nearly half a century a fugitive from justice, a man after whom the officers sought vigilantly for years and for whose arrest large rewards were offered—a man whose hands in the past were often steeped in crime—he then lived in quiet obscurity, asking to be let alone to die in peace.

It appears he did not at first become an outlaw from choice. For a long time he was engaged in bringing whisky into the territory in large quantities, and was very successful in eluding the officers. After a long chase the deputies cornered him once, and he was in such close quarters that he was compelled to kill a deputy to escape. A price was then put on his head, and from that day he plunged into the wildest of crime and became an outlaw whose acts terrorized the whole Southwest. Alone he committed many deeds at which the Cook or Dalton gangs would quail, and many a wild chase he led the deputy marshals and the Indian police over the territory. Finally, wearying of this carnival of crime, he retired to the mountains and settled down to live a quiet life with a wife whose influence and promise to marry him were undoubtedly the greatest motives leading him to give up his wild life.

Entrenched among the wild hills and passes, it is said that several marshals and detectives who had gone to his home in disguise never returned to tell the tale of their adventures, and other officers who scouted in the vicinity received such effective warnings that nothing could ever induce them to return. Deputy marshals and other officers gave him a wide berth, and to the outside world the name of Bill Pigeon, the Cherokee outlaw, is almost forgotten.

CHAPTER XXIII.

DUELS FOUGHT BY INDIANS—ONE WITH RIFLES AND ANOTHER WITH KNIVES.

An old scout recently furnished the *Cincinnati Enquirer* with an account of two Indian duels witnessed by him, which is here reproduced. The first one occurred at Standing Rock Agency, Dakota, in 1876, between Scout **Shave** Head and Chief Crooked Neck of the Hunkpapa Sioux. "It was a performance that would have called for applause from the most critical audience that ever witnessed a Spanish bull fight," says the writer. "Shave Head was one of the Indian police who was killed while attempting the arrest of Sitting Bull in the winter of 1890. In 1876, I was interpreter and chief of scouts at Fort Yates, near Standing Rock Agency, where I had thirty Sioux Indian scouts under my command, who were selected from the friendly bands and quartered at the military post with their families. The military authorities issued rations only to the scouts, while their families drew from the Indian agent. The beef was slaughtered on the east bank of the river, the Indians crossing in boats.

"I usually accompanied the scouts when they went for their beef. About 150 Texas steers were killed every two weeks. These were parcelled out to the several bands, beginning with the largest, who would receive twelve or fifteen head as their share, the next ten or twelve, and so on to the smaller bands, who would get two or three, according to their number. Lastly, single families, not members of bands, were given beef by themselves, one steer to four families, or a quarter to each. The scouts, half breeds and squaw-men, were among this number. The trouble which terminated in the duel between Shave Head and Crooked Neck began over the issue of beef.

"Shave Head, Crooked Neck, Charley Pappan, a half breed, and the Widow McCarty, a squaw who had been married to a white man, were given a quarter each in the last beef issued. Shave Head, Pappan, and the widow immediately began skinning the beef, when Crooked Neck approached the scout, and, placing his hand on his shoulder, pushed him violently aside, saying: 'You belong to the soldiers; you have no right here; go to the fort for your beef.'

"I stood not more than fifty feet away. Shave Head cast one look of defiance at his assailant and then came to me and said, pointing at Crooked Neck: 'That man has driven me away from my beef. If I was not under your command I would know what to do, but now I await your orders. If you leave me free to act he is not man enough to keep me away from my beef.'

"I answered that since the agent had given him a quarter of that beef it was, therefore, his, and he had a perfect right to take it.

"'Then,' said he, 'tell that man to keep away from me.' I answered that Crooked Neck did not belong to my company and I had no authority over him.

"'Very well,' said the scout. 'I shall take my beef,' and rejoining the others he again offered to assist in dressing the beef, only to be again thrust away by Crooked Neck. This time he gave utterance to that savage growl, which, once heard, can never be forgotten, and climbing out of the slaughter pen on the north side, and taking his rifle from his wife, he turned to the left, coming out on that side of the corral facing the river. Crooked Neck, seizing his rifle, went out of the corral on the south side, and, turning to the right, the two combatants met face to face on the west side of the corral. Between them was the agency wagon, which was backed up to the fence to receive the beef. The first shot was fired by Chief Crooked Neck over the rear end of the wagon. The driver, supposing that he was the object of attack, frantically whipped up his mules, leaving a clear field between the two enraged warriors, who were not more than ten yards apart. Talk about an Indian war dance! Here was executed a dance that surpassed anything of the kind I ever saw. Shave Head was the most agile of the two, jumping from side to side, rearing high in the air, and again bending low down to the ground, all the time keeping his eye fixed on his foe and his gun ready for use. The corral had been surrounded by not less than 1,000 Indians, men, women and children, but when the firing began they had surged to one side, leaving the space in the rear of each combatant clear.

"The second shot was again fired by Crooked Neck, but he again missed his mark, and during the instant required by him to throw another cartridge into place, Shave Head, who was still as a statue, took aim and fired. The ball struck Crooked Neck in the hip, which crippled him so that he had but one leg to dance on. As soon as Shave Head fired he resumed his dancing, keeping it up until his antagonist fired again, when he repeated his former tactics, pausing in his dance while he took aim and fired. This time he brought Crooked Neck down with a bullet through his breast. He fell forward on his face, his gun under him. His friends pressed forward, holding up their hands and calling upon the scout to desist—he had killed his man.

"But Shave Head was determined to make it a sure thing. First pointing his gun toward the crowd to warn them back, he advanced to the prostrate Indian and, holding the muzzle of his gun within two feet of his victim, fired three shots into his head. He then resumed his dancing, and facing the crowd he moved backward to the river, and leaping into a boat was rowed to the west side, where I found him later away out on the prairie performing the Indian rite for purification after shedding blood.

"The last duel of which I was a witness was fought with knives. It was in 1870. A party of tourists were visiting the agency at Standing Rock, Dak., and wishing to see an Indian camp by night they applied to me for an escort.

"I gave them three of my best scouts, and soon after dark they started for Wolf Mecklace's camp, four miles up the river. They had been gone about two hours when a warrior came down from the camp and reported that the tourists were giving the Indians whisky. I mounted a horse and rode swiftly to the camp. Tying my horse to a tree, stole softly among the tepees, in one of which I recognized the voice of one of my scouts sent as an escort for the tourists. Entering the tepee, I found the scout Good-Tone Metal, sitting with his back to the door, his face to the fire, which was burning in the middle of the tepee. There was but one other occupant, Kill The Bear, who sat directly opposite the scout, the fire between them. A quart bottle half filled with whisky stood on the ground near the fire at the scout's right hand. Turning to the right as I entered, I took a seat facing the fire midway between the two Indians. I had exacted a promise from all of my scouts not to drink whisky, so I said to Good-Toned Metal, 'Is this the way you keep your promise?'

"'The son of a great man in Washington,' he answered, 'gave me this whisky, and I felt bound to honor him by drinking it. It is good whisky. Take some yourself.'

"'No,' I replied, 'I will not drink from this bottle, nor will any one else;' and reaching over I took the bottle in my hand and tapped it sharply against a stone which lay near the fire, breaking the bottle and spilling the contents.

"Not a word was spoken for fully a minute, when Kill The Bear broke the silence by saying to Good-Toned Metal: 'I thought this white man was your friend.'

"'He is my friend,' responded the latter.

"'Your friend destroyed your whiskey.'

"'He has a right to do as he pleases with my whisky.'

"'Huh!' contemptuously. 'I thought you were a brave man.'

"Kill The Bear no doubt said this with the intention of turning the scout against me, but he made the greatest mistake of his life. Good-Toned Metal had imbibed just enough whisky to make him a dangerous man, and the sneering words of Kill The Bear aroused all the demoniacal savagery of his nature. His face expressing all the ferocity of a wild beast, his eyes flashing defiance upon Kill The Bear, he answered; 'I am brave! Are you?'

"'Yes,' came the reply.

"'Are you brave enough to die?'

"'Yes.'

"'Then draw your knife.'

"Two bright blades flashed in the firelight. Without rising to their feet they came together, fighting over the fire and scattering coals in every direction. Good-Toned Metal, with his knees in the fire, thrust his knife to the hilt into Kill The Bear's neck, severing the great artery at the first blow. At every beat of the heart great streams of blood, spurted out, covering everything in the tepee, myself included. Kill The Bear sank back dead. But the scout was not done.

"His savage instinct was aroused, and he continued to

bury the knife in the flesh of his victim, at each thrust uttering that blood-curdling growl. Indians upon the outside, hearing the disturbance, seized the tepee, and, turning it over, liberated me and exposed the horrifying scene to hundreds who hastily gathered about the place. Yet unmindful of the multitude, and heedless of the fact that his feet were in the fire, the scout continued to wreak his vengeance on the body of the man who had dared to question his bravery. Tiring at last, he rose to his feet, glared wildly about, and seeing a horse near by, he mounted it and rode madly into the hills, where he remained ten days, observing the Indian rites for purification."

SITTING BULL.

CHAPTER XXIV.

SITTING BULL'S LAST FIGHT—THE MYSTERIOUS GHOST DANCE—PRELIMINARIES OF THE LAST ENCOUNTER BETWEEN INDIANS AND GOVERNMENT TROOPS.

The death of Sitting Bull, the famous Sioux chief, was precipitated by a new craze among several tribes of Indians, which it is necessary to briefly describe here, and which led up to Sitting Bull's capture and death. Ten or twelve years ago an Indian by the name of Smohalla advanced the doctrine of the expected advent of a red Savior or Messiah, and the new belief spread rapidly through all the Western tribes, and Red Cloud prophesied that it would spread over all the earth. Smohalla theorized that there would be an upheaval of nature which would destroy the eighty millions of whites in the United States and that the dust of countless dead Indians would spring to life to occupy their former possessions.

The apostles of this new creed instituted a sacred or ghost dance in honor of the dead braves who were to be resurrected, possibly at a moment's notice. The performance of this religious ceremony was similar to the old May-pole dance of our ancestors. Arranged in a circle, about 300 of them, alternately a man and a woman, they went round and round in the same direction, uttering a dirge or ghostly chant. Frequently a dancer would fall exhausted, when he would be carried away. It was claimed that in this swoon the Indian communed with his Messiah. Sitting Bull, the deadly foe of white men, took advantage of this craze to inflame the Indians and prepare for war. He had about three thousand warriors under him at the time the Interior Department transferred the control of the Indians of North Dakota to the War Department, by order of the President. They had possession of all the rifles captured at the Custer massacre and an immense stock of ammunition procured from tradesmen. About three thousand regulars were massed at the Pine Ridge Agency to combat any violence on the part of Sitting Bull's followers, and an order was given to the Indian police to arrest the dangerous old chief. The circumstances attending the carrying out of this order are told by a correspondent of the *Ladies' Home Companion* of Springfield, Ohio, fully and graphically, as follows:

The order directed that the Indian police make the arrest, and that the troops should be near enough to aid in case of a resistance, which was not contemplated by the authorities.

There had been rumors flying around the post and agency for days, that the authorities were going to cut short the so-called "Messiah's coming," if stopping the "ghost dance" would do it, and everyone had been on the *qui vive* as to how it would be effected. Now it was settled. The old medicine-man had been making things lively for some time, down on Grand river, forty miles away, and had been ordered by the agent to cease his dancing, and come into the post and have a talk. But he would have none of the agent's talk or talk from any one else, and danced longer and sang louder than ever before. He claimed that he and the coming Messiah would fix things, and when the latter would come the white man would have to stand from under; so he not only absolutely refused to go to the authorities to talk matters over, but coolly proposed to them that as they were so much interested in his "prayer-meeting," they would better come to his place with lots to eat, and there have a council. Perhaps he might intercede for them with the Great Spirit, and make things more pleasant for them than it would be if he did not interfere to save them from the wrath to come.

So it had gone, nothing definite being settled one way or the other, the disaffected and the curious flocking to Sitting Bull's camp all the time. As they all went with ponies, guns and ammunition, it did look promising for an interesting time ahead for somebody. Now the climax had arrived, and the long interim between the time of the dancing and the various little messages, pacific and otherwise, that had gone between the agent and the rebellious Indians, was to be brought to a sudden close. The powers that be had at last recognized the fact that this so-called "ghost dance," with its attendant evils of discontent and disobedience to all recognized authority, could not go on indefinitely; and so it came that the messenger bearing the momentous telegram from headquarters to the commanding officer went with quicker steps and sober men to that officer's quarters, and delivered the message. How these things get abroad no one knows; but it was a fact that before the official notice of the receipt of the telegram was promulgated, nearly every man, woman and child in the post knew that some movement of importance was going on, and the shrewd guessers were not long in doubt as to the nature and place of the move.

The commanding officer, sitting in his warm and comfortable quarters, was looking over his evening's mail, and blessing the fates that kept him indoors on such a night as this; but thirty years' service prepares a man for anything, and simply telling the messenger, "Very well, I will be at the office immediately," he stopped to don his cape, and in a moment the gray-haired chief was at headquarters. Calling his orderly, he said:

"Give my compliments to the post adjutant, and tell him I want to see him immediately."

On the arrival of the adjutant the colonel said:

"Mr. B, I have received orders to arrest Sitting Bull. Have the officers assemble here at once to receive their instructions."

With a "Certainly, colonel," the soldierly form disappeared, to be followed almost instantly by the clear, martial strains of the bugle, ringing out across the parade-ground, and "officers' call" echoed and re-echoed throughout the garrison, causing sudden silence in the quarters, and making painfully distinct to straining senses, on the alert for the least sign or sound, the shutting of the doors at the officers' quarters, as these gentlemen issued hastily forth, throwing on capes and overcoats and buckling on sword belts.

By this time the officers were all at the colonel's office, prepared for anything that might come. A keen glance at the interested faces around him, and the colonel said:

"Gentlemen, orders from headquarters direct me to secure the person of Sitting Bull. It is thought best to have the Indian police make the arrest. They are in the vicinity of Bull's camp now, and only await orders to bring the chief here. The troops are to co-operate with the police, so if there should be any fighting, you will go to their help, and bring in the body of Bull, dead or alive. The two troops of cavalry will be in readiness to start at midnight to-night.

They will go in light marching order, with two days' cooked rations, and forty rounds of ammunition per man."

Short and to the point were the orders, and the officers dispersed at once to see that their men were ready. Captain Forbes started at once for the barracks of his troop, and entering the orderly-room, said:

"Sergeant, get the men ready for field service; we pull out at midnight to get old Sitting Bull."

The movement was to be conducted as secretly as possible, for if the disaffected Indians at and around the agency got an inkling of what was going on, they would get a courier off at once to Bull, before the police or troops could interfere. And once warned, the wily chief would in a very few hours be safe from all pursuit, and join the hostiles at Pine Ridge. So the column was to pull out at dead of night as quietly as could be. At the stables the troop horses were being carefully looked after. The stable sergeant of Troop N was busy looking up saddle-gear, carbine-slings, girths, and all that goes to make up the complement of the McClennan saddle in the campaign. As the old sergeant walked down between the long line of horses, he stopped at the side of one bearing the euphonious name of "Gorilla." Tradition had it that he had eaten two stalwart troopers once on a time. At least they had been seen in the stable one evening, near "Gorilla's" stall, an 1 as they were never seen by man after that, and as "Gorilla" was known to have maneating tendencies, it was clear enough to N troops at least that they had furnished an equine lunch. The sergeant meditatively regarded the horse for a moment, and then delivered himself thus:

"Ah, ye ould divil, may Sittin' Bull git ye this time, though small thanks would you be gittin' from him, if ye started in to ate the tribe."

And having vented his spleen, the sergeant turned away, and went to look after the harness and gear of the Hotchkiss gun and three-inch rifle, which were to go with the troop.

At the commanding officer's office, men are coming and going in hot haste. Now one of the Indian police has dashed up with a note from the agent, with the latest advices from Sitting Bull's camp. Bull is rampant, but retribution is gathering her forces, and in a few short hours the so-called hero of the Sioux-tribe, their big medicine-man, will be lying stark and stiff, and Custer will be avenged. It is nearing the hour of eleven, the first bustle and confusion of preparing to move out are over, everything is settled, and all are awaiting the hour to start. In the barracks, the men have thrown themselves on their bunks for a few moments' rest, or others are giving the final touches to carbines and revolvers. Along officers' row the lights are twinkling here and there, and the last moments of the ones to go are being given to wife and home. The spirit of peace seems to have folded its wings and taken the old post in its keeping. And some forty miles away, the red demons, all unconscious of their danger, are exulting in their fancied security.

Suddenly there is a commotion at the guard-house, a sound of scuffling, and the door is thrown wide open, permitting a broad, wide glare of light to stream out across the parade. A figure is seen for a second, as it leaps from the door, and vanishes in the darkness. At the same time the hoarse call of the sentry on No. 1 shouts, "Halt!" accompanied almost instantaneously by the loud report of his rifle, which rings out on the wintry air with an electrical effect, bringing everyone up standing. In a moment all is confusion. A crowd is hurrying in the direction of the guard-house, where the guards are quickly falling in. Now the officer of the day comes running up, calling out:

"What is the trouble, sergeant?"

"That man who was confined for selling whisky to the Indians has escaped, sir. He has been nearly wild ever since he heard the news about Sitting Bull, and he wanted to see the commanding officer to get permission to go out to-night as a guide. He says he knows that country well. I told him he could not see the colonel, and he took on bad. Just now he came to the door of his cell, saying he wanted to see the officer of the day, and I opened the door for him, when he threw himself against me, knocking me down, and then got out the door. No. 1 missed him when he fired."

The officer of the day turned quickly to the sentry, saying:

"Which way did he go, Burke?"

"Right down toward the stables, lootenant."

"Take some of the men at once, sergeant, and we will go to the stables to see that he takes no horses. Hurry up there."

The squad double-timed toward the stables, being halted on the way by sentry No. 2, who, on being asked if he had seen any one, replied that just after the shot was fired, he thought he had seen some one running past troop O's quarters, but it was so dark he could not be sure.

Telling No. 2 to keep a sharp lookout, the party kept on to the stables, where No. 3 was stationed, to see and hear from him if anything was wrong on his post. At the stables the sergeant met them with his lanterns, having just come from his quarters, about thirty yards from the corrals, and had seen or heard nothing. They all went over to the entrance of N troop stable, where, after a short inspection, everything was found secure, and the doors locked.

"Where is No. 3," asked the lieutenant, "why don't he challenge?"

Just then an exclamation from the sergeant brought his officer quickly around to one side of the stable, where he was examining something on the ground.

"There is something wrong here, sir. I think it's No. 3. The lantern went out just as I turned the corner."

Striking a match, the lantern was relighted, and as the rays flashed over the little group, a cry of horror went up. The sentry was lying, face downward, on the ground, his rifle beneath him, just as he had fallen, stabbed through the heart. No. 3 would challenge no more.

"Quick, **sergeant,** look carefully through the stables; we may get the murderer before he can escape."

A search soon revealed the fact that the big doors at the south end of troop O's stable were swinging wide, the chains down, and "Pharaoh," the fastest horse in all the eleventh cavalry, the hero of many a race, the joy and pride of O troop, was gone.

There were ominous faces, and many hearts were filled with foreboding in the little command that defiled out of the post at midnight. As the column wound out by the last of the buildings and debouched on the plain, a sigh of relief seemed to go through all those forms enveloped in overcoats and furs—it was the last shaking off of the evil spirits produced by the tragedy of the night. There was no doubt that the assassin was a traitor, as well as a murderer, since the tracks made by the stolen horse led directly from the stable out onto the flat, and thence straight across the country for the Grand river, to tell the Indians the troops were coming.

The stalwart form of the cavalry leader straightened up even more, as glancing ahead into the obscurity, he gave the orders, "By fours, gallop, march," and on went the gallant troopers, straight into—they knew not what, only that there was more than likely to be sharp work cut out for them, and many thoughts were turned back to that fatal day in June, 76, when Custer and his brave and noble band went down before the hordes of the very old chief they were seeking now.

"Lieutenant B," called the major, "take ten men and throw out an advance guard and flankers. Instruct them to give the alarm at once, in case anything suspicious is seen or heard."

And then under his breath he said.

"If the police don't stop that infernal spy, all our work will be in vain, and Bull will get clean away, unpunished."

* * * * * * * *

In front of Sitting Bull's house, in a little valley inclosed by the high bluffs overlooking the Grand river, stood the pole that marked the centre of the circle made by the ghost dance. Around this pole, which was gaily decorated with many colored streamers and ribbons, the old guard of the non-progressive Sioux nation danced and howled to the monotonous tum, tum of the wooden, hide-covered drum, which one of the elect was beating with might and main. As the beating of the drum grew louder and faster, the frenzy of the dance increased, until the jumping, revolving figures more nearly resembled some of the scenes in Dante's purgatory, as they flew with frantic jestures around the ring, than they did Indians holding a dance. The half-naked bodies were streaming with moisture, although the afternoon was waxing colder, as the sun disappeared in the west. So violent was the exercise that the paint, which had originally been laid on the body in stripes and rings of different colors, had run together, producing an effect that was bizarre in the extreme.

Ha! The one in green, with the red stripes down his chest, has succumbed to the vigor of the dance and has fallen senseless in the circle. At this the dance ceased, as if by magic, and a loud chorus of howls announced a critical point in the proceeding. At this juncture the door of Sitting Bull's house opened, and out came the renowned medicine-man of the Sioux. The heavy, thick-set body of the old warrior was clad in the full regalia of the high priest of the "prayer-meeting." He wore a head-dress of buffalo horns, bristling with eagle feathers, and falling over his shoulders and down his back was a long string of hawk and eagle pinions. His 'ghost shirt' covered his brawny chest, and was gaily decorated with scenes from his past life worked in beads and painted on the buck-skin front of the shirt. The bullets of the white man would drop harmless to the ground on hitting this magic shirt, and no harm could come to the wearer.

The "prayer-meeting," for so Sitting Bull insisted on calling the ceremony that less enthusiastic Indians and whites profanely christened "ghost dance," had stopped suddenly, and as Sitting Bull advanced to the circle, the dancers on either side fell back before him, forming a lane down which he went toward the figure of the prostrate dancer. His eyes gleamed red as he glanced sharply at the tense features and rigid form; then straightening up his body to his full height, and raising his hands toward the sky said·

"Our brother is now with the Messiah. He has gone on his long journey. When he returns we will know what the Great Spirit has told him. I have told you we will see our buffalo once more covering the hills and the valleys, where now stand the houses and villages of the whites. These will all disappear, as the mist before the sun, and the red man will rule this land, as did our fathers before us. The Great Spirit holds us in his hand. We are his people. He has promised me that he will destroy all others. Why, then, do ye stand here idle? Your brothers in the South are shedding their blood. Already have they commenced their war of extermination against the whites. Even now I can see the ruddy glow of their fires against the sky. Ye are men. Listen, then, to my words. Our own people have turned against us. Have they not been armed by the Great Father in Washington to fight and kill their own brothers? Even now, as I talk, the police are coming down upon us. Have they not been here and told us to stop our meeting, like the dogs that they are, and made our hearts bad with their talk? Why should we cease our religious dance? This is our religion.

We do not interfere in their meetings. They have oppressed and trod upon us long. Will ye stand it? I have told you this many times. I will now tell you no more. Those of you who are men get your horses and guns, and in the gray of the morning we will start to the aid of our brave brothers in the South, who have begun the fight for you. Kill all the whites. This is our country."

And drawing his blanket around his shoulders, the old chief started to leave the circle, amidst the wild applause of all his followers.

"To the horses! To the horses!" was the cry; but the chief with a gesture restrained them.

"It is now too late in the afternoon to start. See, it is growing dusk, and you are tired with the dance. Wait until morning, and we will then take our wives and children and begin our southward march. Then, too, we have time enough. Our friend, who is trusted by the whites, is even now in their very fort itself, and will let us know when danger threatens. He has helped us many times, and will not desert us now. But see, my brothers, our brother who has died and gone to meet the Great Spirit is with us once more. Hearken to his words."

A second later and all were gathered around the form of the dancer who had fainted, and who, having come to, was sitting upright and glaring wildly around him. Gradually his eyes lost their wild stare, his limbs became less strained, his whole form relaxed, and he seemed himself once more. His voice at first was like the sighing of the zephyr in the tree-top, but became stronger as he continued:

"My brothers, I have seen the Great Spirit. He called me his son, and his heart was glad toward me. He has put into my mouth the words I now speak to you. He says, 'Kill the white man; kill his wife and his children; kill all whose skin is not red, and who speak with a forked tongue, and the heart of the Great Spirit will be glad toward his people. He will then come to rule us, and we will come into our own again.' I have done."

The head of the speaker dropped forward on his breast, and Sitting Bull proceeded to speak:

"You have heard our brother. He has spoken with the tongue of the Great Spirit, and it is good. What do my brothers, Little Assinaboine and Spotted Horn Bull say?"

The two warriors thus addressed advanced to the outskirts of the crowd, then turned, and facing to the setting sun, Spotted Horn Bull, one of the bravest and smartest of all the sub chiefs, said:

"Our big medicine-man, Sitting Bull, has spoken. He said well. Our brother who died went to the Great Spirit and returned to us again, has told us what our medicine-man said. Those of you here who are men will do as he says. Those women amongst you who are wearing men's clothes, and who look like men, will stay behind to cut wood and bring water for the white man." With this sarcastic speech he closed.

Little Assinaboine suddenly, and with a terrific yell, then sprang on a wagon that stood just without the boundary of the yard marked by the houses and corral of Sitting Bull, and brandished his gun in the air. It needed no words to tell that he was for war. Then came a yell, as if a thousand demons had escaped from hell, and let off the pent-up energy of years in one grand effort. Sitting Bull's warriors, evidently, had by unanimous voice declared a war of extermination.

All this time everyone was so intent on watching, and taking part in these immediate events, that no one thought of being interested in anything of minor importance until after the edict had gone forth, and Sitting Bull was giving a few final directions to a little group around him. Crowfoot, Sitting Bull's son, a lusty, vigorous fellow of sixteen, who had been apparently looking for some one among the crowd, ran up to Catch the Bear and asked him what had become of the man who was standing at his side a moment before.

"Why, I don't know," was the response, "why do you ask?"

"I believe it was a spy," said Crowfoot. "He was here all the time, but when I spoke, he paid no attention to me, and kept his blanket so close around him I couldn't see his face. I am sure he was a spy, and I can't find any one else who knew him, but several others noticed him. You don't suppose any of those cursed police would come down here, do you, alone like that?"

A laugh was the response, as though the idea was too absurd to even think of. The police knew perfectly well that all of Bull's people had sworn to kill any policeman on sight that they caught alone, and so the idea of any one policeman venturing into that hornet's nest seemed absurd in the extreme. Nevertheless Sitting Bull looked troubled, and said:

"Crowfoot, my son, mount your horse, and scout through that brush, and look well over toward the hills, for my heart is troubled. I would know who it is that has heard all the secrets of our council."

Crowfoot leaped lightly on his horse, but turned to his father, saying:

"My father, I will find this spy, tie him to my horse's tail, and drag him into your house."

So saying, he spurred up his horse, and dashing into the brush, was quickly out of sight of the others, several of whom had gone down the river on foot, looking for the unknown, while Crowfoot had gone up. The young boaster rode rapidly along the bank of the stream, looking for tracks in the snow. Ah, here it is! A moment and Crowfoot is following the plainly-marked track of a moccasin, through the snow, directly away from the river toward a clump of trees that stood by themselves. He dashed up to this timber, only to be confronted by Bullhead, the captain of the police, who ordered him to give up his gun, revolver and horse. He delivered up his arms to Bullhead, and stood there like the great awkward boy that he was, trembling with shame and fear. Bullhead, coolly buckling Crowfoot's belt of cartridges around his waist over his own, and putting the boy's revolver in his holster, sprang on the horse. Leaning over, he said:

"Boy, go home to your mother. Next time we meet you will not get off so easily."

And off he went at a hard gallop toward the hills.

Filled with humiliation, Crowfoot watched the retreating figure out of sight, and slowly turning away, slunk back down to the river, where he waited until dark, and got back to camp unnoticed. All the others were too busily engaged in their final preparations to steal away in the morning to pay any attention to a boy; so none knew of his adventure with Bullhead.

Bullhead rode rapidly back some miles to where his police were encamped. They had temporary quarters in a log house and were keeping a watchful eye on the hostiles. As Bullhead dismounted, he said:

"My brothers, if you will listen you will hear the war-drum and the shout of death, and the crack of the rifle that betokens for many of us certain death. The Great Spirit has foretold my death; but it will be with a glad heart that I die at the head of these men I see around me now. But enough; we must to work. Shave Head, you and Red Tomahawk will stay with me at present. Red Bear and One Feather, get your horses and ride out to guard the path to the south. Keep your eyes open, while Eagleman and Wakute Mani watch the road from the north, and tell the courier, when he comes from the big chief at the post, that I am here. Let the others rest."

Drawing his lieutenants apart, Bullhead made his dispositions for the night.

The night came on dark and drizzly, and to the single horseman from the post who was urging his steed along the road from the north, all was one impenetrable veil of darkness. He laughed to himself as he thought of his escape, and said aloud:

"They didn't keep me long this time. What a lucky thing it was having that stupid sergeant on guard. Thanks to the darkness, the sentry missed me. I am a little sorry for that poor wretch at the stable, though. What a fool he was to try to stop me. Hey, old horse!" And he slapped the neck of his horse as he spoke; but "Pharaoh," with instinctive aversion, tossed his head and unwillingly proceeded with the murderer and renegade on his back.

The man resumed his musing:

"Those fool officers at the post, how they were taken in! Didn't know I was Sitting Bull's right-hand man all the time, and that I have kept the chief informed of all that was going on," he chuckled to himself. "I would have been there by this time, and Bull would be pulling out now, I reckon, if it hadn't been for the scrape I got into with that dirty corporal, and got caught. That nearly settled the whole business. But I am still in plenty of time, and with the warriors Bull has, together with those of Big Foot and Two Strikes, I can pay off some old scores. But this road don't seem natural. Whoa!"

And pulling up short, he looked around him, but could see nothing that could give him a clue. The fact dawned upon him that he was hopelessly lost.

Taking a sudden resolution, he rode quickly over the prairie, he knew not where. His horse suddenly stopped, nearly unseating the rider. Recovering quickly, he leaned over the saddle to see what had frightened the horse, when he was greeted with a shout to dismount. Instantly the fact was apparent that he had run directly into the arms of the police; and just then one dark form stepped out of the gloom, and grasping the bridle, again ordered the man to dismount. There was only one chance for him, and he knew it, and cursing himself for running into such a trap, he suddenly raised his arm and brought his revolver down with all force, full at the upturned face in front of him. But the motion had been seen, and quick as it was, the other was quicker still, and evading the blow, sprang full on the rider, who had lost his balance from the force of the blow and was completely unseated, and fell heavily to the ground, with the policeman on top. The struggle was brief. The renegade endeavored to possess himself of Wakute Mani's knife, which he wore in his belt; but the policeman had his knees on the other's arms, and he could do nothing save articulate hoarse cries of rage. Wakute Mani drew the knife, and with terrific force brought it down on the unprotected chest of his adversary. One convulsive shudder and all was over. The spy was dead. Sitting Bull would await his coming in vain.

Shortly after, the courier dashed past from the post, and being joined by Wakute Mani and Eagle Man, rode on down into camp, where Bullhead was shortly giving his orders, and not long after the brave band of police had swung into line, and following their leader, were dashing in the direction of Sitting Bull's camp.

* * * * * * * *

On Grand river, the morning of December 15th, 1890, dawned rainy and cheerless. No sign of life was visible at the Indian Camp. The flag-pole standing in the circle made by the ghost dance looked very forlorn in its loneliness. Its gay streamers hung limp and bedraggled to the staff, and the sound of the drum and the dancing figures had disappeared from the scene.

Looking down the valley from the old chief's house, the houses scattered here and there, some clustered close together and others standing alone, keeping company with the lifeless-looking timber and brush, it formed a very striking contrast to the scene in Sitting Bull's camp that bright June morning in 1876, when his tepees covered the hills far and near, and when the hornets swarmed out on Custer and his brave little band, and left not one alive to tell the tale.

But look! What means those creeping figures that, keeping in the shelter of the brush and lurking down through the ravines, looking dim and ghostly in the uncertain light? They are drawing stealthily nearer and nearer to Sitting Bull's house. Not a sound breaks the stillness, and suddenly, as if by magic, a dozen dusky forms spring out of the ground in front of the single door to Bull's long, low house, and a moment later, all unchallenged and unnoticed, it and its sleeping occupants are in the hands of Captain Bullhead and his men. A smile of satisfaction crossed Bullhead's face, and he said as he glanced at the sleeping forms around him: "We have done well."

Posting some of his men near the corral and others at the door to guard against surprise, he advanced to the side of Sitting Bull's bed and looked down at the sleeping form of the old man. He laid his hand heavily on the shoulders of the prostrate form, which rose like a flash at his touch, and seeing Bullhead with his police around him, said:

"Why are you here, Bullhead? And all these men, what do they want?"

"Sitting Bull," said the policeman, "I am come to arrest you, by order of the big chief. Lose no time, but come quickly with me."

For once the old chief was caught napping. If he could only temporize until his followers could come up! He knew the force of the police and that they were far outnumbered by his own warriors, all armed and ready for a fight. Why could he not gain a little time?

At this point, One Feather, who was posted nearer the main village, called out that the men were rousing and the alarm would soon be general. At this, Red Tomahawk and Shavehead advanced to Bull, who was sitting on his bed slowly getting into his clothes.

"Come at once," they said, and half carried him to the door.

"Don't go, my father," suddenly called out Crowfoot, who had slipped unseen around the house, and with rifle and revolver menaced the police. "Your men will soon be here, and we will kill these police dogs!"

"My son, I will go quietly. Cause no disturbance."

At this the police, who had gathered around, turned away, and all started for a wagon which had pulled up a little distance away, and in which the old medicine-man was to be taken to the agency. A chorus of wild yells suddenly broke in on the quiet, and a moment later, a horde of howling, painted Indians was pouring down on the police force from all sides. Little Assinaboine was leading on his men, and crying death to the police. The main body of the police scattered at once to the shelter of the buildings and corrals, where their guns could command the situation, leaving Sitting Bull standing between Shave Head and Bullhead, Red Tomahawk directly in the rear of them, and One Feather immediately in front, distant about twenty yards. This little group stood calm and unmoved, and a moment later Bullhead saw that his position was a good one for a time, as his men were around him, and the way to the wagon was clear. Catch the Bear called out:

"Where are you going with our chief?"

"To the agency," Bullhead answered.

At this Bull Ghost called out:

"Let us kill the police! We are more than they. We will take their own guns and shoot them!"

"My brothers, hold!" cried out Bullhead. "We are not here to kill any one, or be killed, either, but to take our old friend into the post to the big chief, and there he will hold a council, and we will then learn what is right and just."

As he spoke, he drew himself up and looked with a bright, keen glance around him, and motioning quickly to Red Tomahawk, started on with the prisoner.

"What has come over our old war chief?" called out Spotted Horn Bull. "The great chief of the Sioux nation is led away like an old woman, a willing captive."

"Not so!" called out Crowfoot. "My father, give the word."

As though by a preconceived plan, Sitting Bull gave his war-whoop and threw himself violently backward, out of his captors' hands.

Catch the Bear raised and fired his rifle, and the fatal shot rang out clear and loud. The gallant captain of police staggered and fell. Struggling to a sitting posture he said, "You will go, too, Sitting Bull!" and put a bullet through the chief's body. As the latter fell, Red Tomahawk put a bullet through his brain, quelling that restless spirit forever. At the same moment, Shave Head was shot through the heart, and died instantly.

"Come on, my braves!" shouted Catch the Bear. "Kill them all!"

But as he spoke, a sheet of flame rushed out from behind the corral, the houses and other points of vantage, and Catch the Bear and half a dozen of his men fell dead or mortally wounded. The police had awakened at last. It was to be a fight of extermination. No quarter was asked or shown by either side.

Red Bear through it all had never lost sight of Crowfoot, who, keeping well out of harm's way, was pouring shot after shot in the direction of the police. He suddenly darted out and sprang full on the boy, who gave a cry of terror, and dropping his gun, started to run. It was his last effort in life, for a shot from Red Bear's revolver brought him screaming to the ground, and a second shot stretched him lifeless at the threshold of the door, both bullets going through Crowfoot and thence into and through the floor of his father's house.

The hostiles, as Catch the Bear fell, ran quickly to the cover of the brush, trees and anything that would afford shelter. Out of all the men in sight a moment before, not one was to be seen, save the little group of dead and dying that lay where they had fallen, in front of Sitting Bull's house.

The old "medicine-man" lay with his face upturned to the sky, his arms outstretched and with a look of hatred, as he had last glared at Bullhead as he fell. No more would his voice incite the warriors to battle and blood. No more would his voice be heard in the councils of the Sioux. The restless life was gone out, and Custer was avenged.

And now from all points a deadly fire was being poured in

on the devoted band of police. From the brush, from the ravines, from the hills even, came the spiteful crack of the rifle, followed by the spat of the ball as it struck a house or found a lodging in the body of one of the police. The brave little band is being thinned out rapidly.

A courier had been sent back along the road to tell the troops to come on, as Bullhead had ridden down into the valley with his men. Since then nothing had been seen of the courier or his troops. Red Tomahawk, who had succeeded to the command of the police, was fighting away and wondering why the troops did not come in response to the courier's request. What Red Tomahawk did not know was, that about midway between the fight and the troops a riderless horse was standing beside the road, and near him lay his rider, the messenger dispatched for help. A bullet-hole through his head had stopped brave Hawk Man's career forever.

Back on the road the troops impatiently awaited the coming of Hawk Man. Still the minutes dragged slowly by, until the major who had been scanning the country ahead with his glass, said:

"Mr. P, we will wait no longer. Our orders were to wait here for the courier, but we will push on, anyway." And swinging himself to the saddle, he gave the command, "Prepare to mount — mount!" and a moment later the battalion was on a gallop down the road.

As the body of Hawk Man was discovered, a yell of execration went up from the troopers, which was quickly checked by a word from the officers. On went the column at increased speed, and the determined lip and fiercer grasp of carbine and revolver denoted that the spirit of revenge had arisen, and nothing but blood would atone now for that poor policeman's death, in his effort to do his duty and save his comrades.

Red Tomahawk turned to Thunder Iron, who stood beside him, and said:

"Can't you get your horse and get to the white soldiers? I don't know why they are not here now. Hawk Man started back before the fight to bring them up."

Thunder Iron looked grimly out from behind the house where they were sheltered, and said:

"Brother, I will no doubt be killed; but our brave captain is dead or dying, and if help don't come soon, we will all be killed. Brother, good-by; I am going.'

He glanced for an instant over the field, and then made a dash for his horse, which had wandered some distance away, and luckily in the right direction for Thunder Iron. As soon as the hostiles saw his purpose, a hundred rifles were leveled at him, a hundred messengers of death whistled after his flying form. His hat flies suddenly into the air, but the bullet has not hit the man, and unscathed amidst it all, Thunder Iron is on his horse at last, and flying like the wind to bring the troops to the rescue. As he goes, a wild shout of triumph rings out from the indomitable police, and the firing is renewed more briskly than ever.

One Feather was leaning against the back part of Sitting Bull's house, where he could clearly see the open where lay the bodies, when he noticed Spotted Horn Bull suddenly rise from where he lay concealed and begin to work his way cautiously toward the little group of dead and dying, where Sitting Bull and Bullhead lay. "What can he want?" thought One Feather. Then in an instant the errand that Spotted Horn Bull was on flashed through his mind; and his face assumed such an expression of deadly hate that it would have appalled the other had he seen it. But his eye was intent on one single figure prostrate on the ground, and for this, gun in hand, he was making his way. Bullhead, though mortally wounded, was conscious of all that was going on, and to wreak vengeance on his still living body was Spotted Horn Bull's purpose. As he drew closer he said:

"Bullhead, I am going to kill you this time. You will not escape now!" And suddenly rising to his feet, he dropped his gun and rushed forward to brain Bullhead with an ax he held in his hand. His cartridges had given out.

One Feather is there! See how he towers between his prostrate chief and the would-be assassin. Spotted Horn Bull is surprised at this unlooked-for interference. For one fatal instant he hesitates; that instant is his last. The revolver of One Feather speaks, and Spotted Horn Bull falls dead, shot through the heart. A wild cry rings out from a hundred throats, and a storm of bullets hurtles and sings around One Feather, who, hurling his revolver away, stoops

SCALP DANCE.

and lifts Bullhead in his arms and carries him safely out of further harm into the house. Well done, noble One Feather!

But now the ammunition of the police is nearly gone. Flying By holds up his empty belt and hurls it out defiantly toward the enemy. Many others are out of cartridges, but still the little band holds its own. No thought of surrender could be tolerated a moment, even with ten of their number dead or dying, and only about thirty of them left to fight the ever-increasing enemy. It is only a question of time, and a very short time at that, before the few cartridges left will be gone; and then, the slaughter of the police.

But hark! What is that clear, ringing sound borne on the breeze, high and clear above all the noise and tumult of the firing and shouts? Once again the bugle calls out its wild notes, and the eyes of all the combatants are turned to the hills, whence, a second later, with a loud hurrah O Troop comes dashing down to the relief, closely followed by N Troop as a reserve, with the three-inch rifle and Hotchkiss gun rushed into position on the crest of the hills. Once more a blast on the trumpets, and simultaneously fifty carbines belch out smoke and flame, carrying death into the now dismayed ranks of the hostiles, who are preparing to seek safety in flight. Suddenly there comes a lull—dead silence—which lasts for a single second, broken by a crash that wakes all the echoes, and a shell has screamed its way from the cannon and plunged into the stronghold of the savages. A puff of white smoke goes up, followed by a dull, muffled report, and the hostiles are seen fleeing for their lives, and the ground occupied by them so recently covered with their dead or dying.

Red Tomahawk was quick to grasp the changed situation, and as the troops, preceded by their sturdy commander, rode upon the bloody scene, he drew up the little remnant of his band in line and saluted. As for the hostiles, the fragment of Sitting Bull's once numerous host, now dwindled to a handful, had disappeared as the frost before the sun. Utterly thrashed and cowed, they scattered and ran, until a few days later, they had all surrendered, willing captives.

CHAPTER XXV.

SITTING BULL'S ADOPTED BROTHER—STORY OF SCOUT GROUARD AND HIS SIX YEARS' LIFE WITH THE SIOUX INDIANS.

FRANK GROUARD, the Indian scout, who lived in St. Joseph, Mo., at the time this story was given to the public by the Chicago Record, recovered from the surgical operation in which an arrowhead was removed from his groin, after having been imbedded their for nearly a dozen years. The surgeons who cut the flint from his muscles told the scout the operation would probably be fatal, and a few days later he was told that he could not possibly recover; but he had endured so many tortures while he was captive among the Sioux Indians that he laughed at the fears of the physicians and regained his health in spite of their predictions. While the surgeons were operating on him he smoked a cigar, and at no time was he impressed with the idea that the injury would prove fatal, although at one time he was so near death as to be unconscious, and apparently lifeless.

The scout has never been willing to talk freely of his life among the Indians, and all that has been learned of that period has been drawn from him by close questioning in unguarded moments. He was captured by Sitting Bull and a small band of followers when 19 years old, and remained with the Indians during six years, a greater portion of the time in the camp of Sitting Bull, through whose influence he was saved from torture and death. At the time of his capture Grouard was a mail rider between Fort Hall and Fort Peck. On the way to the Indian village he learned the name of his captor, and made up his mind that nothing but torture was in store for him. Great was his surprise when the chief announced in council that he had determined to spare the captive's life, and, greater still, when he was adopted as Sitting Bull's brother.

"No human being who has never been a captive among savages can realize the horrors that constantly surrounded me,' said Grouard. "I was sent to the lodge of Sitting Bull's mother and sister, and to these two savage women I also owe my life. I had never before attempted to live on a meat diet alone, and I found that was the only food the Indians had, without salt or seasoning. I was stricken with a strange illness, and do not know how long I was ill. Nothing would supply my craving for bread, and in my troubled dreams I saw loaves of it just out of reach of my outstretched arms. White Cow divine i the cause of my sickness, and in the spring, when the Indians from the agencies came out to the hostile tribes, she bought small quantities of flour, coffee, salt and pepper, for which she paid an enormous price in ponies and furs. When I awoke one day there was a smell of burning bread and boiling coffee in the teepee, and for a moment I could not realize that I was still a captive. When the flour was all gone White Cow would gather turnips, dry them and pound them into a pulp, from which she would make a porridge. In time I learned to live on a meat diet alone.

"I was closely guarded for sixteen months after my capture, my guards being Little Assiniboine and White Eagle, the latter a cousin of Sitting Bull. It was customary in the spring of the year to move the camp toward the north, to meet the vast herds of buffalo coming down, and in the fall the Indians generally located on the Belle Fourche or Little Missouri river, where game was plentiful. It was on the first hunt that I killed a deer in a running shot at a **great distance** with an old flint-lock gun that had been given me. The feat so pleased Sitting Bull that he presented me with a Hawkins rifle and from that time no restrictions were placed on my movements. I roamed the wilds at will and acquired a thorough and intimate knowledge of every mountain pass, crag, ravine and canyon in the great stretch of country now known as Wyoming, Dakota and Montana.

"My name among the Indians was Standing Bear. It was given to me because I was dressed in a fur overcoat, cap and mittens when captured. In the winter of 1870 I went out with a war party for the first time. The Sioux and the Crows were always at war. About the time we left the Sioux village we struck the trail of a war party of Crows going toward the Sioux camp, with the evident intention of running off as many ponies as they could. We returned to camp and met the Crows, driving them into the bad lands, where they sought shelter in a basin, behind a wall of rocks. The attack was not by Sitting Bull himself, and the rush toward the spot where the Crows were intrenched meant death to many of the Sioux warriors. The chief went in advance of his braves, jumped over the rocks into the pit and had killed a number of Crows before the others arrived to assist him. In point of numbers the war parties were about the same, but all the Crows were killed and only a few of the Sioux. The bodies of the enemies were scalped and left where they were slain. There must have been a hundred dead Indians in that gulch, and it was one of the bloodiest scenes I ever witnessed.

"One of the biggest Indian clean-ups I ever knew anything about occurred a short time before that, on Beaver creek, about midway between Fort Hall and Milk river. Four hundred Gros Ventre Indians were camped there, some of them confined to their lodges with the small-pox. The Blackfeet made a raid on the village and only two of the Gros Ventres escaped alive. We heard of the massacre and a party of us went over there from the Sioux camp. A month later I passed by the place with a hunting party. The half-decomposed bodies of the victims were scattered about in every direction, and were being eaten by wolves and other wild animals. None of them were ever buried. I saw a great many barbarous things while I lived with the Indians, but the scene in the Gros Ventre village after the massacre by the Blackfeet was the most sickening sight I ever witnessed.

"From the time of my capture up to 1872 I was not required to undergo any of the self-inflicted tortures of the Sioux, but after I became one of them to all intents and purposes I knew what to expect. While we were camped where Glendive, Mont., now stands, the whole tribe gathered one day about the sweat and I was informed that I was to be put to the test. All the Indians gathered around, taking positions where they could watch my face. Sitting Bull, No Neck, Gall, Four Horns, Little Assiniboine and other head men of the tribe sat near me smoking their pipes. Four warriors squatted on each side of me and with needles raised up the flesh between the shoulder and elbow on each arm and cut out pieces the size of a pea, taking 480 pieces out of each arm. The skin and flesh were taken off in five rows on each arm. It was not painful at first, but before they were through there was a stream of agony pouring from my arms to my heart that was almost unbearable. I did not open my lips or make a sound while they were torturing me, although the operation lasted four hours. The next time I was tortured all my eyebrows and eyelashes were pulled out. After that I went through the tortures as stoically as the Indians themselves, even including the tortures of the sun dance, when horsehair ropes were tied in the muscles of the breast and back and torn out by sheer force.

"Sitting Bull would never make a treaty with the whites. For the purpose of securing supplies he made a treaty with the Red river half-breeds to bring him such articles as his tribe needed, and when the half-breeds came they brought five sleighloads of whisky. There was nothing but drinking in the village as long as the whisky lasted, and it ended in a terrible fight, from which the half breeds were glad to escape with their lives. The faction opposing Sitting Bull tried to kill him. There were 5,000 Indians in the village at that time, and many were killed. Many lodges were torn down or burned.

"The next spring a Yankton Indian from the agency at Fort Peck came into our camp. I sent a letter by him to the agent, telling him what the Red river half-breeds had done. The agent sent the Yankton back in a few months asking me to come in, as he wished to see me. He also wanted me to bring Sitting Bull in so they could make a treaty with him and get the hostile trade. In a short time Sitting Bull, Little Assiniboine, Black Shield and myself went to Fort Peck, where a big council was held, but Sitting Bull flatly refused to have anything to do with the whites. While we were there the agent told me he wanted me to go with a party to capture the half-breeds who had been selling whisky.

" To get away from Sitting Bull without him finding out where I was going I had to tell him I was going on the warpath to steal horses. I told him I was going up the Missouri. I went instead with some troops to a place on Frenchman's creek, where the half-breeds were camped, and picked out the ones who had taken whisky to the Indians. The soldiers arrested a lot of them. They gave me three horses so I could make Sitting Bull believe I had stolen them. I gave the horses to Sitting Bull, and, as he was very much pleased to think I would go out alone and steal horses, he told every Indian he saw about it. There were some Santee Indians in the camp of the half-breeds and they recognized me. In about ten days they came into our camp and told Sitting Bull all about it. He was the maddest man I ever saw and said he would kill me on sight. His mother kept him from killing me. Gall and the other members of the faction who were opposed to Sitting Bull wanted me to come over on that side of the village, but I would not go. Sitting Bull never spoke to me after that, and when the camp moved I got on one side and he went on the other, so we kept apart. Soon after that I went over to the Ogallala camp with Crazy Horse, and never went back to Sitting Bull's camp again.

"After I went to the camp of Crazy Horse I was still with the hostiles, who never went to the agencies. The agency Indians would come to us, and it was from them that we secured ammunition. One spring we were entirely out of ammunition and our provisions were very low. The Indian village was then on the head of the Rosebud river. We were expecting a party of agency Indians with supplies, and it was decided to send a party out to look for them. We saw what we took to be smoke signals near the mouth of Tongue river, distant about four days' travel. Myself and two Indians started out to bring the agency Indians in. We left the village with one days' rations and no ammunition.

"When we arrived at the mouth of Tongue river we found where a fire had been, but there was no sign of the agency Indians, so there was nothing to do but go back. On the way back to the village all three of us became nearly insane from hunger, having been eight days without a particle of food. We were within twenty miles of the camp when we managed to kill three prairie chickens with a bow and arrows. My companions tore the fowls apart and ate them raw. I roasted the necks and ate sparingly of them. We were ten days in making the trip, and when we reached the village were nothing but skin and bones. The flesh on our faces was so drawn that we were almost unrecognizable. My two companions died in a few days.

"The next year I went into the agency with a party of Indians, but had no opportunity of making my escape. We only stopped a short time, and then went down on Tongue river. All the time I was studying about a plan to escape. The next spring I went out with a party going to Laramie river. It was a war party, and the night they started to make a raid on the ranches I started for the agency. I never went back to the Indians again."

CHAPTER XXVI.

MOQUI INDIANS ON THE WAR-PATH—THEIR LEADERS CAPTURED AND PLACED IN PRISON AT FORT WINGATE, N. M.

Troops sent out to the Moqui Indian reservation in November, 1894, returned in February, 1895, bringing with them 19 prisoners. All of the leading hostiles who were dangerous to the peace of the reservation were put under lock and key at Fort Wingate, New Mexico. There were some celebrated personages among them and, as long as the government keeps them under surveillance, there is no danger of a recurrence of the recent strife in Moqui. The causes that led to the outbreak is told by Lieut. L. M. Brett, adjutant at Fort Wingate.

There are several villages of the Moquis, upon the high mesas, in Arizona. Their reservation is in the northern part of the territory and is distant about 160 miles from Fort Wingate. Oraiba is the largest of their towns and occupies a commanding site, upon a very abrupt bluff, near the center of the reservation.

Several years ago the government provided schools for these Indians, and that was the first step toward the trouble. The tribe almost immediately divided into factions, one progressive and inclined to take advantage of the opportunities offered them and the other averse to the inauguration of an educational era. The split widened, and the following upon either side for a time was about equal, in point of numbers. But Lo-ma-hung-yo-ma, the belligerent chief (who, by the way, was not a chief at all, but simply a leader proclaimed by the dissatisfied faction), so worked upon the minds of the people that his following became very much stronger than that of the rightful chief, Lo-lo-la-mi. Then Lo-ma-hung-yo-ma began a series of abuses and went to the extreme length of seizing the cultivated lands of the friendlies and the confiscation of their personal property. Finally, in June, 1891, a request for troops was received through the department headquarters, and I was sent in command of a small detachment to Oraiba to settle the difficulties, and restore order. We had no idea here that the Moquis would resist the **authority** of the government, and therefore **only ten** men accompanied me on this trip. When we reached **a** point **within** two miles of Oraiba, the Moquis at work **in a field started** to run. **We** headed some of them off and asked what **they** were running for, but they would not give a satisfactory answer. As we did not know whether they were members of the hostile band or not, we did not detain them, but permitted them to go on to Oraiba. I sent a boy to the village to bring Lo-lo-la-mi to our camp, and the old chief came as soon as my message reached him. When he saw the small force of men I had with me, he counselled us not to go into the village, and assured us that we would all be killed. The hostiles, he said, numbered fully 400 men, all well armed and desperate. They were determined to run the tribe their own way, and would not brook the interference of the troops, and especially in such small force as we presented. They had barricaded the narrow streets of the village, and were prepared for a siege. Oraiba is built upon a very high mesa, and the trail leading up to it is very steep and narrow. We were told that we would all be shot down as we ascended the trail, and that we would not be permitted to enter the village at all. I settled that point by capturing ten of Lo-ma-hung-yo-ma's men, who were hovering about, watching us; then I sent word to him that I was coming into town, and that if we were fired upon each soldier would shoot his prisoner on the spot. We went into the village unmolested. I thought there was a good deal of talk about Lo-ma-hung-yo-ma, and was not very much afraid of him. I marched my small force to the center of the village and suddenly found myself surrounded by at least 300 of the Moquis, all armed and ready for fight. Lo-ma-hung-yo-ma (which translated means "bad") informed me that my time had arrived to pray; that I had only five minutes in which to arrange my earthly affairs and take my departure to the happy hunting grounds. It was a predicament I had not thought of, and it looked **very** gloomy for us just about that time. We would have killed some Moquis, but we would have been wiped out as effectually as was poor Custer and his gallant men, in that death trap in the Little Big Horn country.

I thought I would try a 'bluff,' anyhow, and I made him a talk, which was generously interpreted. I told him a great many things that would happen to him if he fired upon us, and concluded by assuring him that, if he killed us, within three days the plains all around and about Oraiba would be teeming with soldiers and that every Moqui in the village would be slaughtered. This last was a contingency he had not thought of. He pondered over it a long time, finally allowing us to retreat slowly from the dangerous pocket into which we had walked. Other troops were sent for and, upon their arrival, Lo-ma-hung-yo-ma and six of his lieutenants were arrested and escorted back to the post. That ended the matter for the time being, and we thought no more of the Moquis. Just one incident occurred there, by the way, that will illustrate how easy it would have been at one time to have precipitated a massacre. Lo-lo-la-mi, the friendly chief, was with us, and, seeing a chance to shoot Lo-ma-hung-yo-ma when that gentleman wasn't looking, he snatched a pistol from the belt of one of my men and leveled it at his enemy. I caught it by the barrel just in time to prevent his firing. That shot would have sealed our fate.

Nothing more was heard from the Moquis until October, 1894. Lo-ma-hung-yo-ma had, in the meantime, been released from prison and had returned to his tribe. Discontent soon broke out, and in the month named a request for troops came through School Superintendent Russell and Captain Constant Williams, Indian agent at Oraiba. In his communication, Captain Williams stated to the Interior Department that the hostiles were again taking the lands and crops away from the other faction, and that a murderous outbreak was likely to occur at any time. Orders were, therefore, issued by Colonel Hunt, commanding the post, directing Captain Frank U. Robinson, Second Cavalry, to proceed, with two troops of cavalry, to Moqui, arrest all the leaders in the disturbance and settle matters to the satisfaction of the local authorities and the Indian agent there. Captain Robinson left Fort Wingate Nov. 17, with Troops G and H of the Second Cavalry and a Hotchkiss gun. The latter was in charge of Lieutenant C. C. Smith, Second Cavalry, and a detachment of four men from K Troop, of the same regiment.

The command reached Keams' Canyon on the 21st of November, where Captain Williams, the Indian agent, joined it. Captain Robinson was informed fully regarding affairs at Oraiba, and prepared to meet certain emergencies which seemed inevitable. The command left Keams' Canyon on the 24th of November, and reached camp at the foot of the mesa upon which Oraiba is situated, at 1 o'clock the next afternoon. Mr. Thomas Keam, a trader, joined the troops here and proved a valuable aid to Captain Robinson, for the reason that he personally knew all of the hostiles and knew everything about the Moquis as far as related to the present trouble. With Mr. Keam was an Indian named Tom Po-la-ka, an interpreter, who was also well acquainted with the hostiles who were wanted by Captain Robinson. Couriers had evidently been sent out to all the surrounding tribes announcing that a great fight was to occur between Lo-ma-hung-yo-ma's men and the soldiers, for Navajos and Moquis from remote villages had flocked to the scene to witness the fight and to pillage the vanquished, whichever way victory might go. The first thing Captain Robinson did was to place these Indians where they would do the least harm.

When everything had been arranged, Captain Robinson moved upon the village. He marched his force to the rear of the town, and there formed in line, with H troop on the right, G troop on the left, and the Hotchkiss gun in the center. In the meantime there was intense excitement in Oraiba. Indians were seen scurrying here, there and everywhere; some were armed, others carried sticks and clubs; Lo-ma-hung-yo-ma and his body guard had barricaded themselves in a strong house and everything seemed ripe for a conflict. The soldiers were ready, too, and only wanted a chance to clean up a few hundred Indians, as they expressed it, just to get a little rifle practice. But Captain Robinson wasn't there to sacrifice life unnecessarily, and before ordering an advance into the streets of the village, criers were sent in, ordering all the Indians to come out where the troops were and hear the orders of the commander. Soon there was a great gathering in the open space in front of the houses, or in the rear of them, rather, and when all had arrived, the names of the Indians who were wanted were read out. As fast as their names were called, they were pointed out by Mr. Keam or Captain Williams, and all save two were under arrest before they knew what was happening. The

arrest of the chief and the medicine man, who were the chief instigators of all the discontent and trouble, left the hostiles without leaders and they did not know how to act. The war was over before it had fairly begun, and there was no chance for a fight, which both sides were spoiling for. The arrest of eighteen prisoners was accomplished within a few minutes, and Captain Robinson returned to his camp at the foot of the mesa. Two Indians, however, could not be found. One of these was Ha-bi-ma, a medicine man who was particularly wanted, and the other a leader in Lo-ma-hung-yoma's band. Several attempts were made to get them, but neither of them was caught until late at night, and then only Ha-bi-ma was found. Lieutenant Sawtell, Second Cavalry, refers to this in his narrative of the campaign. Among other things he said:

"I was left in charge of the camp at the foot of the mesa when the troops went to the village to make the arrests. I had six men with me, and, while I regretted very much not being able to be at the village, yet we had enough to do to keep us awake down there. There was a feeling prevalent everywhere that there would be a big fight. This caused all the roving bands of Navajos and Moquis in the country to come there, and if there had been a battle it is not difficult to guess which side they would have assisted. Whenever one of these bands came within hailing distance of the camp they were stopped and asked to step up to the fire. There I ordered them to be disarmed, and all their guns and pistols were piled up in a heap before the fire. Those who had been armed were kept prisoners until the troops returned from Oraiba. When I saw the troops returning with their prisoners I knew there would be no fight and consequently turned my prisoners loose, after returning their belongings.

"In the evening Captain Robinson directed me to detail a sergeant, a corporal and six men, to go into the village to capture the two Indians who had escaped arrest in the afternoon. It had been reported to us that both of them were in a certain part of the town. I sent Sergeant Henser with six men and another non-commissioned officer to apprehend them. I think Sergeant Henser's adventure, as he narrated it to me, was the most exciting episode of the campaign. My instructions to him were to divide the guard, sending three men with the corporal to one house and taking three men with himself into another house, where the men were supposed to be in hiding. Sergeant Henser caught his man, but the other detail of the guard were less fortunate, for they returned empty handed.

"The Indian boy, who brought us word as to the whereabouts of the two Indians, guided the guard to the houses. One of these was the house in which were kept the ceremonial robes of the Moqui priesthood and it is a house that had never been entered by a white man. The houses, as you know, are entered through the roofs. A ladder reaches the roof from the ground and the doorway is only a scuttle hole in the top of the house. The first room may be three or four stories from the ground, and communication is had with the lower rooms by means of rickety ladders, similar to the one used to scale the outer wall, except shorter. The house was as dark as Egypt and there was no knowing at what moment the soldiers would be shot or stabbed from behind. They got trace of the medicine man in the middle room and the chase led them to the cellar, which was cut out of the solid rock underneath the house. There were two rooms; in one of them a woman was found, standing in the corner. There were masks and robes of all sorts hanging on the walls all about the room. False faces, made from wolf and wildcat heads, masks and head ornaments, painted in the most fantastic and savage manner, weapons, spears, bows, arrows—in fact, everything pertaining to the uses of the priests was stored in this cellar or estufa.

"The entrance to the second room was screened by a hanging blanket of unusual design. The Indian woman, who was evidently the custodian of the place, stood ready to prevent the entrance of the sergeant and his men into that holy of holies. Sergeant Henser thrust the hanging blanket aside, and stepped into the doorway. As he did so he saw a moving figure underneath a pile of priestly wraps, and grabbed it. It proved to be the medicine man, very much alive and full of fight. At the instant he caught the medicine man, the Indian woman on the other side of the doorway sprang upon him like a tiger cat and struck him a furious blow in the back with a bunch of steel-tipped arrows. His heavy overcoat saved him and the blow glanced off. The infuriated ha; snatched up a bow, fitted an arrow to it in the twinkling of an eye, pulled it taut and in another second the brave sergeant would have been killed in his tracks, but for the fortunate arrival of one of his men, who had been searching the other rooms. The soldier took in the situation at a glance, threw himself upon the priestess and diverted her aim. A struggle ensued for the possession of the bow, and eventually the woman was overpowered, but not until she had given the soldier a fight that he would not soon forget. The medicine man was delivered safely at the camp within an hour."

The return of the troops with their prisoners to Fort Wingate was accomplished in three days and a half after leaving Keams' Canyon, the Indians traveling on foot all the way. O e mounted guard was assigned to each of the nineteen Indians. The troopers rode their horses at a trot the greater part of the distance and the Indians ran alongside, the horses easily keeping up the pace for five or six hours at a time. The prisoners were placed in the guard house at Fort Wingate to remain there until disposed of by the Interior Department. They were given a comfortable, clean room, good beds and blankets, three meals of substantial army rations every day and seemed to be perfectly contented. They will profit greatly in every way by being the guests of Uncle Sam.

CHAPTER XXVII.

A TRAGIC CHAPTER IN THE PIONEER HISTORY OF THE UPPER DELAWARE

Among the papers and old documents left by Paul S. Preston of Wayne county, Pa., and now in the possession of his daughter, Anna Preston, of Middletown, N. Y., is a diary kept by his father, Judge Samuel Preston, more than a century ago. Samuel Preston was a Quaker from Philadelphia, and was a pioneer of the upper Delaware Valley, whither he went as a surveyor in the employ of Robert Morris, the financier of the Revolution, and others, while the most of northern Pennsylvania was still comprised in the manors of the descendants of William Penn. In 1787, Preston was exploring and prospecting in what is now Pike county, Pa., near the present village of Shohola. Following is an entry he made in his diary at that time:

July 6, 1787.—Started this morning with Ben Haynes, John Hessum and Felix Hooper. Reached the river before night and crossed in a canoe to Ben Haynes' house in York state. He being lame from running a stub in his foot, I settled with him and paid him. As to his character, he is a Low Dutchman, a great hunter, and well acquainted with the woods. There is a dark stain on his character. * * * One evening, some time ago, there came a panther into his house and took one of the children from out of the cradle and was carrying it off, but his wife, a resolute woman, with the dog, rescued it. The child was much wounded. It is still living. I have seen the scars.

The stealing of this child by the panther has been a favorite tale in the upper Delaware Valley for generations, but the household version of the incident varies much from that in the old Preston diary, and the latter is undoubtedly the true account. As the story is told by the backwoods fireside, Mrs. Haynes, one day when her husband was absent on a hunting trip, took her baby from their cabin, which stood near where the village of Barryville, Sullivan county, N. Y., now is, and went to the creek to do her washing. The baby was but a few months old, and Mrs. Haynes placed it on the ground near where she was at work. **As she was** busy pounding the clothes she heard a cry from her baby, and, looking around, **saw** a large panther moving deliberately off with the child in its mouth. The mother started in pursuit, carrying **her** heavy clothes pounder as a weapon. The panther **did** not move very fast, and Mrs. Haynes soon overtook it. Attacking it with her pounder, she forced the bold beast to drop the child, and a few additional blows from her formidable weapon put it to flight.

The "dark stain" on Ben Haynes' character, mentioned by Samuel Preston in the above entry in his diary, **is a** reference to a cold-blooded murder. One of the historic characters of the Delaware Valley, whose career was one of blood, was Tom Quick, the Indian slayer. When he was a young man Indians killed his father, the first settler at the present site of Milford, Pa., and Tom swore vengeance against all Indians, although he had lived among them, and was almost an Indian himself. For many years he carried on a relentless warfare against them. Tradition says that he killed ninety-nine Indians, and on his death-bed his only regret was that he could not make the number an even hundred. He is cannonized in the Delaware Valley as a hero, but, as a matter of fact, his exploits show him to have been an assassin.

In 1784, the Indians had nearly all been driven from the Delaware Valley. A few solitary and miserable members of a once proud and defiant tribe remained, scattered here and there through the region, living by fishing and hunting and on charity. Among them were two named Huycon and Kanope. In 1784, they appeared near Shohola to hunt and fish. Ben Haynes, who had **himself** been a deadly enemy of the red men, had his cabin on the New York state side of the Delaware, and Tom Quick's cabin was on the Pennsylvania side, up the Shohola creek a mile or so from the river.

Haynes, having discovered the two Indians, went to their camp and invited them to go fishing with him next day in Handsome Eddy, in the Delaware not far below his cabin. The Indians, knowing Haynes of old, were at first suspicious of him, and not inclined to accept the invitation, but he persisted, and seemed so sincere in his offer of hospitality, that they at last accepted his invitation.

After dark that night Ben Haynes paddled his canoe to the Pennsylvania side of the river, and went to Tom Quick's cabin, up the Shohola. He told Quick about the Indians, and the two hunters planned that Tom Quick should hide in the bushes on the river bank at Handsome Eddy, and when Haynes brought the unsuspecting Indians to the rocks to fish, Quick was to shoot one and Haynes to kill the other.

Next day Huycon and Kanope went to Haynes' cabin, and he paddled them to the eddy, and they larded at the rocks and began to fish. Quick, from his ambush, shot Kanope. The bullet passed through the Indian's skull but did not kill him. Huycon saw the flash of Quick's gun, and, jumping into the river, swam toward the New York shore. Haynes finished Kanope as he lay wounded on the rocks, by knocking his brains out with a pine knot. Quick, in the meantime, reloaded his gun and fired at Huycon, who had got well toward the opposite shore. Quick missed him, and before he could load again the Indian had reached the shore and escaped to the woods. Neither of the murderers was ever brought to justice, and for years afterward they boasted of the killing of Kanope, and regretted that his companion escaped them. Yet the memory of Quick is kept green by a fine bronze statue at Milford. It was erected by the late Lieut.-Gov. William Bross of Chicago, who was pleased to give it the heroic title of "The Avenger."

The story of the panther that tried to steal the resolute Mrs. Haynes' baby is not complete without its sequel. The baby grew to manhood. His name was Ben, and he proved to be a worthy son of his father. He became known as one of the most desperate characters along the river. When the lumber business of the Delaware Valley was developed, Young Ben Haynes, as he was known, became a raftsman. He piloted rafts down the then treacherous rapids of the Lackawaxen river. One afternoon he started with a raft from Paupack Eddy, now Hawley, Pa. The freshet was high and strong. Haynes was asked where he intended to stop for supper.

"In hell, maybe!" was his reply.

Perhaps he did, for his raft was wrecked in the fierce rapids known as the Narrows, four miles below the eddy, and he was drowned.

CHAPTER XXVIII.

INDIAN TERRITORY LAWS—THE "NATION" A REFUGE FOR CRIMINALS FROM ALL PARTS OF THE COUNTRY.

During a trip early this year (1895) from Chicago to the Southwest the *Record* correspondent took pains to make some personal observations in the Indian Territory, and came by rail through the strongholds of the Cook gang, near the southern Kansas border. Before leaving Kansas City the writer read of fresh "hold-ups" in the region he proposed to visit, and even the Missouri Pacific passenger agent at Kansas City admitted that his company could not guarantee a safe passage through the Territory. The agent complained bitterly of want of protection by the United States Government, and said that the business of not only his company but each of the other companies running through the Territory had been ruined by a prevailing lawlessness. The last sleeping car sent through the Territory had come back riddled with bullets, and the night train service had been discontinued as a result. Nothing short of martial law, according to the railroad official, would meet the situation, which became more desperate day by day. The express companies declined to receive money or valuables for transmission through the Territory, and business was rapidly being paralyzed.

At Nowata, a small station near the Kansas border, the agent said he had been "held up" a few hours previously by some of the Cook gang and about $100 of the company's money had been stolen. It was the evident purpose of the bandits to hold up the train at that point, but as the latter was some hours late, they robbed the station agent and left before daylight came. At Bragg's, another small station, a group of coffee-colored natives were seen guarding the dead body of an Indian who had been murdered a few hours before. At a third stopping place there was a scrimmage on the station platform, in which the train porter, a burly Creek Indian, scored one or two knockouts and restored quiet before the train left. According to the train officials such incidents as the above are daily witnessed, and it was freely admitted that never before had crime been so rampant in the Territory.

At Fort Smith and Little Rock the correspondent questioned leading officials of the United States courts, with jurisdiction in the Indian Territory, and also leading officials of the Arkansas State Government, as to the most feasible methods of breaking up the gangs of criminals that have brought about this reign of terror. Opinions widely differ, but it is noticeable that the only pleas for a continuance of the present condition of affairs come from United States officials. There are a good many Federal Commissioners, Judges, and other officials whose usefulness would be gone and whose salaries would be stopped if the present tribal relations of the five civilized tribes of Indians were broken up and either Territorial or State Government adopted. Without a single exception, the opinion of all others than Federal officials is in favor of a change. Men who have lived in the Indian Territory for a generation, and others who have lived on its borders and traveled through it for an equally long period, all pronounce the present condition of affairs a disgrace to the national Government.

In a recent magazine article Gov. Fishback of Arkansas, who has lived most of his life at Fort Smith on the border of the "nation," as the Indian Territory is called, says: "This territory in its present condition has become a national pesthouse! It is a disgrace to our country, to civilization, and to humanity!" He takes the Government to task in this way:

"We have entered into treaties with the five civilized tribes as if they were an independent nation, and yet we, at the same time, assert jurisdiction over them as if Indian Territory were a part or parcel of our national domain. We try them in courts just as we try citizens of the United States in any state or territory. This dual jurisdiction makes law and order impossible. If an Indian kills a white man or a white man kills an Indian, he is tried in the United States courts. If an Indian kills an Indian of the same tribe he is tried in the Indian courts. This, with the sparsely settled condition, makes the Territory a safe harbor for criminals. Almost every week I am asked to offer a reward for criminals who commit crime in this state and flee to the nation for refuge.

The Territory has become a school of crime for the younger **Indians.** The recent bands of desperadoes are almost all young men. Our Government's relation to the Indians is a sham. It treats them as foreigners, and at the same time treats them as citizens. It does not protect the real Indian, who has been driven to the wilds and fastnesses by the squaw men and sharpers who now control the Territory. We pretend to protect the poor Indian from robbery by the rich, while in reality we protect nobody but the rich in their robbery of the poor Indian."

A remedy is the next thing. Gov. Fishback and others who consider present conditions a disgrace would welcome either Territorial or State Government for the Territory. No one talks of taking any land from the Indians. It is even proposed to allow the new Indian State, like Texas, to absolutely control its own public domain. All that is asked is that the Indian Territory shall change its form of government and come into line with the rest of the nation either as a Territory or as a State.

Judge Parker, the Federal Judge at Fort Smith, and perhaps the most conservative living authority on our relations with the five civilized tribes, has sentenced more Indian criminals to death than any other Judge, and yet so just is he in the interpretation of Indian treaties and so fearless in the punishment of crime that the Indians regard him as their greatest friend. He says: "Territorial government would not better the condition of the Indian Territory, neither would it repress crime. I favor State government for the Indian Territory, and believe the Indians themselves will ask for it in time, say within ten years. But the process of civilization is slow, and the Indians are not yet ready for state government. There should be no intermediate Territorial process, which would only aggravate present conditions and would overrun the Territory with carpet-baggers and broken-down politicians. I do not believe that crime in the Territory is worse than it was ten or fifteen years ago, and the courts are fully able to cope with it."

On the latter point the preponderance of testimony is against the conclusions of Judge Parker. Traveling men who have regularly visited the "nation" for a dozen years or more say that ten years ago they thought nothing of making collections and carrying large sums of money on their persons. They do not dare do so now, and most of them are walking arsenals.

The Indian Territory is no longer an Indian reservation, and there are four or five whites to every Indian within its borders. Squaw men and adventurers hold sway and have fenced in all the desirable lands, with the consent of the Indians who are too rich to work. The full-blooded Indians live in isolated corners and are rarely seen. The wealth of some of the tribes is remarkable, although the whites absorb most of every Government allowance and rob the Indians by every artifice known. Even after being plundered for years, the Osage Indians in the Territory are worth about $20,000 for every man, woman, and child in the tribe. There are many very rich men among the Cherokees and Chickasaws. But the Indians have already practically surrendered their lands to the whites, and by inviting the latter into the Territory for purposes of tribute have, it is claimed, themselves abrogated their treaty with the United States.

Whatever may be the force of the treaty with the five civilized tribes, it is manifest that law and order cannot be sacrificed. Post-offices are being robbed, mail trains are held up, and inter-state commerce is interrupted by the Territory's gangs of bandits. The United States Government is set at defiance daily, and the public at large do not really understand the situation.

CHAPTER XXIX.

THE FIVE TRIBES OF CIVILIZED INDIANS—PROPOSED LEGISLATION IN CONGRESS TO GIVE THEM TERRITORIAL GOVERNMENT.

It is a difficult matter for Congress to supply legislation of a sort that will at once be acceptable to the Indians and desirable for the Government. The Dawes Commission, appointed to confer with the tribes was unfortunate in not being able to get any counter propositions from the Indians in response to their own. On the day appointed the Indians met the Commissioners, listened attentively to what was said, and asked time for consideration, but promised nothing, and all the indications were against a favorable conclusion.

The proposals submitted to the Five Tribes by the Commissioners were, with slight modifications, the same for each of them. First, all lands except town sites and coal and mineral lands were to be divided in severalty among the citizens of the tribes according to treaties now in force, the land thus taken for homes being made inalienable for twenty-five years, or such longer period as was agreed upon. Each allottee should receive his land without expense, any trespassers being removed. Town sites, coal and minerals already discovered before allotment were to be disposed of by fair and just agreement, protecting the interests both of the tribes and those who had invested in them. All claims against the United States were to be settled, and all invested funds not devoted to school purposes and all moneys found due from the United States or derived from the sale of town sites, coal and minerals were to be divided per capita among the citizens. Finally, a Territorial Government should be formed by Congress over such of the tribes as might consent to it, the present tribal government meanwhile continuing until after the allotment of land and money. For some tribes a board of three persons, one to be a member of the Dawes Commission, another a member of the tribe, and a third selected by those two, was to be appointed upon all questions of citizenship and right to allotments. But in the case of the Cherokee tribe, which, according to a decision of the Interior

Department, is the exclusive judge of who are citizens, this proposal was withdrawn.

State legislation proposed in Congress covers the two main points thus presented, namely, allotment in severalty and a change to Territorial Government. But it proposed to deal with them in a compulsory manner instead of allowing the Indians a voice in the matter. One of the propositions of the Dawes Commission was that an agreement for a Territorial Government, " when made, shall be submitted for ratification to the Cherokee Government, and if ratified by it shall then be submitted to Congress for approval." This appears to be a very fair arrangement in any case.

But the question arises whether, after all, the Indians would ever consent to these two main provisions. It appears that on Jan. 23rd, 1894, the Dawes Commission met, at Muscogee, a commission appointed by Chief Legus C. Perryman of the Creek Nation; but, after a conference, the Creek delegates requested a public meeting at Okmulgee, their capital. At that point, on April 3rd, a number of Creek citizens expressed themselves as desiring the proposed changes on account of the poverty-stricken condition of the common people; but after the Commissioners had addressed the large gathering the Chief followed in the Creek language, which was not interpreted to the Commissioners. They were informed, however, by one who was present, that the Chief told the people that they would each receive a lot of land only 8 feet by 4. It was unfortunate that the Commissioners did not take the precaution to provide themselves with an interpreter, as they would have learned whether the Chief's statement was only a jocose reference to the fact that allotment might yield a burial lot. At all events they found that on a vote the entire meeting " passed over to the side against our propositions." Immediately thereafter the Creek Council met and passed resolutions declining to appoint persons to treat with the Commissioners, or to take any steps looking to the allotment of lands or change of government. Nevertheless, on July 25th, the Dawes Commission sent in the formal propositions already spoken of, but received no answer to them.

The Choctaw Council was addressed in like manner at its capital, Tuskahoma, on Jan. 2th, and afterward the Commissioners, by request, addressed meetings on various points during the spring and summer; but it seems that they were accompanied by three persons appointed by the Choctaw Council who could speak both English and Choctaw, and "were instructed to use their influence to prevent favorable consideration of the propositions submitted." In fact no answer came from the Choctaw Council. Like results followed the labors among the Chickasaws, who were addressed, at the suggestion of Gov. Jonas Wolfe, Feb. 6th, 1894, at Tishomingo, and afterward elsewhere.

The Cherokees were in like manner called upon; but at the outset, on Jan. 30th, 1894, a Commission, instructed to deal with the visitors, informed the latter that their tribal Council had forbidden them to enter upon negotiations looking to allotment or changes of government. Afterward Chief C. J. Harris asked for an extension of the time for answering the propositions until the November meeting of the Cherokee Council, but nothing came of it. The negotiations with the Seminoles were of the same fruitless character.

Taking these facts into consideration, it seems absolutely hopeless to secure either the suggested change of government or severalty allotment without taking compulsory steps or else offering to the Indians inducements greater than have yet been mentioned. The conclusion of the Dawes Commission was in favor of overthrowing the present Governments, on the ground that the Indians themselves had violated the spirit of the treaties allowing lands to be held in common and securing tribal rule.

CHAPTER XXX.

SURVIVORS OF INDIAN WARS—ONLY ABOUT 4,000 VETERANS AND WIDOWS NOW ALIVE.

The report accompanying a bill introduced in Congress to pension the surviving soldiers of the Indian wars whose names are not now borne on the pension rolls, and which was written by Mr. Tawney of Minnesota, contains some interesting statistics. It shows that there still remain of the Seminole war of 1817 only five survivors and 120 widows; of the "La Fevre" Indian war, which occurred sixty-eight years ago, there remain only 14 survivors and 107 widows; of the Sabine war of 1836 there remain only 221 survivors and 155 widows; of the Cayuse war of 1847 there are 144 survivors and 32 widows; of the Texas and New Mexico Indian wars there still survive 1,418 veterans and 800 widows; of the California Indian wars there still survive 476 and 230 widows; of the Indian wars of Oregon and Washington, prior to 1856, there still survive 2,399 and 1,340 widows. In many cases the same man's name appears twice on the rolls, and it is estimated that a proper accounting of the soldiers will show that not more than 4,000 are alive at present.

"The last of these wars," the report continues, "occurred forty years ago, and the estimated age of the survivors is fixed at 65 years, while the estimated age of the Seminole survivors is 94 years. We owe to them largely, if not entirely, the acquisition of the vast empire of the Pacific Northwest. Most of the old survivors are in needy circumstances, while all are in old age, and it is estimated by the Commissioner of Pensions that the pensionable period cannot extend more than about seven years hence. Many of these men were omitted from the act pensioning survivors of Indian wars between 1832 and 1842, and for this reason the latest bill is the more just, since it includes all the survivors of the recognized Indian wars prior to 1856."

CHAPTER XXXI.

INDIAN GAMBLING—A FLIGHT OF ROCKY MOUNTAIN LOCUSTS—A PRAIRIE FIRE.

A YOUNG captive among the Indians told his friends after escape that the tribe holding him were greatly addicted to gambling. They had a variety of games; one was that of the moccasin. It is played by a number of persons divided into two parties. In one of four moccasins, a little stick, or small piece of cloth, is concealed. They are then laid down by the side of each other in a row, and one of the adverse party touches two of the moccasins. If the one he first touches has the thing hidden in it, the player loses eight to the opposite party; if it is not in the second, but in one of the two passed over, he loses two; if it is not in the one he touches first, and is in the last, he wins eight. The articles staked are valued by agreement. A beaver-skin or blanket is valued at ten; sometimes a horse at one hundred. There is another game played with circular counters, one side of them being plain, while the other is painted black. Generally nine are used, but never fewer. They are put together on a large wooden bowl, which is placed upon a blanket, when the two parties playing, numbering perhaps thirty people, sit down in a circle. The game consists in striking the edge of the bowl so as to throw all the counters into the air, and on the manner in which they fall upon the blanket or into the bowl, depends the player's gain or loss. If the player is fortunate in the first instance, he strikes again and again until he misses, when it is passed on to the next. So excited do the Indians become, that they often quarrel desperately. On one occasion the captive was staked by the Indian who considered himself his owner, and he was lost to a chief. The squaw, who had the care of him, on hearing that he had been lost with other property cried, and declared that she would not agree to his being given up. Thereupon several packs of peltries, the whole of his remaining property, were staked in a fresh game by his owner, who won, and the captive remained with his Indian mother.

One of the strange sights that frequently came over the

vision of Indians and on several memorable occasions has been witnessed by settlers, to their sorrow, **in the region** of the Rock Mountains, was the army of locusts *en route* over the plains. The horizon at first wears an unearthly **ashen** hue, giving one the impression of an approaching storm. Presently it seems as if the whole air is filled with light silvery **clouds**, and what looks at first like flakes of snow falling turn **out to** be numberless large insects with wings. The number in **the** air in a short time becomes so great that at intervals they perceptibly lessen the light of the sun. In looking upward as near to the sun as the light will permit, the sky continually changes color from blue to silvery white, ashy gray, and lead color, according to the density of the masses of insects. Opposite to the sun the prevailing hue is silvery white, perceptibly flashing. The hum produced by the vibration of so many million wings is quite indescribable, and is more like what some people call a ringing in the ears, than any other sound that is anything like it. The sight is very awe-producing to the mind. At first the locusts take short **flights,** but as the day increases, cloud after cloud arise from **the** prairie and pursue their way in the direction of the win**d.** Later in the day, they settle down upon the leaves of shrubs and grass to rest after their long flights. The whole district where they alight presents a curious appearance, for they cut the grass uniformly to one inch from the ground. If they settle on any cultivated ground, the entire crops of corn, wheat or rye is destroyed. They leave nothing green behind them, and even devour such things as woolen garments, skins and leather with the most astonishing rapidity. Though they fly very high in the air when on their journeys, they pitch usually on the ground by preference. Occasionally the forests are stripped of their leaves, and are left with a thoroughly wintry aspect, by these rapacious insects. In 1875, **great** deprivation was caused by the ravages of the locusts in a certain meridian of the West. It has been asserted that locusts boiled, and afterward stewed with a few **vegetables and a little** butter, pepper, salt and vinegar, make **an excellent fricassee.** This kind of meat might have satisfied **John the Baptist,** but **no one** need be alarmed that locusts **will ever become a staple** article of food in **the United States.**

For the benefit of those who **never** witnessed **a** genuine prairie fire a vivid description of one is here published. The **story** is told by a **camping** party. About half **a** mile away appeared what looked like a vast burning lake about a mile in width and **extending to** a much greater distance. Presently, beyond **it**, another began to blaze up, increasing with terrible rapidity; **and, further off** a third bright light was seen, which also began quickly to extend itself. Nothing, save a volcanic eruption, could surpass it in grandeur. The flames rose to an extraordinary height, rushing over the ground with the speed of race horses, and devouring every **tree and** shrub in the course. The wind blew it away **from us; but we** could surmise how fearful would have been our doom had we been on foot traveling across that part of the country. We should have had no chance of escape, for the intervals which at first existed between these lakes of fire quickly filled up. The conflagration swept on to the westward, gradually also creeping up toward us. We continued watching it, unable to tear ourselves away from the spot. It was grand and awful in the extreme. To arrest its progress would have been utterly beyond the power of human beings. The Indians have a paradoxical way of saying they have "put out fire" when they mean they have just started one. They frequently committed this destructive act simply as a **signal** to let their friends know that they had found buffalo. Streams of water or marshes, or a heavy **rainfall, are the** only extinguishers of prairie fires.

THE SCOUTS AND THE SIOUX.

A mount-inclosed valley, close sprinkled with fair flowers,
As if a shattered rainbow had fallen there in showers;
Bright-plumaged birds were warbling their songs among the trees,
Or fluttering their tiny wings in the cooling western breeze.
The cottonwoods, by mountain's base, on every side high tower,
And the dreamy haze in silence marks the sleepy noontide hour.
East, south and north, to meet the clouds the lofty mounts arise,
Guarding this little valley—a wild Western Paradise.
Pure and untrampled as it looks, this lovely flower-strewn sod—
One scarce would think that e'er, by man, had such a sward been trod;
But yonder, see those wild mustangs by lariat held in check,
Tearing up the fairest flora, which fairies might bedeck;

INDIAN MASSACRES.

And near a camp-fire's smoke, we see men standing all around—
'Tis strange, for from them has not come a single word or sound.
Standing by cottonwood, with arms close-folded on his breast,
Gazing with his eagle eyes up to the mountain's crest,
Tall and commanding is his form, and graceful is his mien;
As fair in face, as noble, has seldom here been seen.
A score or more of frontiersmen recline upon the ground,
But starting soon upon their feet, by sudden snort and bound!
A horse has sure been frightened by strange scent on the breeze,
And glances now by all are cast beneath the towering trees.
A quiet sign their leader gives, and mustangs now are brought,
And, by swift-circling lasso, a loose one fast is caught.
Then thundering round the mountain's dark adamantine side,
A hundred hideous, painted, and fierce Sioux warriors ride;
While, from their throats, the well-known and horrible death-knell,
The wild blood-curdling war-whoop, and the fierce and fiendish yell,
Strike the ears of all, now ready to fight, and e'en to die,
In that mount-inclosed valley, beneath that blood-red sky!
Now rings throughout the open, on all sides clear and shrill,
The dreaded battle-cry of him whom men call Buffalo Bill!
On, like a whirlwind, then they dash—the brave scouts of the plains,
Their rifle-barrels soft caressed by mustang's flying manes!
On, like an avalanche, they sweep through the tall prairie grass;
Down, fast upon them, swooping, the dread and savage mass!
Wild yells of fierce bravado come, and taunts of deep despair;
While, through the battle-smoke there flaunts each feathered tuft of
    hair.
And loudly rings the war-cry of fearless Buffalo Bill;
And loudly rings the savage yells, which make the blood run chill!
The gurgling death-cry mingles with the mustang's shrillest scream,
And sound of dull and sodden falls and bowie's brightest gleam.
At length there slowly rises the smoke from heaps of slain,
Whose wild war-cries will never more ring on the air again.
Then, panting and bespattered from the showers of foam and blood,
The scouts have once more halted 'neath the shady cottonwood.
In haste they are re-loading, and preparing for a sally,
While the scattered foe, now desperate, are yelling in the valley.
Again are heard revolvers, with their rattling, sharp report;
Again the scouts are seen to charge down on that wild cohort.
Sioux fall around, like dead reeds, when fiercest northers blow,
And rapid sink in death before their hated pale-face foe!
Sad, smothered now is music from the mountain's rippling rill,
But wild hurrahs instead are heard from our brave Buffalo Bill,
Who, through the thickest carnage charged ever in the van,
And cheered faint hearts around him, since first the fight began.

Deeply demoralized, **the Sioux** fly fast with bated breath,
And glances cast **of** terror along that vale of death;
While the victors **quick** dismounted, and looking all around,
On their dead and mangled enemies, whose corses strewed **the** ground.
"**I had** sworn I would avenge them"—were the words of Buffalo Bill—
"The mothers and their infants they slew at Medicine Hill.
Our work is done—done nobly—I looked for that from you;
Boys, when a cause is just, you need but stand **firm** and true!"
—"*Buckskin Sam,*" *in Beadle's Weekly.*

CHAPTER XXXII.

THE MOUNTAIN MEADOWS MASSACRE—THE MORMON CHURCH THE INSTIGATOR—A SCENE OF HORROR.

The massacre of 1857 by the Indians, instigated by Mormon rulers, for baseness of motive and fiendish ferocity of execution has no parallel in the history of civilized nations. A party of emigrants from Arkansas to California, numbering nearly 150 persons, pursued their uneventful journey until they arrived at the Mormon settlements of Utah. On all sides there seemed to be a premeditated agreement to refuse the emigrants the slightest courtesy or any information. Even money, so potent everywhere, would purchase no delicacy for the children, medicine for the sick, or food for themselves and their starving animals. The party journeyed wearily onward until they reached the Mountain Meadows, in Washington county, 325 miles from Salt Lake City. This was an oasis, indeed, with verdant grasses and crystal springs of water. In order to recruit their stock, it was decided to remain on the beautiful spot a few days, not suspecting any danger; but they were doomed to encounter a fate as horrible as it was unlooked for and undeserved.

The Mormon spies reported to their superiors this fatal decision of the emigrating party, and the Indians, who had been incited to fury against these unfortunate people, were led on to the attack. Among them were fifty or sixty Mormons disguised as Indians. The force was led by John D. Lee, and several fiendish associates, one of them being a Mormon bishop. Having surrounded the unsuspecting emigrants on the 12th of September, the next morning, at dawn, they made a furious attack upon them, killing seven and wounding sixteen, three of them fatally. Although taken unawares, they made a noble defense, and the savages and their allies were beaten off with severe loss. None of the Mormons were killed, but several Indians were. Infuriated at the loss of their warriors, runners were sent out to various tribes for reinforcements, and Mormon militia were hurried forward also to render certain the annihilation of the heroic men who bravely held their corral against overwhelming numbers of their assailants So successfully had the Mormons disguised themselves that two of the Arkansans slipped through the Indian lines the next night and were making their way back to Cedar City to ask help from the Mormons, when they were met by some of the faithful. Their errand was stated to these fiends, when one of them instantly shot one of the messengers. The other was wounded, but managed to get back to the corral with the report that they could more hopefully look for mercy from the Indians than the Mormons. After the first attack on Tuesday the emigrants drew their wagons close together, and dug a rifle pit in their midst, and from this the emigrants poured out a deadly fire on the hordes of savages whenever they attempted a charge. On Thursday, just at daylight, another furious attack was made by the combined forces, but it proved disastrous to the besiegers. One band of Indians left in disgust, and drove off some of the emigrants' cattle.

The same day one of the leading Mormons crossed the valley to get on higher ground to spy out the best method of attack. The emigrants saw his movements, and also perceived that he was a white man. Two little girls were sent out to him with a flag of truce, to implore terms for the doomed train, but were unrecognized. He satisfied himself that some other method than assault would have to be resorted to dislodge the emigrants. That night there was a Mormon council held, at which it was decided that on the morrow the Arkansans should be decoyed from their fortress, and all of them who were old enough to talk were to be butchered. The arrangements agreed upon were, that John D. Lee was to treat with the emigrants under a flag of truce. He was to demand that all of the young children were to be put into one wagon, the wounded into another, and the arms into a third. They were then to be protected from the Indians and conveyed in safety back to Cedar City, where they could wait until the arrival of some other train and go through to California with it. The three wagons were to be driven without halt past the Mormons and savages, who had been concealed in a growth of scrub cedars, over a quarter of a mile from where they had dug the rifle pit. Following the wagon were to come the women and youth. These were to pass the Mormon militia and not to halt until in the midst of the cedar thickets, where the Indians were hidden. The men were to be halted opposite the militia, who were to form a line on the right of the emigrants with their guns lying across their left arms ready for instant action. The march was then to be resumed until the three wagons had cleared the cedar thicket and the women were in the midst of it, with the men about a hundred yards behind them. A signal was then to be given, at which the militia was to shoot the unarmed men, the Indians to rise from their ambush and butcher the women and the larger children, while Lee and others were to murder the wounded. The emigrants accepted the terms proposed. The arms and ammunition were surrendered.

While all were moving forward in the order stated, the signal was given. After a moment of deep silence, there came a report of a single gun, and the carnival of murder had begun. Before the echoes of that gun, or the death moan of its victim had died away, there came the fierce rattle of musketry, the shrieks of the wounded and the groans of dying men. Further up the line toward the wagons, where the red savages had waited, was heard their blood curdling whoops and the screams of women and children. Bow and rifle, spear and tomahawk, were doing the infamous work of the Mormon church. Childhood and age; the matron and maiden; the hoary octogenarian and tiny prattler, and babes at the breast were ruthlessly butchered. Nearly every one of the male emigrants was killed by the first fire; but strange to say three escaped death and made their way almost to the borders of California before they were overtaken and killed. Two girls escaped into the cedar brush, but were trailed by an Indian chief, who wanted to save them. Lee cut the throat of one, and commanded the chief to shoot the other. When the massacre was complete the dead bodies were robbed of money and jewelry, and the Indians carried away all the clothing stripped from the victims. The next day the corpses were thrown into ditches and covered lightly with dirt, which was entirely washed off by the next spring, and their flesh and bones became food for beasts of prey and carrion birds.

Nearly 20 years after this horrible massacre the Mormon church surrendered Lee to suffer for this terrible crime. On March 23rd, 1877, he was taken to the meadows and shot to death—the laws of Utah Territory giving the condemned a choice of death by hanging or shooting. A single life to atone for the murder of one hundred and thirty-five souls!